WITHDRAWN
WRIGHT STATE UNIVERSITY LIBRARIES

THE CRAFT OF TONAL COUNTERPOINT

THE CRAFT OF TONAL COUNTERPOINT

Second Edition

Thomas Benjamin

Routledge
New York • London

MT
55
.B446
2003

Published in 2003 by
Routledge
29 West 35th Street
New York, NY 10001
www.routledge-ny.com

Published in Great Britain by
Routledge
11 New Fetter Lane
London EC4P 4EE
www.routledge.co.uk

Copyright © 2003 by Taylor & Francis Books, Inc.

Routledge is an imprint of the Taylor & Francis Group.
Printed in the United States of America on acid-free paper.

This book is a revised edition of *Counterpoint in the Style of J. S. Bach,*
originally published in 1986 by Schirmer Books.

All rights reserved. No part of this book may be reprinted or reproduced or utilized in
any form or by any electronic, mechanical, or other means, now known or hereafter
invented, including photocopying and recording, or in any information storage or retrieval
system, without permission in writing from the publishers.

10   9   8   7   6   5   4   3   2   1

Library of Congress Cataloging-in-Publication Data
Benjamin, Thomas.
    The craft of tonal counterpoint / Thomas Benjamin.
        p. cm.
Rev. ed. of: Counterpoint in the style of J.S. Bach. c1986.
Includes bibliographical references (p.   ) and index.
"Anthology (all works are by J.S. Bach)" : p.
    ISBN 0-415-94391-4 (pbk. : alk. paper)
1. Counterpoint—Textbooks. 2. Bach, Johann Sebastian,
1685–1750—Criticism and interpretation. 3. Musical analysis—Music
collections. I. Benjamin, Thomas. Counterpoint in the style of J.S.
Bach. II. Bach, Johann Sebastian, 1685–1750. Selections. III. Title.
    MT55.B446 2003
    781.2'86—dc21
                                              2003012527

CONTENTS

*This book is gratefully dedicated to my supportive and witty colleagues
in theory and composition at the University of Houston's School
of Music, the Peabody Conservatory of the Johns Hopkins University,
and to a few special friends who have been of more help to me
over the years than they will probably ever know,
first among them my dear wife and best friend, Carol.*

ACKNOWLEDGMENTS

I would like to acknowledge the assistance of the University of Houston in awarding me a Faculty Development Leave Grant, which was used to underwrite the year's leave during which the original edition of this book was written, and a Publication Subvention Grant to help with clerical costs. I am also indebted to my students of counterpoint at the University of Houston's School of Music, the National Music Camp (Interlochen), and at the Peabody Conservatory. Painstaking and thoughtful criticisms of the manuscript were received from Bruce B. Campbell, Robert Lynn, Bruce E. Miller, Robert Nelson, Anthony T. Rauche, Randall Shin, Eileen Soskin, Dan M. Urquhart, and Thomas Warburton. The reader must ascribe to my pigheadedness any errors of omission or commission remaining in the book. Linda Watson provided helpful critiques of several of the graphic reductions, and Laura Neidlinger, Carol Benjamin, and Elaine Gerdine lent steady hands at the computer, and fine editorial skills. Major thanks are also due my supportive and helpful commissioning editors, Maribeth Payne (first edition), Richard Carlin (current edition), editorial assistants Robert Byrne and Emily Vail, and production editor Lisa Vecchione.

PREFACE TO THE SECOND EDITION

In the roughly seventeen years since the first edition of this book appeared, a great deal has changed in the field of music theory, and several intelligent and interesting new textbooks for the study of tonal counterpoint have appeared. At the same time, the continuing popularity of this text, as well as the need to update its explanations and exercises, has encouraged the author to undertake a revision.

My original reasons for writing this book still seem valid. Of the several other texts in this field currently available, all seem, while in many ways estimable, problematic as regards their pedagogy. Some strike me as insufficient in the ordering, rigor, or comprehensiveness of their exercises; crucial conceptual or skills-developing steps may be omitted. Other texts seem unfocused and diffuse in terms of musical style: works by vastly disparate composers are thrown together in a way that seems likely to confuse the student. Still others appear to be aimed at the already expert theorist of music, and are so tied to specific metatheoretical concepts and language that many students will be sure to find them mystifying.

The danger of such approaches is to complicate technical and stylistic matters by wrapping them in theoretical constructs, reinforcing the tendency of most music students to assume that "music theory" is an abstruse and mystical discipline divorced from their own experience of music—in other words, that "music theory" is an undertaking entirely separate from musical practice, and from their own lives and needs as practicing musicians.

The attempt in the current edition is to construct a book that the intelligent student can read and understand, with some help from the instructor. It focuses on the work of Johann Sebastian Bach, and aims to be practical and useful as a study of both style and technique through performance, listening, analysis, and writing. It reflects current thinking about tonal music in its emphasis on structural harmony and line, structural-pitch reduction, linear-intervallic patterning, and so on, but presents these concepts in what I hope is a practical and immediately applicable way, as free as possible from abstract theorizing, and always focused on the music itself.

Those students and instructors who wish more background information on Bach's life and output and other issues of music history, theory, and literature are referred throughout the text to appropriate resources.

NOTES TO THE INSTRUCTOR

This book seeks to provide a great deal of fine music for performance, listening, analysis, and model making; straightforward explanations of technical and aesthetic matters; and a multiplicity of exercises in listening, analysis, and writing that are both technically sound and musically satisfying. The approach taken here is style-specific; the examples are drawn from the instrumental music of Johann Sebastian Bach, especially his keyboard music. But the techniques covered transfer easily to other media within the Bach style, at the instructor's option. It is, of course, also true that composers of Bach's time considered performing media to be to some extent interchangeable. The emphasis on the music of one composer allows this text to be used not only as a study of contrapuntal technique but also as a model of style analysis that is procedurally transferable to the music of other composers and historical periods. The instructor is free to focus as much as the course goals allow on matters of style in addition to the more purely technical aspects (to the degree to which style and technique can in fact be distinguished from each other).

This text is based on a study of musical practice, and the student is directed in the analytical exercises to deal with the music itself. It is clear that any meaningful study of music must be solidly based on experience in listening, performing, analyzing, and writing; it is urged that each class period include performances—recorded or live—of the music under study, and a discussion of what has been heard, including reference to issues of music history and literature, and performance practice. Some instructors may even wish to combine this text with a survey of the music of Bach, and listening assignments and tests would be most appropriate. As we all know, technical studies tend to be bloodless and abstract unless constantly connected with musical experiences; such connections, made explicit by the instructor, will tend to validate and clarify these studies.

On a more specific note, this book makes no use of a strict species approach. A multiplicity of analytic and written exercises provides ample practice in technique within a realistic musical context. In the interests of ease of reading, modern clefs are used throughout. The explanatory material is written as simply and practically as possible. Considerable generalization as regards both style and technique is inevitable, though, and I hope that in the search for directness and comprehensibility no outright errors have been made. It should be made clear to the student, in any case, that this book presents a picture of Bach's most typical practices (and, by extension, of the other masters of tonal counterpoint), and that there are exceptions to these practices. The language chosen is intended to be as positive as possible and avoids burdening teacher and student with a multiplicity of "rules" and prohibitions beyond those that seem unavoidable. It is urged that the word *rules* be avoided, and that such terms as *practices* or *typical procedures* be used.

To be properly prepared for this study, the student should be somewhat conversant with common practice theory, including basic four-voice part-writing principles and practices.[1] It will save class time if students know figured bass symbology, chord nomenclature, the basics of voice leading (including doubling), and principles of harmonic progression. According to the reports of Johann Philipp Kirnberger and others, Bach in his own teaching started his students with four-voice harmonic studies, using figured bass realization as the basis for written exercises. The sense of integration of vertical and horizontal aspects gained from such studies will prove invaluable as a background to contrapuntal study.

---

1. A brief review of harmony (including chord vocabulary and functions, cadences, inversions, nonharmonic tones, figured bass symbols, and modulation) is found in the appendix and will be a helpful resource for students.

The instructor need not feel locked into the order of presentation given here, though chapters 1 and 2 should be taken in order. (It is important to note also that certain terms and abbreviations mentioned in the introduction and chapter 1 will appear in later chapters.) As time permits, the chapters on chromaticism, canon, chorale prelude, and passacaglia may be shuffled or omitted to suit the instructor's needs and the course goals. The instructor should not feel limited by the music presented in the anthology; it can be supplemented by other works of his or her own choosing.

Following are a few practical suggestions, based on my classroom experience and in no way intended as prescriptive, for presentation of the material.

1. *Listening and performance.* As suggested earlier, it is most important that each class session include some listening examples and if possible live performances of the works under study. This can lead to discussion of such fruitful issues as performance practice, music history, cultural history, and so on.

2. *Background information.* Although this text by design does not deal with the historical or biographical background, the instructor may choose to present such information in the interests of establishing a style-historic context; he or she may assign information gathering in the form of class reports by students. Such reports might include such topics as the life and works of Bach and his major contemporaries; a survey of the output of Bach; cultural and political currents in the German Baroque; national influences on Bach; the history and development of various musical genres and forms; and so on. A basic bibliography begins on page 295; it is intended as a starting place for such background studies. Appropriate articles in *The New Grove Dictionary of Music and Musicians* (see bibliography) are cited throughout.

3. *Listening list.* It is suggested that a listening list of Bach's major works be distributed to students, and that they be made responsible for a listening (recognition) familiarity with the works on it, perhaps by way of periodic listening quizzes. All typical genres and media should be represented.

4. *Classroom process suggestions.* In class it is always a good procedure to vary the format, avoiding too much lecturing and ensuring that each student is actively engaged in the learning process. This can be accomplished by having students perform, discuss, and critique each other's written and analytic work; having them work at the board individually or in small teams; and assigning brief in-class writing exercises critiqued on the spot by the instructor. A very helpful classroom activity involves the solving of a problem—from the current or upcoming assignment—by the instructor, with student input. This modeling of the compositional process will prove invaluable for the student and will improve both the efficiency and the quality of his or her own work. Critiquing of individual student work in each class period, either with the class seated around the keyboard or with the aid of an onscreen projection, will be of great value.

5. *Possible omissions and reorderings.* There are far more exercises here than any class is likely to have time for, so the instructor will need to be selective in assignments. Such selection will be based on the background and abilities of the class and the aims of the course. If the focus of the course is on analysis, it will be possible to use the Directed Study section of each chapter, along with the exercises in analysis found at the end of each chapter, in conjunction with this volume's anthology. Such classes will omit the written exercises. In classes where the writing of counterpoint is the goal, a sampling of all the exercise types within each chapter is recommended. As far as possible, the written exercises in each chapter should be done in the order in which they are given.

   It is also possible to omit the Directed Study and/or Sample Analysis sections, if that better fits a given instructor's style, as the Discussion sections contain all the essential information. Or, the Directed Study sections may be taken up at the end of each chapter.

Further, some slight reordering of the chapters will be possible. Chapters 13 and 14 can be taken up earlier in the course of study if desired (following chapters 9 or 11) or they can be omitted. Chapters 3 and 4 may be postponed or omitted if necessary, depending on the course goals and the time available.

6. *Student writing.* The musicality of all student writing should be emphasized in addition to its technical proficiency; emphasis on this aspect will pay dividends in terms of student commitment to quality work. Technique, style, and "playability" should be stressed in discussing written work, and all work should be played and discussed in class, when time permits.

7. *Linear reductions.* This book depends to some extent on linear reductive principles, but it is not an orthodox Schenkerian text. The approach taken here focuses on the central issues of shape and direction through the analysis and composing-out of the structural-pitch framework, employing an informal system of reduction. The instructor is, of course, free to use whatever terminology and analytic system he or she prefers.

8. *General suggestions for analysis.* It is important to stress the general musical principles operating in the music to be studied and not merely the individual details of the technique. The fundamental musical laws operating behind the surface should be pointed out at every opportunity, including all the sources of shape; the organic nature of musical logic; the mutual interactions of all elements, and such basic dualities as continuity/articulation, tension/relaxation, unity/variety, and so on. Reference to Jan LaRue's *Guidelines for Style Analysis* (see bibliography), as appropriate, will be useful in assuring that the student is aware of organic processes and not just discrete events.

9. *Definitions.* A glossary of musical terms, also new to this edition, is given, starting on page 290. This is intended as a practical reference tool only, and in no way substitutes for the comprehensive treatment of technical matters found in the text. The table of contents and index provide reference to detailed discussions of technique. The glossary includes cross-references to many standard alternative terms.

10. *Ear training and improvisation.* Beyond analysis and writing, many exercises in this text may be used for ear training, sight-reading or sight-singing, and improvisation. It is always wise to work as much by ear as possible, in order to draw students away from excessive dependence on musical notation, and improve their aural acuity and musicianship.

    For instance, the error-detection exercises found throughout the text may be done by ear, using the piano. Solutions to the sequence-writing exercises in chapters 1 and 2 can be improvised vocally or instrumentally, by the class or by individual students, as can the melody-writing exercises at the end of chapter 1. The exercises concluding chapter 2 will prove particularly useful for sight-singing, or improvisation at the keyboard or on individual instruments.

    All exercises that can be easily sung should be, using solfège or any system of the instructor's choosing.

11. *Harmony.* Classes needing any review of tonal harmony, including chord functions, figured bass symbols, and nonharmonic tone definitions are referred to appendix 1. Even those students somewhat conversant with common practice harmony will benefit from a class session devoted to review. Several central points made there should be emphasized in all discussions of harmony:

    A. The distinction between *structural harmony* and *embellishing harmony* is important to an understanding of tonality. It is suggested that in their analyses students be taught to distinguish between structural (prolonged) harmonies and those of less structural significance, either by circling the principal chords (and pointing out main prolongations), or providing a two-level harmonic analysis:

	Phrase 1				HC	Phrase 2					PAC
Layer 1 (details):	I	vi	ii⁶	(I$^6_4$)	$\bar{V}^7$	V	vi	IV	(I$^6_4$)	V7	$\bar{I}^1$
Layer 2 (structure):	I (prolonged)				V	V		(prolonged)			I

It may also prove useful to reinforce this distinction by using the symbols T (tonic), D (any structurally important dominant function chord), and PD (any important predominant chord, whether IV, ii, IV7, ii7, or some chromatic substitute), and roman numerals for other chords.

B. *Linear "chords."* It is important to introduce the concept of linear sonorities (those arising from linear motion, especially from simultaneous nonharmonic tones) early in the course—best, perhaps, in chapters 1 and 2. Many weak or dependent harmonic effects are best understood as of linear origin, most obviously the $^6_4$ "chords," which can almost always be heard and explained as linear in origin and effect, the result of passing, neighboring or suspensive dissonance. The "cadential $^6_4$ chord," for instance, can be analyzed as (I$^6_4$), or simply as V with two nonharmonic tones.

12. *Other important concepts:*

A. The notion of *linear-intervallic patterns,* as found in Schenker's writing and well explained in Forte/Gilbert (see bibliography), is very useful in both analysis and writing, and is highly recommended as a tool. It is taken up in the introduction, in chapter 2, and elsewhere in the text.

B. A high degree of *scale-degree pattern* awareness is central to both understanding and accurately hearing tonal music. Explaining harmonization in terms of scale-degree formulae in the harmonized voice is very helpful to students. Equally important is understanding harmony in terms of bass line formulas. The common bass-line patterns should be explored, memorized, and practiced as early as possible; they are found in chapter 2, associated with cadential formulas, the descending T–D tetrachord, and typical sequential harmonic patterns (such as the circle of fifths and the descending chain of thirds). The association of bass scale-degree patterns with certain typical chord-inversion formulas is of great help with both analytic and written work.

Indeed, the cultivation of the student's awareness of *all aspects of patterning* in this music will be a central concern of your pedagogy in this course. The more this awareness can be refined and generalized, the more the student's aural acuity, skill in writing and analyzing, and level of performance will benefit.

NOTES TO THE STUDENT

What can you expect to gain from a course in the analysis and writing of counterpoint? First, such a study should make you a more accomplished and discriminating musician, whether as listener, performer, or composer. It can teach you what to listen for in a passacaglia, for example, or what to bring out in performing an invention, or how to compose a convincing fugue. It can help you to understand compositional technique and can enhance your own creative abilities. There is an excitement in composing good music that is hard to match in any other musical activity, even when this music is written in a borrowed style. Contrapuntal studies are essential for theorists, composers, and keyboard players (especially harpsichordists and organists), and for any serious student of music who wishes to refine his or her musicianship.[1]

The study of the music of Johann Sebastian Bach (1685–1750[2]) is an excellent way to learn how to grasp the underlying principles of all good counterpoint. The musical principles and processes as applied by Bach are common to music in general. For instance, the means by which a composer keeps one voice distinct from the others around it are essentially the same for, say, Bach, Béla Bartók, and Orlando di Lasso.

Additionally, this book can be read as a model of how to approach and understand the music of any composer; it can be used, in other words, as a model for style analysis. There is little about musical style that is mysterious. Any style can be learned with study and application. One learns a composer's music best through maximum exposure to it by listening, performing, analyzing, and writing. And through such exposure one often reaches an appreciation of the intellectual discipline that any creative art demands, and of the fact that in great music we find a perfect mixture of intuition, spirit, and intellect. In the case of a composer as great as Bach, this combination of craft and genius is especially awe inspiring. There is no more contradiction between technique and instinct for a composer than there is for a performer. The technique must be in perfect working order to serve as a vehicle for the musical instinct.

Finally, as a reason to study counterpoint, there is simply the satisfaction of being creative, of producing something that was not there before. You will be asked in this book to write music that is not only technically "correct" but also musically satisfying and as close as possible to the style of Bach. This will require familiarity with *the sound of Bach's music*. It is not possible to get to know a composer's music simply by memorizing a lot of rules. You need to *immerse* yourself in the music, as listener and/or performer. Play and/or listen to all the music assigned for analysis, and always play your own written work, both while working on it and after it is completed.[3]

---

1. For more background on counterpoint in general, see *The New Grove Dictionary of Music and Musicians,* "Counterpoint," vol. 4.
2. A good introduction to Bach's life and works may be found in *The New Grove Dictionary of Music and Musicians,* "Bach, Johann Sebastian," vol. 1.
3. It is excellent ear and mind training to work away from the keyboard, going to it only to check your work.

INTRODUCTION

Almost all music is to some degree contrapuntal. Even music that is usually studied for its harmonic content is often equally linear in conception and effect. The distinction usually made between harmony (the chordal or vertical aspect) and counterpoint (the linear aspect, the ways in which independent voices interrelate) is a pedagogical convention not supported by actual musical practice. In most polyphonic music, one can say only that there are both horizontal and vertical controls present (as well as many other kinds of controlling elements). Thus, we will concern ourselves in this book with both chord and line, and with how they influence each other.

This study is rooted in musical practice, not in abstractions, and is based on the instrumental music of Johann Sebastian Bach, with emphasis on the keyboard music. Why Bach? Because in his music we find an ideal coordination of strong, directional harmonic progression and energetic, interdependent lines, all of this suffused with greatness of spirit and largeness of musical conception. His mastery of harmony, melodic and motivic processes, and extended contrapuntal composition is of an extremely high order, yet his astounding technique is always at the service of musical ends, never an end in itself. Only in the greatest performers and composers do we sense this perfect unity and balance of technique and expression. Bach represents a culmination of musical trends in the Baroque era, a composer who pulls together in his work at least three separate national styles, and brings to their highest point all the contrapuntal forms he inherited. He exerted a tremendous influence on later composers. Wolfgang Amadeus Mozart exclaimed, on hearing a Bach motet for the first time, "Now, there is something one can learn from!" Ludwig van Beethoven said; "Not Bach [brook] but Meer [sea] should be his name"; and Robert Schumann advised the young musician, "Let the Well-Tempered Clavier be your daily bread. Then you will certainly become a solid musician."

DIRECTED STUDY

In the Directed Study sections of this book you will be asked to perform, listen to, and think carefully about a variety of musical excerpts. Though you will be focusing on one aspect of the music at a time, still it is important to be aware of the ways in which the musical elements work together to produce an effect. For instance, a climactic effect may well be achieved through intensification of several aspects: a rising line, lengthening phrase structure, increasingly chromatic or dissonant harmony, more active rhythm, and thickening texture. Music in which all the elements work together toward the same result is said to exhibit *concinnity*.[1] The music of the great composers always displays a high degree of concinnity.

A NOTE ON GRAPHIC ANALYSIS

The system of graphic analysis used here requires a brief introduction. The approach has been suggested by but is not an orthodox version of the linear reductive system developed by

---

1. This useful term, adopted from the vocabulary of rhetoric by Jan LaRue in *Guidelines for Style Analysis* (see bibliography), may be defined as a property of close agreement (in both logic and style) among all the elements of an artwork.

Heinrich Schenker (1868–1935).[2] Schenker realized that the conventional "analytic" tools of his time were merely descriptive of discrete events, taking into account neither the fact that music has shape and direction nor that some tonal events are more important structurally than others. His system grew out of an attempt to show graphically the fundamental pitch structure of a work. His writing suggests that a musical work consists of layers (*Schichten*) that can be peeled away, onionlike, to reveal a skeletal inner structure, the *Ursatz*. The Ursatz forms a background or skeleton for the work, over which we hear the middleground and foreground (surface) levels of activity. Schenker's mature work posits a small repertoire of fundamental structural lines in common practice music (including that of Bach) that descend stepwise during the work from some member of the tonic triad to the tonic note. According to Schenker, it can be shown that many works represent a working out in time of the descent from, say, the mediant to the tonic note, 3–(2)–1. All other notes in the melody serve to ornament, expand, prolong, and connect between the pitches of this fundamental melody (*Urlinie*). Such ornamentations consist mainly of triad arpeggiations, passing tones, and neighbors.

This book employs the following symbols:

1. The *principal structural pitches* (notes of departure and arrival) are shown as ♩. Structural pitches are usually notes of the tonic triad.
2. *Secondary pitches* are shown as o for main *arpeggiations* (again, usually of the tonic triad), and ● for *neighbor* (N) and *passing notes* (P), and other events of lesser structural importance.
3. The main localized melodic *motions* are shown as ⌒. These motions involve scales, passing tones, neighbors, or dominant-to-tonic leaps.
4. *Octave transfers and prolongations* of principal pitches are shown as ⌒→.

In making your own graphic reductions, keep the following points in mind:

A. Bass lines are patterned, often involving descending scalar motions outlining octaves, fourths, or fifths. Such bass patterns are highly standardized and normally gravitate toward the strongest tonal scale degrees, $\hat{1}$, $\hat{4}$, and $\hat{5}$, thus emphasizing the principal harmonic functions of tonal music. The principal arrival points in the bass (especially on $\hat{1}$ and $\hat{5}$) outline the *structural harmony,* to which all other harmony is subsidiary.
B. The structural pitches of melodies form patterns, emphasizing the pitches of the tonic triad.
C. Strong counterpoint is formed between the structural pitches of the outer voices. This fundamental outer-voice framework will be satisfying and solid when extracted and played by itself. A typical outer-voice framework consists of a series of descending scalar structural pitches forming parallel tenths between the voices (see *linear-intervallic patterns,* p. xxii).
D. Notes that will tend to sound most important (structural) are tonic triad members and/or those notes placed on strong beats, or of longest duration. The initial notes of sequence units tend to be heard as structural.

The following excerpts and their graphic reductions are taken from chapters 2 and 4. These reductions may be discussed in class, if the instructor wishes, as they are intended to exemplify and clarify the analytic concepts discussed above. In this discussion, alternative reductions may be considered. Several more elaborate graphic reductions are to be found throughout the text.

2. Those wishing more information on Schenker and his theories are directed to The Forte/Gilbert and Parks books (see bibliography) and the following articles in *The New Grove Dictionary of Music and Musicians:* "Analysis, III" (vol. 1) and "Schenker, Heinrich" (vol. 16).

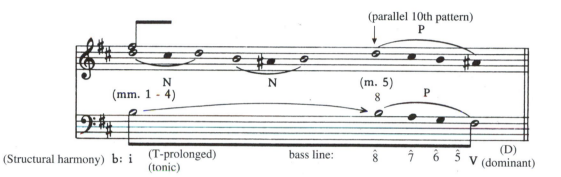

Linear Intervallic Patterns (LIPs). One of the most powerful and practical of all Schenker's contributions to musical understanding was the observation that between pairs of voices, especially outer voices in sequences, there is a pattern of harmonic intervals that seems the main organizing principle in such passages. While this was not his exclusive discovery, he codified the principal patterns and pointed out their extensive use in tonal music.

The very common 10-10 pattern (equivalent to 3-3 or 17-17) in example 1, mm. 5–8, has already been pointed out. Many other such patterns will be noted as they occur in the music. It will be very helpful in your own analyzing and writing to keep LIPs in mind at all times, and indeed to keep in mind all aspects of *patterning,* which is central to the music of Bach and his contemporaries.

Here are some of the most common linear intervallic patterns:

Ex. I - 3

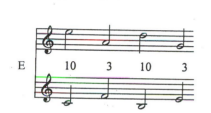

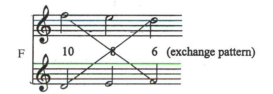

The LIPs are typically ornamented with motivic figures:

exchange pattern   6   3   6   3   10   10

CHAPTER 1

LINE AND OTHER ELEMENTS OF STYLE

Here are a number of melodies drawn from the instrumental works of Bach. Perform each one a number of times.[1]

Ex. 1–1   Orchestral Suite in B minor, Rondeau

Ex. 1–2   French Suite V, Sarabande

Ex. 1–4   English Suite V, Passepied I

Ex. 1–5   Viola da Gamba Movement in G Major, Fourth Movement

Ex. 1–6   Orchestral Suite in C Major, Menuet I

Ex. 1–7   Violin Sonata in A Major, Second Movement

Ex. 1–8   Viola da Gamba Sonata in G Major, First Movement

Adagio

Ex. 1–10   Viola da Gamba Sonata in D Major, Fourth Movement

Ex. 1–11   Partita I for Solo Violin, Courante

SHAPE; TONAL FRAMEWORK; RANGE AND TESSITURA

Most effective musical lines are clearly shaped. Bach's music derives much of its strength from being clearly directed toward melodic and harmonic *goals*. An effective melody makes a clear overall *contour*, which we can represent graphically as a line. The overall shape will normally seem balanced and in repose, with ascending curves balanced by descending curves; this will often be mirrored in the localized, bar-by-bar shapes. In short, the same *shaping processes (gestures)* often control all aspects of melodic structure when the music is of high quality.

Note in example 1-13 the tonally and metrically clear starting point, the swift rise to the tonic octave and the more gradual fall to the dominant note in a strong cadence. This is but one of many possible melodic shapes; you will have observed several others in the music at the beginning of this chapter. The *climactic point* may or may not be obvious in a given melody; it may be a low rather than a high note; it often occurs near the end of a phrase, with the line then falling quickly into a strong cadence (see especially exs. 1-2, 1-3, and 1-11). A climactic note may be emphasized by its length, height or depth, identity as a strong scale degree (such as tonic or dominant), metrical position, and by reiteration and return. Often it is approached by a leap from below, and may be a tied or dotted value (see ex. 1-13, m. 3). Following the main climactic note, there may be a secondary high point or two, and a scalar descent, as in ex. 1-13.

The *tonal framework* formed by the most emphasized low and high notes will tend to clarify the tonality. The framework of the excerpt above can be heard as e^1 to a^2, or a^1 to a^2, both emphasizing the key of A major. Typical tonal frameworks are:

High note:	dominant	tonic	mediant	mediant	tonic
Low note:	dominant	dominant	dominant	tonic	tonic

There is often one note outside the framework, related as a neighbor note to the high or low pitch, as for example:

Ex. 1-14

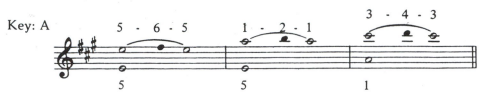

Key: A

Range is primarily a function of instrument and idiom, although melodies encompassing more than a twelfth (unless involving compound line) are quite rare. The *tessitura* (the "heart" or most often used portion of the range) is typically about an octave.

Your written work should (at the discretion of your instructor) be playable in two hands and conform to the range of Bach's writing in the *Well-Tempered Clavier,* great C to C³,—that is, from two octaves below "middle C" to two octaves above it.

What will not be found here, or in any well-shaped music, are shapes that seem aimless, flat, too wide-ranging, or jagged. One rarely finds unidirectional contours such as ╱ or ╲ , steep or jagged outlines like ∧∧∧∧∧, or narrow, oscillating patterns such as ⌒⌒⌒ (which arise from overemphasis on one pitch or one part of the range). These shapes may be made to work on a localized scale only if incorporated in a larger-scale directed contour. For example, mm. 3–5 of example 1-13 oscillate around a², but only as an incidental detail in a clear overall shape.

___

Exercises

1. Perform and critique the newly composed "melodies" on p. 34 in terms of shape and tonal framework.
2. Identify the range and tonal framework in examples 1-1 to 1-12. Which scale degrees are involved in these frameworks? Identify the tessitura (this is often a somewhat subjective judgment).
3. Identify the climactic moments in melodies selected from examples 1-1 to 1-12. Discuss how these are achieved (approached, emphasized, left). Represent the contour of each of these melodies with a line drawing, and compare the contours of several melodies.
4. Perform in class other lines by Bach, perhaps from works you already know or are preparing for performance, and discuss them in terms of shape and framework, as well as performance-practice issues.

STRUCTURAL PITCHES

Sample Analysis (of Example 1-13)[2]

Ex. 1-15   Violin Sonata in A Major, First Movement

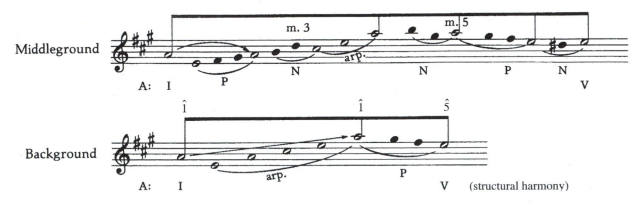

There is no question that some pitches are perceived as more fundamental than others, as more "structural." We can easily show these hierarchies of pitch in some such graphic way as in example 1-15. It should be emphasized that such reductions are to some extent subjective, based as they are on each individual's hearing of and thinking about a given work. Awareness of the directed shapes formed by the structural pitches is important to our understanding of the shaping processes in music, and our ability to hear, perform, and write musically.

The shapes formed by these fundamental pitches are usually simple and easy to hear. They are what makes this music so clear in its contours. Observe in example 1-15 the simplicity of the underlying shape: a prolonged tonic note (with the dominant note below it), an arpeggiated rise along the tonic triad to the tonic note an octave higher; the prolongation by surrounding and reiteration of the tonic octave (a^2); and the stepwise fall to the new, temporary tonic (e^2).

The secondary pitches very often form *tonic triad arpeggiations,* or ascending or (more often) descending *scales* starting from and ending on strong scale degrees, most often the notes of the tonic triad. Principal structural pitches are often separated by intervals of an octave (tonic to tonic, or dominant to dominant), or a perfect fourth or fifth (involving the tonic and dominant notes). For example, observe in example 1-15 the octave outline formed by the two a's, and the tonic-dominant P4 descent (a^2 to e^2). The whole melody could be further reduced to a fundamental skeletal outline, thus:

Ex. 1–16

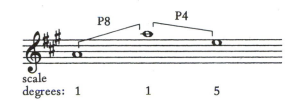

Ornamentation of or between structural pitches can be accomplished by scaler (passing), neighboring or arpeggiated motion. All of these methods are inherent in this melody.

Filling In (Motivic) Figures

Bach and his contemporaries employed certain melodic figures to fill in between structural pitches.[3] Some of the most typical are shown in the following example. Any given movement will be highly unified by use of a limited number of such figures, as appropriate to the genre, scoring, tempo, and *affect* (expressive character) of the work.

Ex. 1–17

Secondary structural interval filled in: | Some typical ornamental (motivic) filling-in figures:

EXAMPLES IN COMPOUND METER

Structural interval: Filling-in figures:

These are not by any means the only filling-in figures available in the style. The choice of a particular figure will depend on factors of harmony, counterpoint, scale, and the overall motivic content of any given work. This will be discussed later.

Notice that each of these figures is an expansion and/or ornamentation of neighboring or passing processes. As suggested earlier, successive structural pitches will be connected by arpeggiated or scalar filling-in figures. Single structural pitches will often be prolonged by neighboring motion.

Analyze the lines at the beginning of this chapter in terms of structural pitches. The individual voices of the polyphonic works found later in this book may, at the discretion of the instructor, also be so analyzed. At least two structural levels should be shown (primary and secondary pitches). Some melodies will be clearer than others in terms of structural line. After each reduction is made, the filling-in figures should be written down and discussed. Be aware of all types of prolongation and filling in: neighbors, scales, and arpeggios. Note also how the principal implied harmonies are prolonged and clarified through the primary structural pitches. Some lines involve octave transfer, or may be compound (see pp. 30–32).

PHRASE AND CADENCE

Sample Analysis

Ex. 1–18   Orchestral Suite in C Major, Gavotte I[4]

IAC = imperfect authentic cadence
PAC = perfect authentic cadence
(see Appendix 1 for definitions of cadences)

Comments on Example 1-18

The *phrase structure,* due no doubt to the fact that this is a dance movement, is quite regular, organized by groups of four measures (except for the last eight measures, which seem more continuous and developmental). The strongest cadences are placed every eight measures. The authentic cadences in mm. 4 and 12 sound less than final, due to the trills and the weak-beat arrival of the tonic note. The four-measure phrases may be further broken down into two-measure subphrases. On a larger formal level, successive four-measure phrases may form eight-measure groups or *periods* (mm. 1–8 form a period, as do mm. 9–16).[5]

The first eight measures are especially simple harmonically and melodically, without many leaps, or any syncopes or other rhythmic irregularities. They seem expository and stable.

The following measures seem more developmental: modulatory, less conjunct (stepwise), and containing a longer phrase (phrase 5).

The cadences are clear as to key and type, even without references to the harmony. The cadential melodic figures move by step, usually falling, into the goal note.

Flow and flexibility are attained by continuing the motion over internal cadence points (ex. 1-18, mm. 4, 12) and by the use of syncopating ties (mm. 17, 19). The motion stops completely only at the strongest cadences, which articulate the main formal divisions (mm. 8, 16, 24).

Discussion

All levels of formal structure in this music reveal the influence of their ultimate origin in dance. As humans are bipedal, many aspects of time in music (rhythm, meter, phrase, and finally form) tend to occur in twos and multiples of two: a gesture and a balancing or opposing gesture; action and reaction. Dance movements, such as the gavotte in example 1-18, will tend clearly to show their historical dance antecedents. More abstract works, especially those based on imitation, will tend to be less regular at all levels of formal structure.

While the underlying phrase structure is basically regular, its effect is often less obvious on the musical surface than in more consistently homophonic music. Phrase is a controlling element in the melody in example 1-19. Notice in it the variety of rhythmic values, the distinct articulations every four measures, and its essential vocality (as against the instrumental flavor of the Bach excerpts).

Ex. 1-19   Franz Joseph Haydn, Symphony No. 104, First Movement

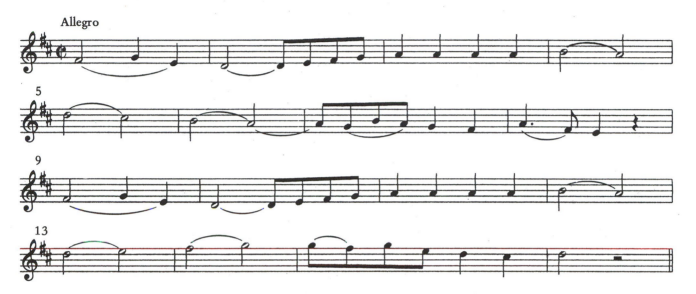

Compared to this music, that of Bach is usually less obviously built around the phrase and is more continuous (pulsatile). It is far less likely to use the phrase as the main unit (module) for development, employing instead the spinning out (*Fortspinnung* is the German term) of motivic fragments by means of various manipulations: repetition, inversion, sequence, and so on. See, for instance, examples 1-3, 1-4, 1-9, 1-10, and 1-11.

CADENCE FIGURES

Cadences (breathing places that articulate the ends of phrases) are principal articulating and form-clarifying devices of this music. In any music, insufficient use of cadential effects may lead to an inarticulate or too continuous result. Overuse of cadences will result in a discontinuous effect. Bach's music is beautifully balanced between these extremes. Bach is careful to continue motion over most internal cadences, weakening them just enough for continuity. Only at main cadences is the motion allowed to stop.

Principal cadential points in this style are emphasized by:

- placement of the melodic and harmonic arrival on a strong beat;
- use of melodic figures that lead smoothly to and emphasize the melodic goal note;
- choice of the strongest harmonies (tonic and dominant) in the strongest position (root), emphasized by harmonically clear and supportive bass lines.

All the cadential melodic figures you have heard so far have been variants of the two basic cadential shapes in tonal music:

Ex. 1-20

I. From above:

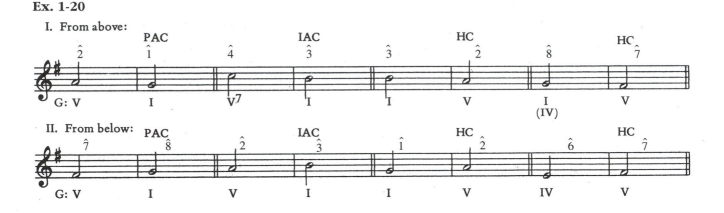

II. From below:

Both of these archetypal shapes approach the goal note by step. The word *cadence* comes from the Latin *cadere*, "to fall," and in fact the cadential gesture in most melodies is a falling one. In this style, the goal note is normally placed on a strong beat, though it may also follow an on-the-beat dissonance such as a suspension, passing tone or appoggiatura, especially in slow movements. Some characteristic ornamentations in the Bach style of these fundamental cadences are seen in example 1-21. These ornament an authentic cadence in G major, with structural pitches on scale degrees 2-1 or 7-8.

Ex. 1–21

Other cadence figures will be found, but will on examination prove simply to be variants of the above figurations.[6]

Exercises

1. Investigate phrase structure and cadence figurations in the poorly composed melodies on p. 34. Critique these aspects.
2. Analyze other music, as assigned by the instructor, from the anthology, focusing on phrase structure and cadences. Be especially aware of any irregular phrases, the use of motion to cover internal cadences, and the use of ties and evaded cadences to make the phrasing more flexible and continuous. Analyze cadences by frequency, placement, type, and melodic figures.
3. Ornament the following fundamental cadences in the Bach style, using mixed note values, including eighths and sixteenths. All are authentic unless otherwise marked. Use as your models cadences from works in this book, or other Bach pieces you know.

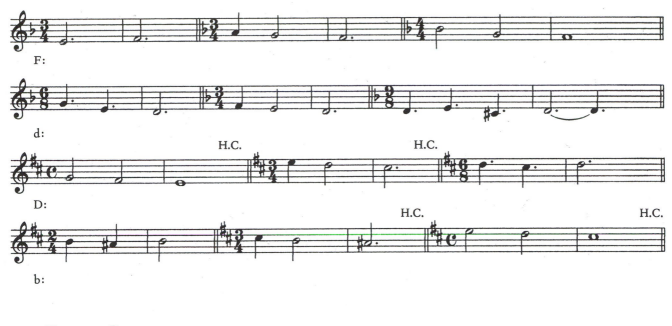

Meter and Rhythm

Sample Analysis

Ex. 1–22

Viola da Gamba Sonata in G Minor

Comments on Example 1-22

The meter is clarified through the grouping of melodic and rhythmic patterns into two- or four-beat units, through changes of pattern that normally occur on strong beats, through sequential units of four beats each (mm. 3–4), implied chord change on the strong beats, and placement of the cadence on beat 1 (m. 9).

Rhythm, while very regular, avoids squareness by the use of the ties in m. 7 and by the off-beat-accenting motive in m. 8, beats 1 and 2. Phrase structure is slightly irregular (nine measures; the "extra" measure is m. 7).

Only two different rhythmic values are employed: a basic unit of motion (♪) and one faster, adjacent value (♫). The last note is, as usual, longer. Until m. 7, only three different rhythmic figures or motives are employed.

Discussion

Rhythm and meter in Bach's style, and especially in faster, dance-dominated movements, are highly regular. Meter is rarely obscured, and the strong beats are emphasized through the regular placement of rhythmic patterns (including sequential units), strong-beat placement of cadences, and by harmonic rhythm. There is a feeling of pulse, continuity, and drive, and often an increase in rhythmic activity through the phrase, with the most complex and quickest rhythms placed toward the end of the phrase (see ex. 1-22, mm. 5–8). Rhythmic activity usually slows at the cadence, avoiding a feeling of abruptness (m. 8, beats 3 and 4). This succession of shorter, more varied rhythmic units followed by longer, more continuous ones (mm. 1–4, versus mm. 5–6) gives many melodies a sense of "rhythmic crescendo," which supports the harmonic and linear processes driving toward the cadence.

Normally there is a basic unit of motion (sometimes termed *impulse*), and one adjacent note value on each side of it. That is, if the motion unit is ♪, there will be ♫ subdivisions, and, at cadence points, longer values (♩). Slower, expressive movements will often exhibit greater variety of note values, less clear meter, more flexibility of rhythm, more ornamentation, and greater use of ties and syncopes.

The faster note values are in general found on the weak beats, or weak parts of beats. This is an important aspect of the style. Further, the quickest notes are most often treated by step (as scalar figures), rather than by skip. The change back to slower values usually occurs on a strong beat or the strong part of a beat (see ex. 1-22, mm. 2, 3, 4, and 8), approached by step.

Rhythm is an essential component of motivic coherence in this style, and rhythmic figures are highly restricted and consistent within a given melody (see ex. 1-22). Such distinctive figures as triplets (within a simple meter) and dotted figures are used consistently, or not at all. The one typical exception to this is that a dotted figure may occur as part of a cadential figuration, and only there, in a piece that otherwise does not employ dotted rhythms (see the cadence examples, p. 12).

As this is a continuous, *motoric* style, rests are used sparingly. Brief rests on the strong part of a beat lend metric flexibility. A voice will usually cadence before a longer rest. The longer the rest, the more the tendency of the resting voice to reenter with important thematic material.

Ties and *syncopes* occur quite often, and are a distinctive feature of the Bach style, giving flexibility to the rhythmic structure. Ties are normally found in 1:1 ratios (such as ♩ : ♩ or ♩ : ♪), 2:1, and 4:1 in simple meters, and 1:1, 3:1, and 3:2 in compound meters. Reverse-ratio ties, such as 1:2, are very rare. The first note of a tied value is very rarely the shortest value in a movement. Exceptions to these observations may be found principally in very slow, expressive movements (see pp. 173 and 174). Syncopes are used freely, but they rarely involve the shortest note value, as this gives an awkward effect (again, excepting works in very slow tempos). For typical examples, see examples 1-5 and 1-13.

Hemiola is rare in this style. Its most typical occurrences come at cadential points in some triple-meter dances, where one feels a shift from 3/4 to 3/2, as in the following minuet.

Ex. 1–23   English Suite IV, Menuet I

The reversed dotted figure is also avoided (♫♩. or ♪ ♩.).

Exercises

1. Critique the lines on p. 34 in terms of meter and rhythm.
2. Perform and analyze works from the anthology, as assigned by the instructor, being aware of factors of both regularity and flexibility in meter and rhythm.
3. Critique the following phrase in terms of the Bach style:

4. As a class, discuss and prepare a list of the distinctive rhythmic features of the Bach style.
5. Perform in class any Bach movement you know, and lead a discussion of its rhythmic aspects.

MELODIC INTERVALS; DETAILS OF LINE

Bach's is essentially a smooth and balanced style. Most melodies tend to move predominantly by step, depending on the performing medium and movement type. Obviously, instrumental music will tend to be more wide-ranging and arpeggiated in its figures, while vocal music will be more conjunct (stepwise). Recall that Bach's works are highly unified by motif (figure), as appropriate to the genre, instrumentation, tempo, and affect of any given movement.

Both scalar and neighboring patterns are common. Unidirectional scales tend to be mechanical and are rarely allowed to continue for more than seven or eight notes. Neighboring figures are problematic because of their inherent lack of direction and are rarely carried on for long at the same pitch level. The lower-neighbor figure is more common than the upper. Series of steps are followed most often by continuing the stepwise motion into the next beat, or by leap in the opposite direction.

Ex. 1–24

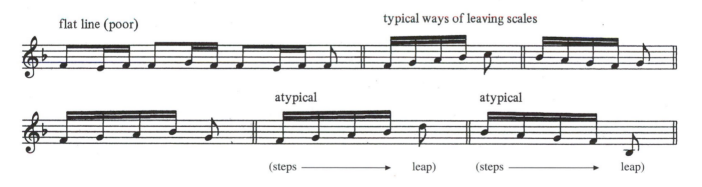

It is the function of stepwise figures to prolong and/or connect structural pitches, as well as to provide motivic content. Some characteristic figures are given on pp. 7–8. Several additional neighboring and filling-in figures are shown in example 1-25, articulating simple structural-pitch frameworks. The choice of a particular pattern will of course depend on considerations of metric, motivic, expressive (affective), and harmonic context.

Ex. 1-25

Structural interval: Filling-in figures:

Leaps are treated with care in this style. All melodic intervals up to the octave are used, but with some restrictions. The m7 is normally found as an ascending interval; the M7 is extremely rare. Intervals larger than a fifth often imply the presence of a *compound line* (see p. 30.) The P8 is most often used to adjust register (avoiding extremes of range), to accommodate a change of direction in line, or to change spacing or avoid voice-crossing in a contrapuntal context. Leaps are most often found from the strong part of a beat to the weak, or from strong to weak beats (except in the bass voice which, when treated as harmonic support, leaps more freely than the others). They most often occur between tones of the same chord. The larger the leap, the more compelling the tendency to follow it by motion, most often stepwise, in the opposite direction. Sixths and sevenths almost always resolve by opposite motion, unless involved in a compound line. Thirds are often not balanced, but larger intervals usually are. Leaps into melodic or harmonic tendency tones are most often resolved by opposing motion. If a line moves in one direction by a mixture of leaps and steps, the leaps usually precede the steps.

Ex. 1-26

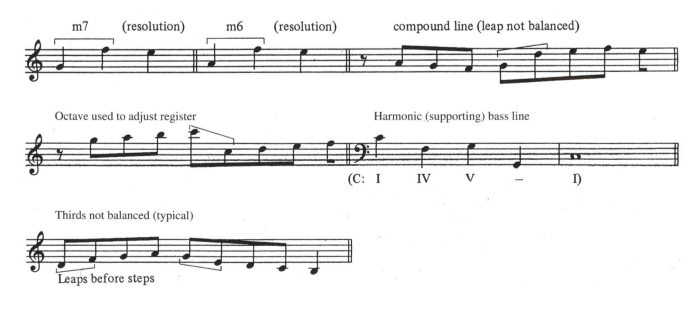

Successive leaps usually form chord outlines—that is, arpeggiated triads or seventh chords. The arpeggiation rarely exceeds an octave in range. Such arpeggiations are usually balanced by opposing scalar motion. The implied chords must be functional harmonics within the key. Occasionally, successive leaps will not form a chord outline. In such a case, either a compound line is involved or the last note of the figure is an appoggiatura or incomplete neighbor tone (i.n.t.).

Ex. 1-27

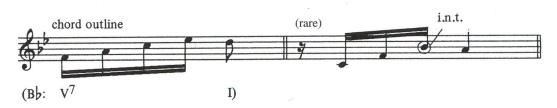

Repeated-note figures are used with care, as they can easily interrupt the sense of direction. When used, they are treated consistently as part of the motivic fabric or they may be found as part of the cadential anticipation figure.

Ex. 1-28

Augmented and diminished intervals are treated with great care, as they are dissonant and require specific resolutions. Briefly stated, diminished intervals resolve *inward*, augmented *outward*. The most common are the A4, d5, d7, and A2. They are nearly always found in association with dominant harmony (V[7] or vii°[7]). The A4 and d5 are used quite frequently and are carefully resolved (either immediately or very soon thereafter). The A2 is much rarer and is normally associated with vii°[7], descending in quick note values (see p. 20).

Ex. 1-29

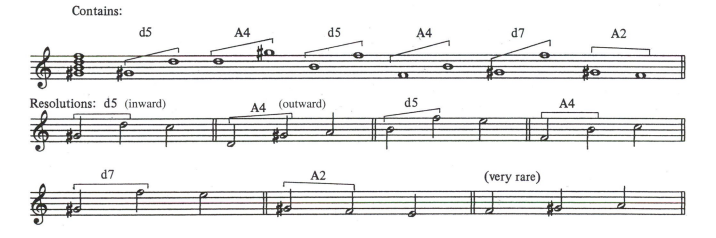

Not only are direct dissonant intervals resolved, but stepwise or arpeggiated lines implying these intervals are treated with the same restrictions.

Ex. 1–30

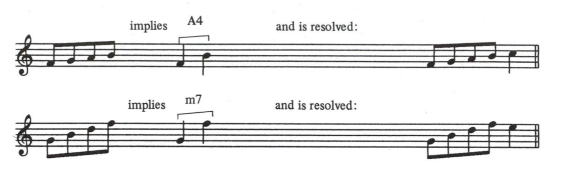

Exercises

1. Perform and critique the "melodies" on p. 34 in terms of the incidence and treatment of leaps and stepwise figures.
2. Critique the following melodic fragments.

3. Identify and resolve the following intervals and lines. These may be done vocally, as ear-training exercises, as long as a key-context is established first, for each exercise.

SCALES; CHROMATICISM; TENDENCY TONES
Sample Analysis, Minor Mode

Ex. 1–31   Musical Offering: Trio Sonata in C Minor, Second Movement

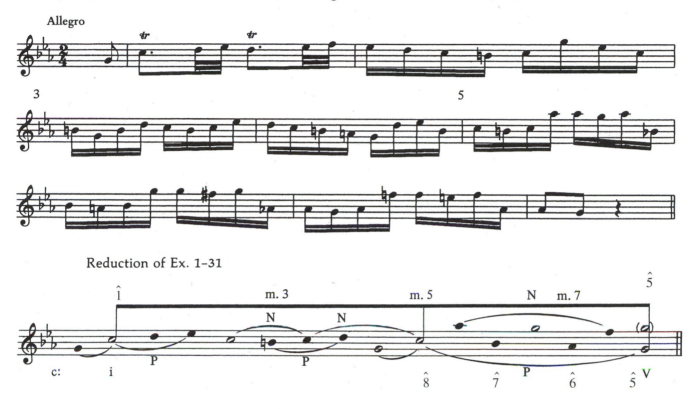

Reduction of Ex. 1–31

Comments on Example 1-31

The leading tone (B♮) ascends to the tonic (mm. 2, 3, 5) and is associated with dominant harmony. It is also used as part of a downward scale, where the harmony is clearly dominant (m. 4).

The raised submediant (A♮) is used to avoid the A2 between A♭ and B♮ (m. 4).

The subtonic (B♭) is used to lead away (down) from the tonic (mm. 5, 6).

The submediant (A♭) leads down to the dominant note (mm. 7–8).

Note the descending tonic-dominant structural line (c²–g¹) formed by the downbeats of mm. 5–8. The natural (or descending melodic) minor form is used here: C–B♭–A♭–G ($\hat{8}\ \hat{7}\ \hat{6}\ \hat{5}$).

Discussion

In the Bach style (and in tonal music generally), the minor scale is used in specific, restricted ways, depending on factors of line and harmony.

1. The *leading tone* is used to lead up to the tonic note, especially when the underlying harmony is dominant or tonic. It may also be used as part of a scale leading down from tonic to submediant, when dominant harmony is implied.

2. The *subtonic* usually leads down from tonic to submediant, as in the natural minor scale, when the underlying harmony is not dominant. The subtonic is almost never used as a lower neighbor to the tonic (except, rarely, with subdominant harmony).

3. The *raised submediant* is used either to lead up to the leading tone (as in ascending melodic minor), or as part of a descending line following the leading tone (avoiding the A2), associated with dominant harmony. It is almost never used as an upper neighbor to the dominant note.
4. The *submediant* (as in natural minor) leads down to the dominant note. It may follow the leading tone (creating an A2) or the subtonic, or may occur as an upper neighbor to the dominant.
5. The A2 between the leading tone and the submediant (as in harmonic minor) is occasionally used, normally descending in quick notes, and always with dominant harmony.

Ex. 1-32

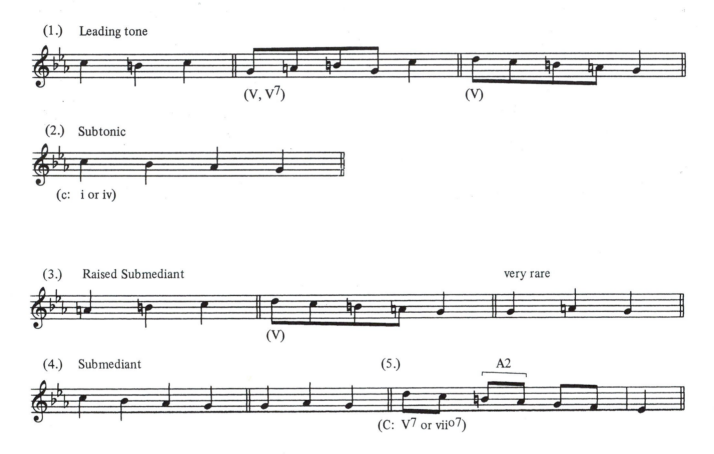

(1.) Leading tone

(V, V⁷) (V)

(2.) Subtonic

(c: i or iv)

(3.) Raised Submediant   very rare

(V)

(4.) Submediant   (5.)   A2

(C: V⁷ or vii°⁷)

It is also possible here to think in terms of the three conventional minor scale forms, though it must be understood that these have more theoretical than actual validity. The C minor scale, in actual musical practice, is:

Ex. 1-33

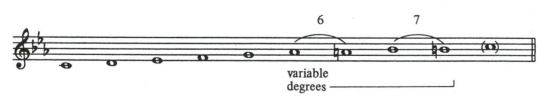

6   7

variable
degrees

The melodic minor is used most often with tonic harmony, the harmonic or ascending melodic minor with dominant, and the natural minor with the other diatonic triads, thus:

CHORD	SCALE FORM
i	melodic
V, V⁷	harmonic or ascending melodic
vii°⁷	harmonic .
ii°, III, iv, VI	natural

Ex. 1-34

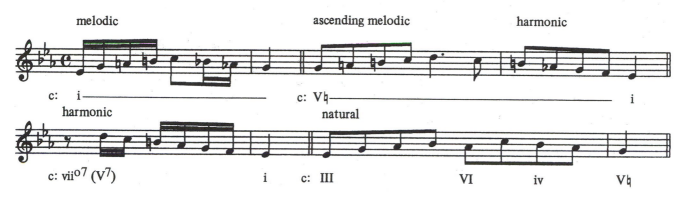

There are no such problems with the major scale, as it contains no variable degrees. Any accidentals will imply either modulation, altered chords such as secondary dominants, or non-harmonic tones, such as an occasional chromatic lower neighbor.

No scales other than major and minor are in common use in Bach.[7] Thus, use of the pentatonic scale is very rare, and whole-tone scale effects are uncommon except as incidental to the ascending melodic minor.

Ex. 1-35

Chromaticism. The use of chromatic scale segments is examined in detail later, but a brief note is appropriate here. Bach uses chromatically altered notes (the two variable degrees in minor are to be considered diatonic) with great care. A few points on their typical use follow:

1. Altered notes usually resolve in the direction of their alteration; that is, raised notes resolve up, lowered notes resolve down. See example 1-31 for several typical examples.
2. Altered notes may be either chord tones or, less commonly, nonchord tones (such as the f♯² in m. 6 and the e² in m. 7 of example 1-31, both of which are lower neighbors).
3. In his highly expressive, slow music, Bach often makes considerable use of both functional and nonfunctional chromaticism. This will be discussed separately later, in chapters 3 and 9.

Tendency Tones. It is difficult to generalize about the resolving tendencies of scale degrees, as this is very much a matter of context, but a few comments can be made here.

1. The leading tone, when in dominant harmony, usually resolves to the tonic.
2. The subdominant note usually resolves to the mediant when in a descending scale line, or as an upper neighbor or following an ascending leap.
3. The submediant in minor has a strong tendency to resolve to dominant.
4. As noted above, chromatic notes normally resolve in the direction of their alteration.

Ex. 1–36

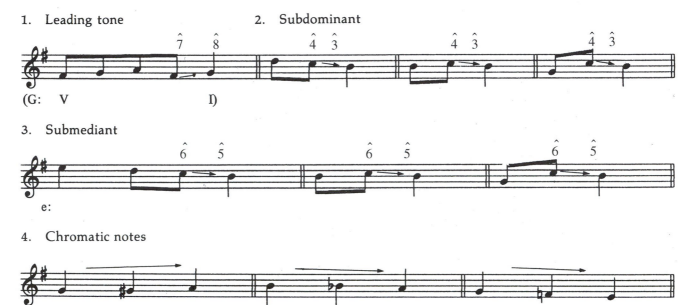

Tendency tones may resolve by *transfer* in another octave or another voice, or their resolution may be slightly *delayed*. The last voice to have a tendency tone will resolve it. Note the compound lines (typical) in the first two parts of example 1-37.

Ex. 1–37

Octave transfer of resolution (leading tone)   Delayed resolution of chord seventh

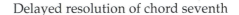

Last voice resolves leading tone.

In writing, it is necessary both to resolve melodic tendency tones normally, and to avoid overusing them. The leading tone in particular will become tedious if overemphasized in a line and will interfere with the sense of direction in a melody. The notes most often emphasized in a line are the tonic triad pitches (these will tend to be the primary structural pitches).

Exercises

1. In the Error-Detection exercises, p. 34, identify all the errors of scale, accidental, and tendency tone resolution.
2. Perform music from the anthology, as assigned by the instructor, and analyze the use of the minor scale degree variants, the function of any chromatic notes, and the resolution of melodic tendency tones.
3. Critique the following lines in terms of the treatment of the minor and other scales, and the resolution of tendency tones. Suggest ways of correcting the problems you find. These may be done by ear, away from the notation.

4. Resolve the following melodic fragments. Where alternative solutions seem possible, suggest these. These may also be done by ear, or by singing.

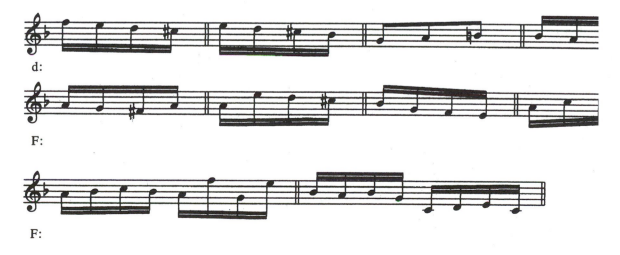

Nonharmonic (Nonchord) Tones

The investigation of the incidence and usage of nonharmonic tones is crucial to the understanding of Bach's music.[8] Their frequency of use, and the conditions of introduction, length, metric placement, and resolution, as well as whether they are diatonic or chromatic, all contribute toward a definition of this style. Bach's usage can be summarized as follows. (In this summary, dissonant and consonant nonharmonic tones are considered together.)

1. *Passing tones* (p.t.) are freely used. They fill in leaps of thirds and fourths between chord tones, by step. In this style, passing tones tend to be short, diatonic, and more often unaccented than accented (though the accented descending passing tone occurs often). They may freely ascend or descend. Two successive passing tones in a scalar figure form a common idiom.

2. *Neighbor (Auxiliary) tones* (n.t.) are also quite common, the lower neighbor more so. Like passing tones, these are normally short, unaccented, and diatonic (though the chromatic lower neighbor is possible).

3. *Anticipations* (ant.) are typical only at cadences.

4. *Suspensions* (susp.) are widely used and are a principal expressive device. They will be treated in detail in chapter 2.

5. *Appoggiaturas* (app.) are quite rare in this style, being more characteristic of later music. They are almost always diatonic and rarely last for more than one beat. The unaccented appoggiatura (called by some theorists a *cambiata*) is referred to here as an incomplete neighbor tone (i.n.t.).

6. *Escape tones* (e.t.) are fairly rare in this music. They are typically very short and are always diatonic.

7. *Pedal point* is a special device which will be taken up later. It will suffice for now to point out that pedal effects are largely restricted to the dominant and tonic notes, whether in a bass line or as part of a compound line. Pedal point is debatably nonharmonic, as it is typically the upper voices rather than the pedal that are heard as nonharmonic. In any case, the pedal note always begins and ends as a consonance.

Ex. 1–38

Some nonharmonic tones in the Bach style:

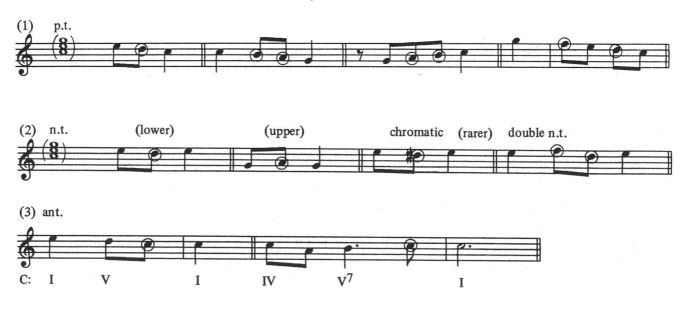

It is important to note that passing and neighboring tones may exist either on the surface (decorative or foreground) level of structure, or, as we have seen in the graphic analyses, on the middleground level. Review the analysis of example 1-31 to see typical passing and neighboring tones on the middleground level.

Exercises

1. Perform the following melody, and locate and identify the nonharmonic tones.
2. Define, in terms of approach, resolution, length, and metrical placement the following nonharmonic tones, as used in the Bach style:
   - passing tone
   - neighbor
   - escape tone
   - anticipation
   - appoggiatura
   - suspension
3. Locate and identify the nonharmonic tones in the examples beginning this chapter.
4. Perform other works of Bach in class, and lead a discussion of the nonharmonic tones, noting their frequency, length, and metric placement.

MEANS OF COHERENCE

Sample Analysis

Ex. 1–39   Flute Sonata in E Minor

Comments on Example 1-39

This melody arises from a restricted set of motivic materials, identifiable by both their rhythmic and melodic properties. How one perceives motivic content is to some extent subjective; we could hear five or more distinct ideas here, or just two ideas with their variants and extensions. The first four measures are spun out of what are identified as "a" and "b" motifs. Motif "c" (m.5) could be understood as an extension of "a" into a scale; "b‴" as a distinct idea or as derived from "b" by rhythm and shape (leap). The "d" idea may be experienced as derived from "a" and "a´," thus:

Ex. 1–40

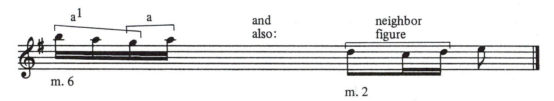

Note that the localized structural pitches of "d" are the same as for m. 1.

Ex. 1–41

Observe also how, in m. 9, the "b" motif gives rise to a typical cadential figure. In m. 10 we find both fragmentation and alternation of "d" and "b´." The "e" motif may be derived from "a‴" but is more likely heard as merely related informally by rhythm. In purely rhythmic terms, there are really only two ideas: groups of eighths and groups of sixteenths.

Transformation or *development processes* include *inversion* ("a´" is an inversion of a"), *sequence* (mm. 1–3, 6–8, 10-11, 12–13, *fragmentation* (m. 10), and *extension* (m. 5, beats 1 and 2, extends "a"; m. 8, beats 3 and 4, extends "d" and returns to "c"). You may also have noticed the highly organized descending structural pitch lines in the above melody and may wish to prepare a graphic analysis of them.

Discussion

Bach's is a highly coherent style on every level, and perhaps most clearly on the motivic one. Movements are "spun out" of the opening materials. As was mentioned on p. 11, the unit or module out of which this music grows is more characteristically the motif than the phrase. Motifs often consist of three- to five-note patterns, identifiable by their rhythm and their shape or interval content. Growth or development processes applied to these motivic units, or *cells,* include repetition; alternation of two different motifs; return after intervening material; sequences (see below for detail); fragmentation, inversion, diminution or augmentation of rhythm; retrogression; and combinations of these devices. Some of these are demonstrated below.

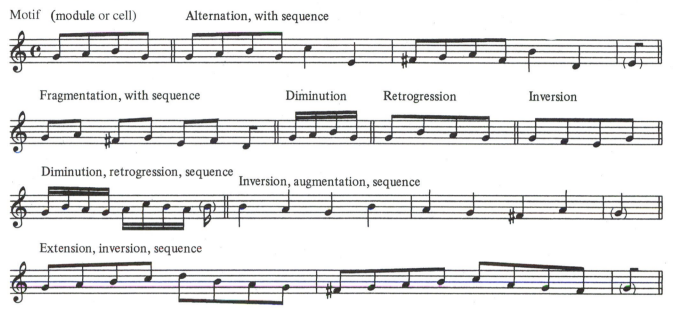

Ex. 1–42

Motif (module or cell) Alternation, with sequence

Fragmentation, with sequence Diminution Retrogression Inversion

Diminution, retrogression, sequence Inversion, augmentation, sequence

Extension, inversion, sequence

Exercise 6A on p. 37 may be done at this time.

Sequence is the most frequently used device for development in the music of Bach and his contemporaries.[9] The power of sequence lies in the fact that it embodies the two basic artistic principles of *unity* and *variety*—unity through repetition of figure, and variety through transposition. The aesthetic danger is that sequence (like repetition), if overused, leads quickly to a mechanical effect. Bach's use of sequence is quite special. The sequence unit (the melodic figure used as the basis for the sequence) is rarely heard more than three times in succession, especially if it is a relatively long unit (one measure or more). The sequence comes in a natural way out of the preceding material and is also left smoothly, most often not at the end of a unit but after the first note (or in the middle) of the next unit. In other words, the unit is typically heard twice in its entirety, with the third iteration only begun.

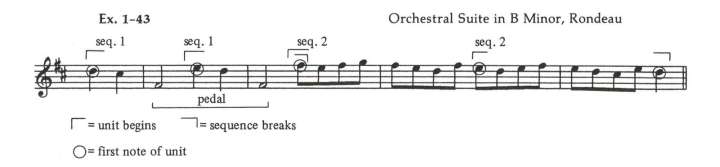

Ex. 1–43 Orchestral Suite in B Minor, Rondeau

seq. 1 seq. 1 seq. 2 seq. 2

pedal

⌐ = unit begins ¬= sequence breaks

◯ = first note of unit

The excerpt in example 1-43 begins with a *pedal sequence* in which the upper notes are sequential (rising by step), and the lower note (F♯) is a dominant pedal. A true sequence begins in m. 2, with a two-beat unit, transposed down by step. The unit is heard twice, ending with the note (d², m. 4) that would have begun the next unit were the sequence to have continued, thus ending the sequence very smoothly. The f♯² in m. 2 is both the expected subsequent note of sequence 1 and the initial note of sequence 2, a subtle *interlocking* of the two sequences. Note the clear pattern formed by the initial note of each unit, a scalar expansion of the note d².

Ex. 1-44

Here, as is normally the case, the initial note of each unit is heard as a structural pitch.

Ex. 1-45

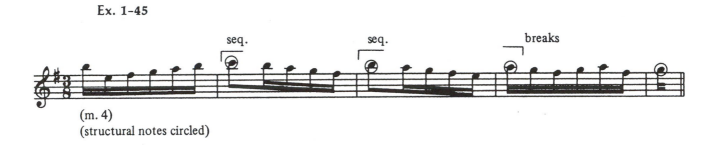

(m. 4)
(structural notes circled)

In example 1-45 a sequence begins in m. 5 (the second measure of the example) with a one-measure unit transposed down by step and heard twice. Notice that the sequence is very smoothly introduced by scale and breaks smoothly, the a² beginning m. 7 being the first note of the potential continuation of the sequence. The first note of each unit forms, typically, a very clear scalar outline.

In Bach, as compared to many of his contemporaries, the sequential unit is often relatively long and complex, sometimes two measures in length, and it often contains at least two motivic ideas in alternation (see example 1-46, mm. 5–8). The *transposition factor* (the interval by which the figure is successively transposed) varies with the musical context. Sequences are often transposed down by step or third, up by step (especially building toward climactic points), or by fourth or fifth around the circle of fifths. Once a certain transposition factor is introduced, that factor continues through the sequence, although there is an occasional exception in which the transposition changes in midsequence for linear or harmonic reasons. There are also occasional cases of what we might call pseudo-sequence, in which the rhythm is consistent from unit to unit, but the shape of the units or the intervals within them may vary slightly (see example 1-46, mm. 1–4).

Sample Sequence Analysis

Ex. 1–46   Sechs Kleine Präludien, No. 2

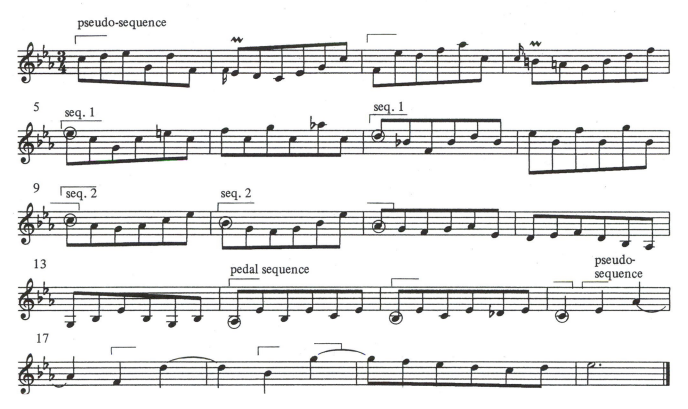

Symbology:

The beginning of each unit is shown as ⌐

The first note of each unit is circled, to indicate transposition: ◯.

The point at which the sequence breaks is shown as ⌐ .

Ex. 1–47

Reduction of Ex. 1–46, mm. 5–20.

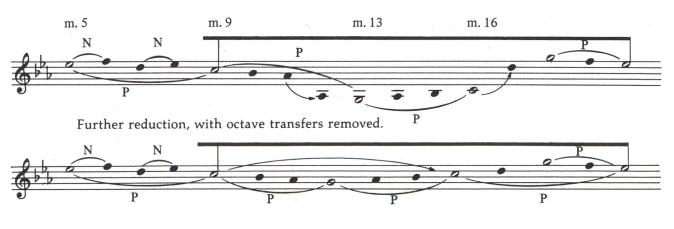

Further reduction, with octave transfers removed.

Comments

Measures 1–4 constitute a *pseudosequence* in that mm. 2 and 4 are nearly sequential, but mm. 1 and 3 are not.

A sequence begins at m. 5. It employs a two-measure unit with two different figures (very typical of Bach), heard a total of two times and transposed down by step.

Another sequence begins at m. 9. If the preceding sequence were to have continued, its next unit would have begun on the note c² in m. 9, which is in fact the first note of the second sequence. This *interlocking* of sequences is highly typical.

The second sequence has a one-measure unit, transposed down by step. This halving of the length of the second unit is also characteristic, and contributes greatly to the sense of drive or acceleration through the phrase. This unit is heard twice and again comes to the note that would have begun the third iteration (the a♭¹ at the beginning of m. 11).

Measures 14–15 have a pedal sequence, in which one implied voice is sequential while the other voice is a pedal point.

The first note of each sequential unit in mm. 5–11 forms a clearly directed descending step-wise structural line, emphasizing the new tonic note, E♭.

Exercises

1. Analyze all the sequences in the melodies beginning this chapter, as shown in example 1-46.
2. Analyze in music from the anthology, as assigned by the instructor, the motivic content and the processes of unification and variation employed, including a detailed analysis of the sequences.
3. Exercises 2–4 on pp. 34–35 may be done, in whole or part, at this time.
4. Bring into class, and perform, works of Bach; lead a discussion of motivic unity; find any instances of repetition, fragmentation, extension, inversion, and sequence.

COMPOUND LINE

Ex. 1–48   Suite III for Solo Cello, Bourrée I

Sample Analyses

Ex. 1-48A Two-voice reduction

Ex. 1-48B Three-voice reduction

Comments on Example 1-48

This music implies two, or even three, voices. One could hear an upper and a lower voice, and possibly also an independent middle voice, shown in example 1-48B in parentheses. It is often difficult in these cases to be sure which voice is represented by which note, or how many individual voices there are.

The voices are to some degree independent in terms of motivic material.

Each voice is well-shaped and motivically consistent.

Measures 1–4 constitute a near sequence in which both voices move down by step. This we will call a *type 1 compound line*.

In mm. 5–6 the lower voice is sequential but the upper voice has a pedal point. This is a *type 2 compound line*.

Discussion

Baroque instrumental music is characterized in part by the frequent use of a *compound line*. A great deal of keyboard music makes use of this device, as does much of the music written for such solo instruments as flute, violin, or cello, giving these the ability to play *implied counterpoint*. Sometimes the number of implied voices is clear; often it is not, or the voices are heard as sharing some of the same pitches. (The final d in m. 7 of ex. 1-48 may be such a note.) Each voice is musically satisfying, directional, and coherent.

There are two basic types of compound line sequences, as shown above. In type 1 (mm. 1–4), both voices move by the same transposition interval. In type 2 (mm. 5–6), one voice is a pedal point (and the sequence thus a *pedal sequence*).

Ex. 1-49

Type I

Type II

Further, the two voices may share the same motivic material, or may not, as shown in example 1-50.

Ex. 1-50

a.

(same material)

b.

(different material)

Exercise

1. Analyze more instances of compound line, as found in the examples beginning this chapter (examples 1-9 to 1-12 all contain some use of compound line), and also from the anthology, as directed by the instructor.

SUGGESTIONS FOR MELODIC WRITING

Rhythm

- clear meter through consistent placement of rhythmic motifs, patterns
- consistent flow; motivic (patterned) rhythm
- increase of motion through phrase
- change to slower motion on strong beats
- change to faster motion on weak beats (or parts of beats)
- short rests on strong part of beat
- lines cadence before longer rests
- usual ties (1:1, 2:1, 4:1, and in compound meters 3:1 and 3:2)
- no ties from shortest value; no reverse ties (1:2)
- idiomatic use of syncopation
- squareness avoided through use of rests, ties, syncopes
- motion slows toward cadence points
- motion does not stop at internal cadences

Scale

- only typical scales used
- idiomatic use of minor scale
- all tendency tones resolved normally
- idiomatic use of chromaticism (if any)
- tendency tones not emphasized in line (especially leading tone)
- whole-tone, pentatonic, or modal scale effects avoided

Line

- clear structural pitch outline
- typical stylistic figures employed for filling in between structural pitches or prolonging them
- clear phrase structure
- scale passages left by step
- idiomatic use of compound line
- repeated notes used only if motivic
- balanced use of leaps, steps
- clear and balanced contour
- larger leaps balanced by opposing melodic motion
- well-placed climax and clear approach to cadences
- typical cadential idioms, approached smoothly and set up beforehand
- no lines that are too disjunct, steep, abrupt, or flat
- successive leaps in one direction form chordal outlines
- all dissonant intervals and chromatic notes resolved
- sequences employed idiomatically
- consistent and restricted motivic material
- strong beat usually approached by step

MELODIC WRITING CHECKLIST

1. Be sure you fully understand and can apply all the points on the preceding Suggestions for Melodic Writing list before beginning the exercises below.
2. As you write, analyze all the following aspects:
   A. Structural pitches. Circle and connect with lines, or provide a structural-pitch graph, unless one has already been provided as part of the exercise.
   B. Chords and nonharmonic tones. Analyze implied harmony with Roman numerals; identify all nonharmonic tones. Analyze cadences.
   C. Sequences. Analyze all sequences as shown in this chapter.
   D. Motifs. Show on the music, or in a separate table, all motivic material, including rhythmic motifs.
3. Remember that you are writing *music,* not "theory exercises." Your work should be musically satisfying, even though it will be rather simple at the early stages of your study. Play all your work to make sure it is correctly notated and sounds as you intended. Work away from an instrument, "singing" the line internally in your head; then check the result at an instrument.

Cumulative Exercises for Melody

1. Error Detection Exercises. Play the lines below and locate and discuss the technical/stylistic errors in them. The Suggestions for Melodic Writing and the Melodic Writing Checklist above will be useful as reference materials. In all the error detection exercises, there are a great many errors. Exercise a, for instance, has more than 20 errors of style and technique.

2. Sequence writing exercises. Review the material on sequences, pp. 27–30. Continue the following sequential patterns (sequence units), using a total of two or three iterations. End the sequence smoothly and continue for one or two more measures, ending in a typical cadence idiom. Some of these may be allowed to modulate. Analyze the harmony and nonharmonic tones, and circle the structural pitches (the first note of each unit will normally be structural). Solutions can also be improvised vocally or instrumentally in class.

Example:
A. Given unit

B. One possible result:

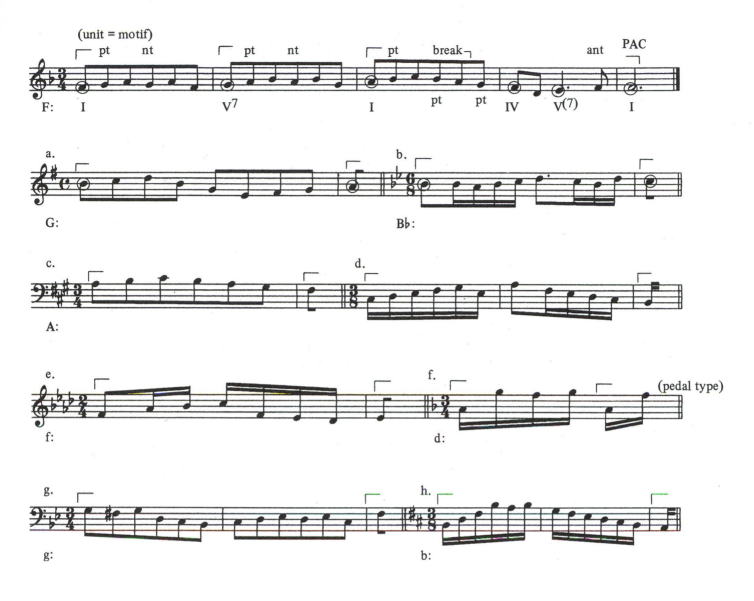

3. Sequences, based on given structural pitches. Construct or improvise sequences based on the following structural pitch frameworks. Break the sequence after the first note or two of the third iteration and continue for two to four more measures to an authentic cadence. Some may be allowed to modulate. Choose a variety of meters. Analyze fully. Refer constantly to the Suggestions and Checklist, pp. 32–33.
   A. Given framework:

𝆸 = principal structural pitch
● = secondary pitch

B. One possible result:

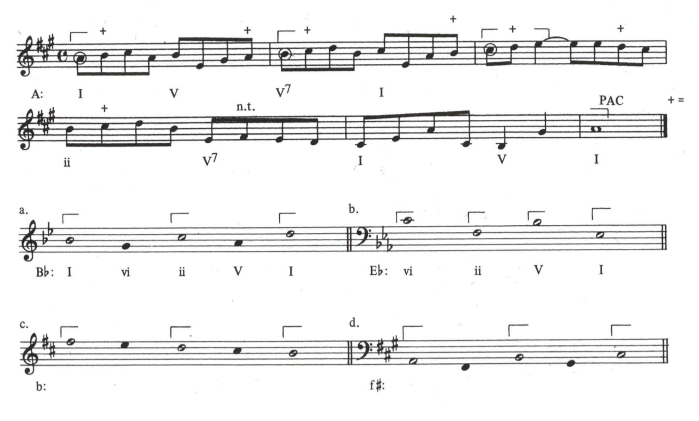

4. Sequences, based on given harmonic progressions. Compose sequences based on these chord frameworks, continuing to a cadence. Analyze fully.

a. D: ⌐vi ⌐ii ⌐V i
b. F: ⌐I V ⌐vi iii ⌐IV I V
c. G: ⌐I IV ⌐vii° iii ⌐vi ii V
d. g: ⌐i iv ⌐VII III ⌐VI ii° V

5. Compose or improvise melodies in the Bach style for instruments available in the class, based on the following pitch frameworks, and using mostly eighth notes. Analyze fully, including structural and ornamental pitches. Choose your own tempo and performance medium. Sequences are shown as ⌐. Have the Suggestions and Checklist pages (pp. 32–33) in front of you as you do this work.

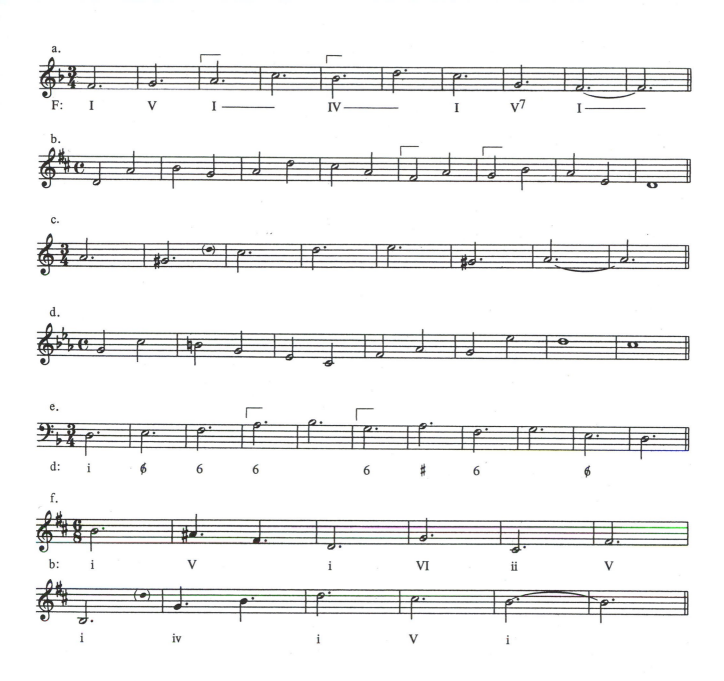

6. A. Write out these manipulations of the following motifs: inversion, retrogression, augmentation, diminution, fragmentation, extension.
   B. Treat these transformations by sequence.

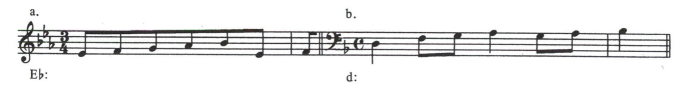

7. Spin out melodies of about 8–16 measures from the given motivic material, using instruments available in the class. End in a strong cadence. Analyze fully.

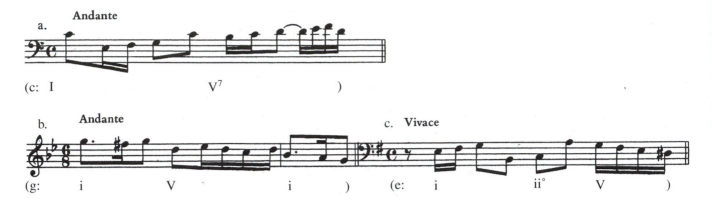

8. Write melodies in the style of Bach for instruments available in class, using the following formats (which may be slightly varied as needed). These formats may also be used for improvisation.

	Clef	Key	Meter	Tempo	Length	Modulate to:
a.	𝄞	D	C	Allegro	16 mm.	dominant
b.	𝄢	b	$\frac{3}{4}$	Andante	8 mm.	relative
c.	𝄞	B♭	₵	Moderato	16 mm.	relative
d.	𝄢	F	$\frac{6}{8}$	Adagio	8 mm.	dominant

Notes

1. The instructor is reminded that throughout the discussions in chapter 1, classes needing review of common practice theory—including harmonic functions, nonharmonic tones, cadences, modulation, and figured bass symbols—should refer to the materials on pp. 283 ff.

   Some instructors may wish to reserve discussion of those melodies employing extensive compound line (particularly exs. 1-9 and 1-11) for the section in this chapter dealing with that technique, pp. 30–32.

2. Refer to p. xx for an explanation of symbols.

3. The term *figure* is used here as synonymous with melodic or motivic *pattern*. It should not be confused with the more specific use of the term to denote particular expressive melodic devices such as the *Seufzer* or "sigh motif." See *The New Grove Dictionary of Music and Musicians,* "Affections, Doctrine of the" (vol. 1), "Figures, Doctrine of Musical" (vol. 6), "Motif" (vol. 12), and "Rhetoric and Music, III" (vol. 15).

4. Only the outer voices (oboe I and continuo) are given here. The continuo part is given only for clarification of the cadences: it is not suggested that the contrapuntal relationship between the voices be discussed at this point.

5. A period consists of two successive phrases, usually of equal length, the second one completing the musical idea begun by the first. The cadence ending the first phrase will be to some degree inconclusive (HC or IAC); the second cadence will be more final, usually a PAC. Cadence definitions are given in Appendix 1.

6. See also *The New Grove Dictionary of Music and Musicians,* "Cadence," vol. 3.

7. There are instances in which Bach uses an incomplete key signature for a work in a minor key, implying a vestigial sense of modality (most often a Dorian mode). In such works, though, accidentals obscure the feeling of modality. In other isolated examples Bach, in the course of harmonizing a modal chorale, will employ a somewhat modal harmonization (this often happens with Phrygian chorale melodies).

8. Classes needing to review the definitions of nonharmonic tones and any other aspects of harmony at this stage of study are again referred to the review materials on pp. 283 ff.

9. *Sequence* can be briefly defined as the repetition of a melodic pattern at a new pitch level.

CHAPTER 2

NONIMITATIVE TWO-VOICE WRITING

Perform the following two-voice music of Bach, repeating each passage until you are familiar with it. Then play each voice by itself to gain an appreciation of the individual lines. These excerpts can be performed, as Bach intended, on a keyboard instrument (preferably harpsichord), or on two separate instruments such as flute (or violin or oboe) and cello (or bassoon)—whatever is available in the class.

Ex. 2–1   French Suite II, Menuet

Ex. 2-4   French Suite III, Menuet (mm. 1–16)

Ex. 2-5   English Suite III, Gavotte I (mm. 1–8)

GENERAL OBSERVATIONS

Directed Study

Based on what you hear and see in examples 2-1 through 2-5, what would you say it is, in general terms, that makes this good counterpoint?[1] Are the voices individually satisfying? Do they make sense as independent musical lines? Are they always of equal interest and importance, or are there moments when one voice seems supportive? If so, under what conditions does this happen? In what ways do the voices relate, in terms of the musical materials they share? In what ways, generally speaking, are they kept distinct from each other?

Discussion

The music of Bach embodies all the fundamental principles of good counterpoint. These include:

1. *Integrity* of the individual voices. Each voice is a satisfying line with the characteristics of melody discussed in chapter 1. Each is coherent motivically, well-shaped, and clear in meter and harmony.

2. *Equality or near equality* of both voices. There are times at which one voice will dominate because of its rhythmic activity, but there is little feeling overall that the lower voice is merely harmonic or figurative support. This will, of course, vary to some degree with the movement under discussion.

    We are dealing now with nonimitative dance movements, which will tend to be somewhat more homophonic than imitative works. Compare, for instance, examples 2-4 and 2-5 above in terms of the function and importance of the lower voice.

3. *Consistency* of materials between the voices. Even when the same materials are not literally shared, as they would be in imitative works, still both voices will share the same general thematic content, especially when both are of equal importance. For instance, in example 2-1, the voices both have some of the same musical ideas, but they also have their own independent motifs. One might understand the motivic content of mm. 1–4 as follows:

Ex. 2–6

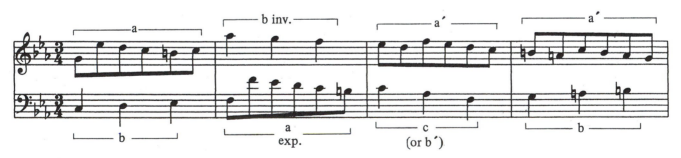

There will in any case be substantial metric, intervallic, and harmonic agreement between the voices.

4. Considerable *independence* of line. While the voices must interrelate successfully, they must also exhibit individual identity. They will be to some extent distinct from each other in terms of rhythmic activity, shape, and (at times) motivic content.

SPECIFIC DETAILS OF VOICE RELATIONSHIPS

Contour (Shape); Relative Motion

Directed Study

Look at how, in the music beginning this chapter, the general contours of the voices relate to each other. Note the overall melodic shapes within each four- and eight-bar phrase, each two-bar group, and finally within each bar. Prepare contour graphs of the voices, as suggested on p. 44.

Next, consider these relationships in more detail. Count from beat to beat, and also from the end of each divided beat to the beginning of the next, the incidence of the four possible relative-motion types: contrary, oblique, similar, and parallel (see example 2-8). Use the format suggested in example 2-7, or one given by the instructor. Prepare a summary of your findings. What generalizations can you make concerning the use and relative frequency of the four types? Focus especially on parallel motion. Which intervals are used consecutively? Which are not?

Sample Analysis and Discussion

Ex. 2–7   French Suite II, Courante (mm. 1–24)

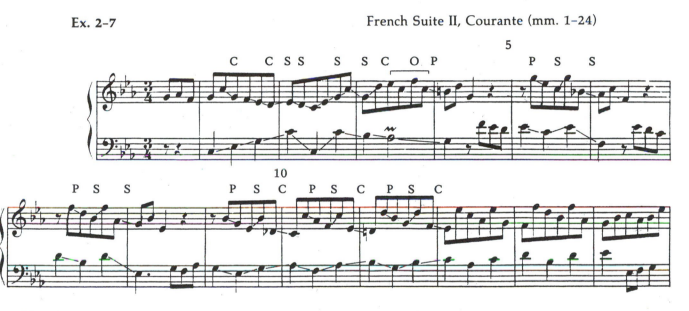

Here is a contour graph of Ex. 2–7, mm. 1–4:

Upper voice:
Lower voice:

Notice that the shapes of the two lines contain both similar and contrary elements. The voices will usually exhibit some degree of independence of shape, as contours that are too consistently similar will not make for effective counterpoint.

In example 2-7 the beat-to-beat relative motions have been shown for mm. 1–11, symbolized as c (contrary), s (similar), o (oblique), and p (parallel). These four types can be shown in a simplified form as follows[2]:

Ex. 2–8

In contrary motion, the voices move in opposite directions; in similar, the same direction but by different melodic intervals; in oblique, one is stationary while the other moves; and in parallel, both move in the same direction by the same interval type.

In the music at the beginning of this chapter there is a mixture of all these directional types, with no strong preponderance of any one.[3] One might suppose that contrary motion would prevail, as this best distinguishes one voice from another. But the attempt to achieve constant contrary motion will result in poor lines. Oblique motion, resulting as it does when one voice become stationary, should not be overused, and will occur largely in passages involving pedal point. Similar motion is freely used, with the following cautions:

1. Both voices in a two-voice texture will rarely leap in similar motion into a P5 or P8. This is known as *direct fifths* or *direct octaves*, and is heard as detracting from the independence of the voices, due perhaps to the acoustically "open" sound of the P5 and P8.
2. Both voices will occasionally move by similar motion into a P8 or P5 if the upper voice moves *by step*. This is especially typical at cadences.

Ex. 2–9

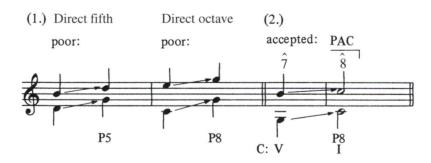

It is in the matter of parallel motion that Bach exercised the most care. His practice can be reduced to the following observations:

1. Parallel (consecutive) thirds and sixths (and their compounds, tenths and thirteenths) are freely used, though it is unusual to find a total of more than five or six in succession, as this detracts seriously from independence. The second idiom below is avoided, unless the implied tritone can be resolved.

Ex. 2-10

poor: (too many parallels)

poor: A4   A4   acceptable: A4

A4 not resolved   A4 resolved

2. *Parallel dissonant intervals,* such as fourths, sevenths and seconds, are very rare in two-voice writing. They occasionally occur as the result of nonharmonic tone activity, as shown in example 2-11.

Ex. 2-11

not normally found in two voices: possible:

P4 A4 (resolved)   or   M7   m7

p.t.   n.t.

3. *Parallel perfect fifths* are not found in his music, nor are fifths by contrary motion.[4] Further, fifths on successive *strong* beats (or strong parts of beats) are not used, though fifths falling on successive *weak* beats (or parts) are possible.

Ex. 2-12

A. Not found: contrary fifths
parallel fifths

consecutive strong fifths   or

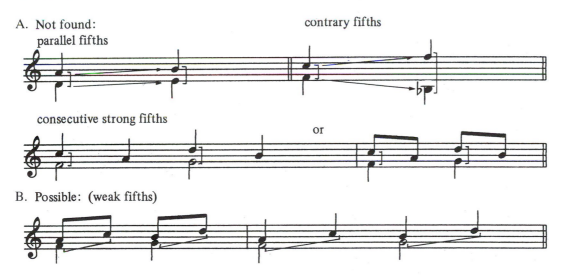

B. Possible: (weak fifths)

4. *Unequal fifths* are occasionally found, though rarely in two-voice texture. They almost always progress as follows: P5 → d5 → 3.

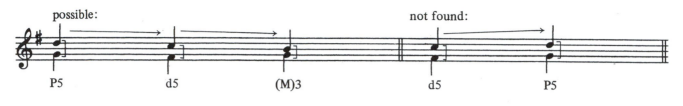

P5   d5   (M)3   d5   P5

5. *Parallel* or *contrary octaves* or *unisons* are also avoided as even more harmful to linear independence than parallel fifths. These parallel motions between independent voices should not be confused with the *acoustical doubling* at the octave or unison of a *single voice* for textural relief and strengthening of line, as so often happens in piano and orchestral writing.

Ex. 2–14

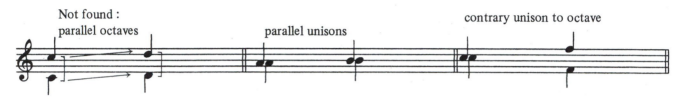

6. Nonharmonic tones cannot be employed to correct an otherwise objectionable parallel motion, as the underlying poor counterpoint is still apparent to the ear:

Ex. 2–15

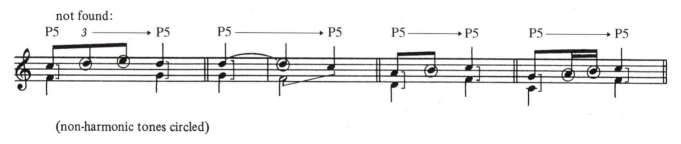

(non-harmonic tones circled)

Exercises

1. Perform and analyze excerpts from two voice works found in the anthology, pp. 301 ff. Analyze the directional and intervallic relationships between voices. Be especially alert to any parallel intervals; how are they treated?
2. Write in two voices, on two staves (bass and treble), brief, isolated examples showing:
   direct fifths
   direct octaves

parallel dissonances
parallel and contrary fifths
parallel and contrary octaves
incorrectly treated unequal fifths

3. Locate and explain the errors of line and counterpoint in the following example. There are at least eleven errors.

Rhythmic Relationship

Directed Study

In the musical excerpts beginning this chapter, observe how the voices relate rhythmically to one another. Are both voices equally active? Note where they move in the same values; for how many beats does this continue? When they do not move in the same value, what is the usual ratio between their values? Is the subdivision unit (eighth or sixteenth note) normally present in at least one voice? Is it often present simultaneously in both voices? Do the voices share some of the same rhythmic motifs? Is there any feeling of acceleration in rhythmic activity through the phrase?

Discussion

The rhythmic aspect of two-voice counterpoint in this style is not complex. You have observed that, in examples 2-1 through 2-5, the two voices are of roughly equal activity, except when the lower voice functions as a relatively slow-moving bass line (as in example 2-4, parts of example 2-1, and in general at cadential points). The bass line may become active at internal cadences, carrying the motion into the next phrase (example 2-1, first ending; example 2-4, m. 8). Otherwise, there is considerable equality of rhythmic importance and a tendency to share between the voices all important rhythmic material, quite often by a process of alternation (example 2-1, mm. 1–2; example 2-5, mm. 1–4). The voices rarely progress in the same note values for more than a few beats. In these cases they usually share the subdivision value (the largest division of the beat) nearing cadence points, for the effect of a rhythmic and textural climax (example 2-2, mm. 11–12; example 2-4, m. 8; example 2-5, m. 7). The subdivision value, once established, is always present in at least one voice, except at strong authentic cadences (example 2-1, second ending; example 2-4, m. 16). The steady motion (*resultant rhythm* or *macrorhythm*) that results is an essential feature of the style.

The preponderant ratio of values between the voices is 2:1, with one voice using the beat unit and the other the subdivision (that is, quarters against eighths, or eighths against sixteenths). In compound meters, obviously, the usual ratio will be 3:1 (for instance, a beat unit of ♩. and a subdivision unit of ♪). We will concentrate in our written work initially on these basic ratios.

As noted in chapter 1, the tie into, or short rest on, the beginning of a beat in one voice is a very useful device for ensuring flexibility, as long as the other voice moves into that beat. If both voices constantly move into each beat, the result will be plodding and overemphatic; but if neither voice moves, the pulse will be absent, an unstylistic effect.

Exercises

Perform and prepare outlines of the rhythms of several selected two-voice excerpts, as assigned by the instructor. The following suggested format shows a rhythmic outline of example 2-1, mm. 1–3.

Then perform these outlines in class, conducting the meter and intoning the rhythms on a neutral syllable such as "ta." Perform each voice separately, then both voices together. Discuss what you observe.

Spacing; Crossing; Overlapping; Range

Directed Study

In the examples beginning this chapter and in music selected from the anthology, note the distance the voices generally are from each other. What is the widest interval you observe? Do they often remain widely separated (say, more than two octaves distance)? Are the voices kept distinct from each other by registrar placement? Are their registers allowed to become and remain very close (say, within an octave) for long? Do you observe any crossing of voices? What are the highest and lowest pitches used? What is the range, generally speaking, of each voice?

Discussion

Bach is very careful to keep the voices in separate registers. Wide spacings predominate in his two-voice keyboard writing. The voices are often two to three octaves apart, though they rarely remain very widely spaced for more than a measure or two at a time, tending to come back together by contrary motion. The extreme registers are used to set up a "registral tension" that is released through the answering use of the middle registers (example 2-3, mm. 1–4; example 2-5, mm. 1–3). On the other hand, the voices rarely share a register for long, as this makes it difficult for the ear to distinguish them. Both voices will occasionally rise together into their highest registers for a climactic effect (example 2-2, mm. 3–6). Voice crossing in two voices is very rare, as it obscures the voices. Likewise, overlapping is to be avoided at this stage.[5]

Ex. 2–16

In two-voice writing, whether for keyboard or high and low instruments, it will be well to consider the two voices as having roughly these ranges:

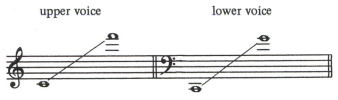

upper voice   lower voice

The upper voice may occasionally go slightly lower, and the lower voice slightly higher, but not for sustained passages. The outer limits (Great C to f³) are those of most of Bach's keyboards and should be strictly observed. Obviously, when writing for specific instruments available in the class, their particular ranges will have to be observed.

Vertical (Harmonic) Intervals

Directed Study

Make an analysis of the harmonic intervals between the voices in some of the excerpts above, as selected by the instructor. Note first the intervals on the beginning of each beat, then those within the beat (if there are subdivisions present). Which intervals predominate? Which are not found, or are found only rarely? Of these rarer intervals, note carefully where they fall metrically: are they in short or long values, weak or strong metrically? Where are the perfect intervals (P1, P5, P8, and their compounds) placed? How are dissonant intervals (A and d intervals; seconds, sevenths, P4) treated in terms of length, strength, approach, resolution? Can you analyze these dissonances as typical nonharmonic tones?

Sample Analysis

Ex. 2-18   French Suite II, Menuet (mm. 1-8)

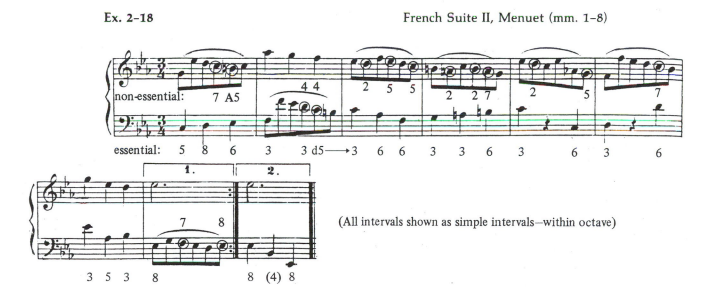

(All intervals shown as simple intervals—within octave)

Comments on example 2-18

The most used essential intervals are the major and minor thirds and sixths (and their compounds), the so-called imperfect consonances.

The perfect consonances (P5, P8, P1) are found at the beginning and cadence, and on weak beats or parts of beats.[6]

The circled tones are those that might be heard as nonessential (nonharmonic) tones, depending on one's perception of the underlying harmonic structure.

Note the large number of weak-beat dissonances (seconds, sevenths, fourths). Passing tones predominate.[7]

The only essential diminished interval (the d5 in m. 2) resolves normally (to a third, m. 3, beat 1).

Discussion

The control of harmonic intervals is a major contributor to the coherence of this music; it is also a chief source of its forward propulsion through the *principle of tension and release*. Considerable attention must be paid to it in analytical and written work.

Example 2-18 is characteristic of Bach in its repertoire of harmonic intervals. This repertoire can be summarized as follows:

1. *Imperfect consonances* predominate, especially on strong beats and beginnings of beats. A two-voice skeletal structure of successive major and minor tenths (or seventeenths) often lies behind the surface of this music, as will be demonstrated later. The imperfect consonances are the M3, m3, M6, m6, and their compounds. These intervals are pleasing to the ear, yet not totally lacking in harmonic tension. They are stable, yet not so stable as to be static. The only restriction on their use is, as noted earlier, that there should not be too many parallel thirds or sixths in succession.

2. *Perfect consonances* are found mainly at beginnings and cadences, or on weak beats or parts of beats. The unison and octave in particular are avoided as lacking in harmonic tension and thus are not useful in distinguishing the voices. Perfect consonances are very rarely used in succession (although the succession P5→P8 is often found at authentic cadences, where the upper voice moves from $\hat{2}$ to $\hat{1}$.

3. *Dissonances* are a chief source of tension in this music and contribute greatly to its effectiveness. The aural requirement for the release of this tension helps drive the music forward. Still, as this is an essentially consonant style, dissonances are used with considerable care. For Bach, the dissonant (tense, unstable) harmonic intervals are: all d and A intervals (most often the d5 and A4), seconds, sevenths, the P4, and their compounds.[8] All dissonant intervals are treated as involving nonharmonic tones or chord sevenths, and are thus approached and left in precisely controlled ways, as discussed in chapter 1.

Ex. 2-19

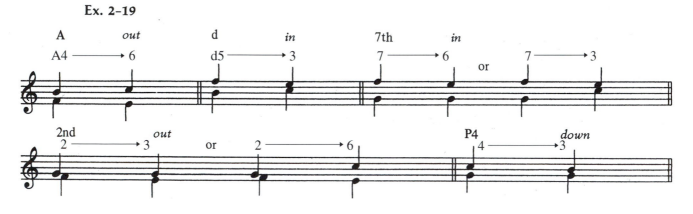

To review:
These strict resolutions are subject to the usual variations of delay and transfer discussed on p. 22.

Some comments on detail follow.

The d and A intervals, as well as the M2 and m7 are often associated with dominant harmony (V7 or vii°7) and may thus be essential intervals (that is, involving chord tones). Note in example 2-19 that all the dissonant intervals (except the P4) are part of a dominant seventh chord built on G.

In two voice writing, the A2 and d7 are rarely used as harmonic intervals; they resolve to the P4 and P5, respectively.

Ex. 2–20

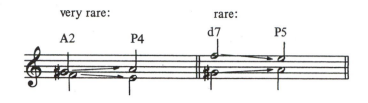

It must be kept in mind that the P4 is a dissonance in two-voice writing, normally requiring resolution into a third. It is usually heard and treated as a nonharmonic tone, or may (more rarely) be found in a $\frac{6}{4}$ effect, or associated with an arpeggiated triad. See p. 57 for more details. Typical treatments of the P4:

Ex. 2–21

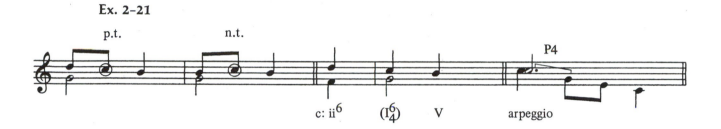

With very few exceptions, dissonances resolve *by step* to *imperfect consonances*. This is an issue of harmonic tension, as a phrase typically moves from perfect consonance to imperfect to dissonance back to imperfect, and finally returns at the cadence to perfect, embodying the tension-relaxation principle.

Perfect consonance	Imperfect consonance	Dissonance	Imperfect consonance	Perfect consonance

Tension level:

Here is a table of intervals, showing the typical usages[9]:

	Consonances (Stable)
M3, m3, M6, m6	freely used, except not as final sonority in this style
P5	beginning; weak beats or parts of beats; half cadences
P8, P1	same as P5, though slightly rarer; final cadences

Most Common Dissonances (Unstable)	
Interval	*Usual resolution to:*
P4	third
M2, m2	third or sixth
M7, m7	sixth or third
A4	sixth
d5	third

Exercises

1. Prepare tables of intervals as found in selected two-voice works from the anthology or from example 2, 1–5. Note statistically the relative frequency of the various interval types and their length and metric strength. Note the resolutions of all dissonances. The following tabular format may be employed:

Interval type	Frequency	Metric placement	Usual length	Resolution
P4	5 times	weak beat or part	♩ or ♪	into third
d5	1 time	weak part of beat	♪	into third

2. Critique the following examples in terms of the incidence and treatment of harmonic intervals.

a.

b.

3. Critique the error-detection exercises on p. 66 in terms of the frequency and treatment of harmonic intervals.
4. Resolve the following intervals; analyze all intervals. This can be done as an ear-training exercise.

Harmony and Nonharmonic Tones

Directed Study

Analyze the harmony in selected excerpts from the beginning of this chapter and from selected two-voice works in the anthology (excepting works with a great deal of chromaticism).[10] Be aware of such matters as cadences, harmonic rhythm, chord vocabulary and function, chord inversions, clarity of harmonic structure (is it always clear what the harmonies are?), use of altered chords, modulation (where; to what keys; by what means?), and doubling and nonharmonic tones. At this point, appendix 1 (p. 283), and the introduction (p. xix) may be reviewed.

Sample Analysis   (+ = nonharmonic tone)

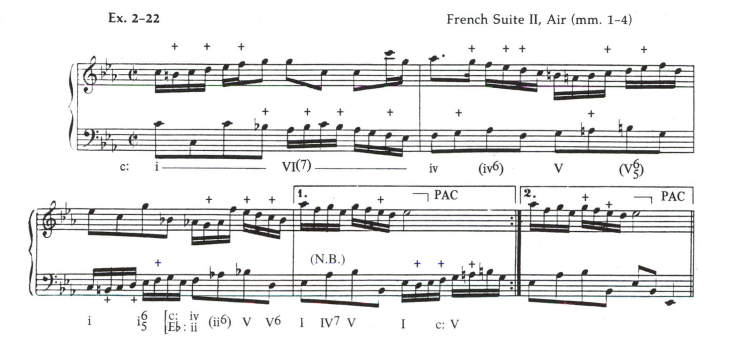

Ex. 2–22   French Suite II, Air (mm. 1–4)

Comments on example 2-22

The vocabulary is entirely diatonic. There is a common-chord modulation in m. 3 to the relative major, and a remodulation in the first ending, returning to tonic. The cadence in m. 4 is a PAC in E♭.

The harmonic rhythm is slow (every two beats) in mm. 1–2, increasing in speed in mm. 3–4.

The progressions are typical, largely based on the downward chain of thirds and the circle of fifths (roots: C–A♭–F–G–C–F–B♭–E♭). All chords have their common resolutions.

Most chords are in root position; all strong beats have root position chords. The first inversion usages are typical for the style and are placed on weak beats or parts of beats.

The harmony is generally unambiguous, though the presence of some passing tones in the lower voice (m. 1, beat 2; m. 2, off beats 1 and 2) might lead to some disagreements about analysis. Measure 4, beat 1, because of a subtle "out of phase" effect caused by the nonharmonic tones, is slightly vague as to harmony. Discuss this bar in class.

Most chords are represented by a root in the lower voice on a strong beat. Doubling is most often of the root. There are a root and a third present on *almost* every beat.

In the following reduction, notice the simplicity and linear/harmonic/intervallic strength of the two-voice skeleton, and the placement of vertical tenths (or seventeenths) on most strong beats. Play the reduction, then the excerpt again.

Ex. 2–23

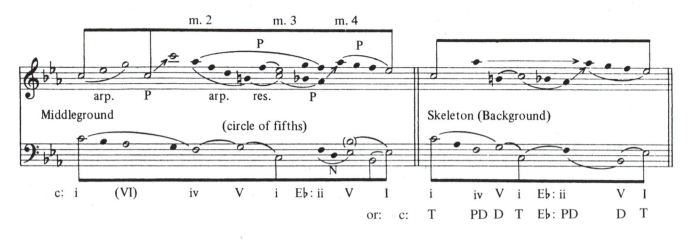

Discussion

A review of harmony and related elements is given on pp. 283 ff. This material must be mastered. A few additional comments are appropriate at this point.

1. Remember that common progression predominates in this music; that the harmonic rhythm is quite regular, often accelerating toward the cadence; that chords change on strong beats; that diatonic chords make up most of the vocabulary; and that modulations are most often to the dominant and relative keys.

2. Bach's harmonic vocabulary is more complex, dissonant, and highly colored (through the use of altered chords, especially diminished sevenths) than that of most of his contemporaries, yet tension rather than color is the principal motivation for the harmony. A typical phrase or section starts consonantly and diatonically, grows more complex as the music moves forward (moving away from tonic harmony; introducing more dissonance, seventh chords, altered chords), and becomes again relatively stable (triadic, diatonic, tonally clear) at the cadence. Thus, the harmonic/tensional shape of the phrase can be roughly graphed as ⌢, a mirror of and supporting element for the other shaping processes in this music, such as line, rhythmic activity, and texture.

3. **Harmonic Clarity; Doubling**. The harmony is largely unambiguous, due to contextual factors. Yet in two-voice textures some ambiguity may occur. For instance, the harmonic interval a^1–c^2 can imply triads or seventh chords, built on a^1 or f^1, or a seventh chord built on d^1. Context alone will determine which of these possibilities is heard.

Ex. 2–24

As you have seen, a third (tenth) usually implies the root and third of a triad. In two voices, this is the most common sound, especially on the beat. A third from chord third to chord fifth is also found quite often. The P5 from root to fifth is rarely used on a strong beat or fraction, as the sound of the "open" fifth is relatively weak. A unison or octave will usually imply a doubled chord root, found most often at beginnings and at cadences. Thus, the sonorities that may imply a C-major triad are as follows:

Ex. 2-25

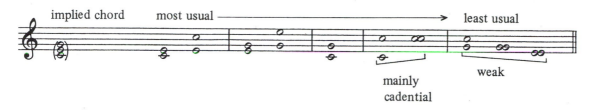

DOUBLING. Any note of a chord or scale may of course be doubled, yet it is possible to generalize somewhat. Chord roots are most often doubled, other chord members less so. Strong scale degrees (especially 1, 4, and 5; less so 2, 3, and 6) are freely doubled. Above all, *tendency tones are rarely doubled* in thin textures, especially on the beat; that is, one rarely finds a doubling of the leading tone, or of any accidental, or of the seventh or ninth of a chord. Unusual doublings are typically due to factors of line. In such cases these doublings are brief and metrically weak.

4. **Cadences**. We have already studied the typical cadential melodic figures in this style (see pp. 11–12). It is now appropriate to investigate bass-line cadential idioms. You have noticed in the music beginning this chapter that the bass voice has very specific and limited melodic/harmonic functions approaching a cadence. Some of the most common cadential bass lines in this style are:

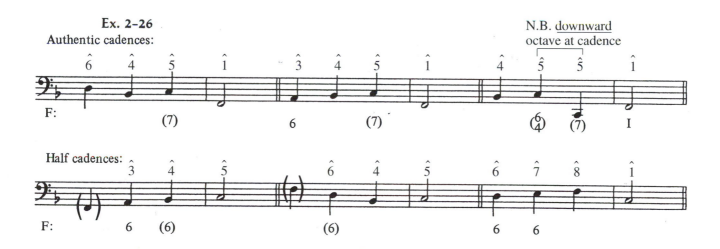

5. Inversions.

A. First inversion. You have observed in the music under study that first inversions are used quite often.[11] First inversion is necessary for (indeed, may be said to arise out of) strong bass lines, and has the additional advantage of "lightening" the harmony and increasing forward momentum. Overuse of root position results in disjunct and awkward bass lines and overstable harmony, lacking in momentum. While root position chords tend to occupy the strong beats, first inversion is widely used elsewhere (that is, weak beats and fractions), and in mid-phrase even on strong beats. Phrases tend to begin and end with root position triads for stability. Any triad may be used in first inversion, but the most usual are I^6, V^6, ii^6, and vii^{o6}. In other words, vi and iii are quite rare in this style. Some typical idioms follow:

(parenthetic notes are optional)

In the idioms above, V^6_5 may substitute for V^6, and ii^6_5 for ii^6. Note that in the majority of these idioms the bass in the first inversion chord resolves *by step* (often up) into the root or third of the following chord. Observe the strongly linear character of these bass lines.

B. Second inversion. Second inversion ($^6_4$) triads are used very sparingly in this music. This is especially true in two voices, since the triad can only be hinted at and since the fourth is a dissonant interval. Most often, as in example 2 28, $^6_4$ effects occur within simple prolongations of T, D, or PD harmony. The only triads found in second inversion in most Bach works are I$^6_4$, V$^6_4$, and (more rarely) IV$^6_4$; their occurrences are limited to the following idioms:

Ex. 2-28

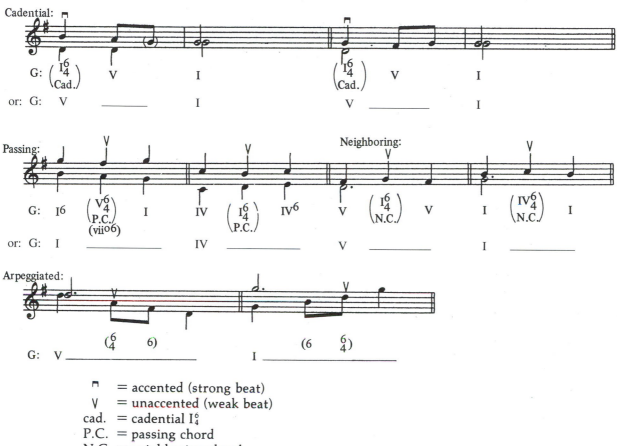

⊓   = accented (strong beat)
∨   = unaccented (weak beat)
cad. = cadential I$^6_4$
P.C. = passing chord
N.C. = neighboring chord

Some theorists doubt that the "$^6_4$ chord" can even be said to exist in this music, especially in thin textures. This is expressed through the use of parentheses around the analytic symbols for these chords. Parentheses are often used when linear chords (those arising from nonharmonic tones) are implied. In such cases, the notes implying the $^6_4$ can often be appropriately analyzed as nonharmonic tones, at the instructor's discretion.[12]

In your own writing, be sure to use $^6_4$ implications very carefully, and always analyze every such chord you write in terms of its function, as above. Always remember that the P4 is a dissonance.

6. **Seventh chords; altered chords.** A seventh chord may be built on any scale degree. The most usual in this style are V[7], vii°[7] (much more often than vii°[7]), and ii[7] (especially in first inversion, at cadences). Seventh chords built on other scale degrees are possible, but are characteristic only in diatonic circle-of-fifths sequences. Again, they are more common in thicker textures. They are most often found in root position and first inver-

sion (especially V^6_5 and ii$^6_5$), although the V^7 may be found in every possible position in Bach. The following is a framework model of a diatonic circle-of-fifths sequence, alternating triads and diatonic seventh chords. Observe in example 2-29 that the upper voice alternately sounds the third of one chord and then the seventh of the next chord, and moves down by step. Note also the common linear-intervallic pattern 10–7–10–7. This is very typical part writing of the circle-of-fifths sequence. Note too that every other note of a circle-of-fifths bass line forms a descending scalar line.

Ex. 2–29

Here are three of the many possible motivic elaborations of the framework above:

Ex. 2–30

Even though Bach uses the altered chords shown on the chart on p. 283, it is best at this stage of study to employ them only sparingly in one's writing, limiting usage to an occasional secondary dominant chord, resolved normally.

7. **Nonharmonic tones** (more detail). In your harmonic analysis of the excerpts beginning this chapter, you have noticed the types of nonharmonic tones discussed in chapter 1 (pp. 23–24). A few further points should now be made:

A. Not all nonharmonic tones are dissonant, nor are all dissonances nonharmonic,[13] as is shown in the following sketch:

Ex. 2–31

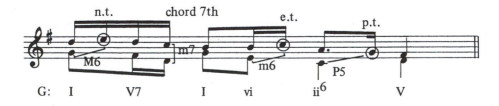

The Craft of Tonal Counterpoint

B. Multiple nonharmonic tones may produce momentary ambiguities of harmonic implication. Therefore, be careful in your own writing to use only those nonharmonic tone idioms employed by Bach, and only in the ways in which he uses them, in terms of length, accentuation, and resolution.

C. Except for the escape tone, all nonharmonic tones resolve *stepwise*, and all involve relatively short notes (except for the pedal point, which is debatably nonharmonic). The only accented nonharmonic tones are the suspension, accented passing tone, and appoggiatura.

D. Simultaneously moving nonharmonic tones are most often consonant with each other

Ex. 2–32

When nonharmonic tones in both voices dissonate, the result can easily obscure the harmony and cause too much harmonic tension. Such cases occur typically with short, weak notes.

8. **The suspension figure.** The suspension is a powerful device for producing expressive tension, embodying as it does the essential aesthetic principle of tension and release. It is one of the accented dissonances, and therefore is especially striking. Because it displaces an expected chord tone in time, it gives metric flexibility while creating psychological tension through delayed resolution.

   Suspensions are rather more complex than the other nonharmonic tones, requiring three elements: a consonant *preparation* note (P), dissonance on the same pitch on a strong beat, which is the *suspension* note (S), and *resolution* (R) by step, normally down.

Ex. 2–33

Suspensions are categorized by the intervals formed between the voices at the points of dissonance and resolution. The 7-6, 4-3, and 2-3 (lower voice) suspensions are by far the most common in two voices; the 9-8 is less so. The 2-1 is very rare, as it has the effect of obscuring the voices; the 6-5 is not a true suspension, as the sixth is not a dissonance, and is therefore little used.

Ex. 2-34

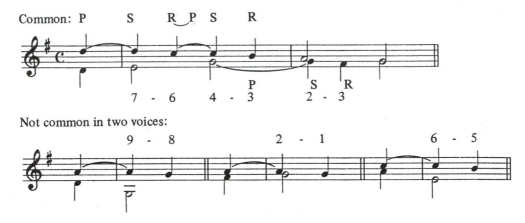

Common: P   S   R P S   R

7 - 6   4 - 3   2 - 3
                  P   S R

Not common in two voices:

9 - 8   2 - 1   6 - 5

Here are some technical details regarding the treatment of suspensions in this style.

A. Suspensions are often *ornamented* at the point of resolution. Some of Bach's characteristic ornaments are shown below in brackets, ornamenting example 2-34. Both the leap down to a consonant note before the resolution ①, and the lower-neighbor figure ②, are typical.

Ex. 2-35

B. *Suspension chains* are fairly common in Bach. These are normally part of a sequential passage, and thus should not be carried on too long. Note the descending stepwise structure, characteristic of passages employing suspensions.

Ex. 2-36

LIP: 7 - 6   7 - 6   7 - 6   (shown unornamented)

C. Another common variant is to let the consonant (the nonsuspending) voice move at the point of resolution, often leaping up a fourth or down a fifth in a series of circle-of-fifths sequential progressions. This leap is always to a note consonant with the resolution.

Ex. 2-37

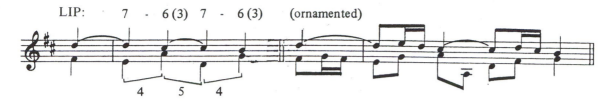

LIP: 7 - 6 (3) 7 - 6 (3)   (ornamented)

4   5   4

D. *Ties.* It will be recalled that ties are commonly used in a ratio of 1:1, 2:1, 3:1, or 4:1. Thus, the note of preparation will be at least as long as the suspension. In few cases is the preparation shorter than an eighth note.

Ex. 2-38

Common: 2:1   1:1   4:1   not found: 1:2   1:2

prep. too short

E. The *upward-resolving* suspension (or "retardation," as some term it) is rare in Bach, reserved mainly for very slow, expressive movements. It becomes very common later in the Viennese classical style.

These are some common mistakes in the use of suspensions:
    i.   using a suspension to attempt to avoid an incorrect parallelism ①
    ii.   a 4-3 suspension using an A4 rather than a P4 ②
    iii   leaping into a resolution ③
    iv.   a dissonant resolution ④
    v.   upward resolution (rare) ⑤
    vi.   incorrect metric placement (dissonance on *weak* beat) ⑥

Ex. 2-39

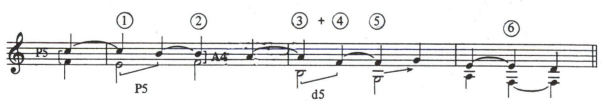

① ② ③ + ④ ⑤ ⑥

P5   P5   A4   d5

A NOTE ON COMPOUND METER

Most of the music examined thus far has been in simple meters, with durational ratios between voices of 1:1, 2:1, and 4:1. There are no new technical observations concerning 3:1 counterpoint. A few brief examples will suffice, shown as elaborations of 1:1 models. In the examples below, note the use of passing, neighboring, and (more rarely) arpeggiated motion to prolong or connect between the model pitches. These elaborations are, of course, only some of those possible in the style; the choice of a particular figure will as always depend on factors of motif, harmony, genre, tempo, and affect. Motivic unity and consistency within a given movement continue to be of primary importance.

Ex. 2-40

Exercises

1. Analyze two-voice works selected from the anthology, focusing on harmony and non-harmonic tones, as suggested on pp. 49 ff. Be sure to attempt two-voice structural pitch reductions, as these are revealing of underlying linear organization. Also analyze the structural harmony, cadences, and all instances of *patterning* (linear-intervallic patterns and sequence).

2. Determine which triads and seventh chords could be implied by the interval d^1–f^1.

3. In the key of B♭, which note is least likely to be doubled? Which note in G minor? Which notes on both keys are most likely to be doubled?

4. Write authentic and half cadence bass lines (of three or four notes) in the keys of D, c, B♭ and e. Use figured bass symbols and analyze the implied harmonies. Show scale degrees.

5. Write bass lines in the keys of d and F, showing eight typical first inversion usages in each key. Use figured bass symbols and show scale degrees.

6. Embellish example 2-37 with eighth and sixteenth notes, showing several typical ornamentations of the suspensions. Work for a clear sequence and limited motivic content.

7. Compose a brief two-voice example in a simple texture, showing the 4-3, 7-6, and 2-3 suspensions, with typically ornamented resolutions.

8. Find and discuss the many technical errors in the following example.

9. Embellish the following frameworks with eighth and a few sixteenth notes, using a variety of nonharmonic tone types, including suspensions. Analyze fully, including harmonic intervals, harmony, and nonharmonic tones.

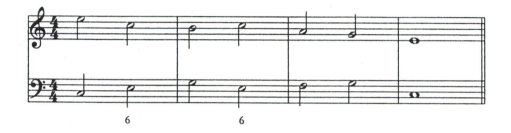

10. Exercises 16 and 17 on p. 73 may be done at this time. Be sure to use, and analyze, only the stylistically appropriate nonharmonic tones, including suspensions with ornamented resolutions.

CONTRAPUNTAL ANALYSIS CHECKLIST

Note: Several of the items on this checklist have not yet been discussed and will be covered later.

Relation of Voices

- number of independent voices
- motivic relationship of voices
- function of bass line: motivic? imitative?
- rhythmic relation of voices
- directional relation of voices; overall contours and localized relations
- harmonic intervals formed between voices; which occur on strong beats?

- any instances of linear-intervallic patterns?
- invertible counterpoint
- textural changes
- treatment of dissonant harmonic intervals
- imitation: pitch and time interval between entrances. Length of imitation.

Line and Form

- melodic intervals used; which predominate?
- phrase and period structure
- cadence formulas, including scale degree formulas in both voices
- overall form, including major cadence points
- how are structural pitches ornamented or connected?
- motivic structure
- sequence: length of unit, transposition interval and direction, number of times unit is repeated
- local and overall contour of line; placement of climax
- compound line
- rhythmic structure: motifs, motion approaching cadence

Harmony

- chord vocabulary and placement in phrase, including inversions; analyze structural harmony
- harmonic rhythm; does it change anywhere?
- cadence types and placement
- nonharmonic tone usage—types, frequency, and placement in meter
- modulations: where, by what means and to which tonal areas?

Special Devices

- pedal point
- stretto
- inversion
- retrogression
- augmentation
- diminution

ESSENTIALS OF TWO-VOICE COUNTERPOINT

1. Rhythmic relationships—1:1, 2:1, 4:1, and (in compound meters) 3:1 and 3:2 are to be used.
2. Motion relationships—available are parallel, similar, oblique, contrary. A mix of all types is typical. Parallels—imperfect consonances only; no parallel perfect consonances or dissonances. Avoid extended use of parallel thirds or sixths.
3. Harmonic intervals—use mostly imperfect consonances. Perfect consonances occur mainly at beginnings and cadences, or on weak beats, using strong scale degrees (1, 4, 5). Treat all dissonances correctly in the usual nonharmonic tone idioms. Resolve all d and A intervals. The P4 is a dissonance. Make use of the LIPs, where possible.
4. Harmony—must be clear, functional, with regular (patterned) harmonic rhythm. Be aware of scale-degree/harmonic formulae, especially in the bass. Use inversions idiomatically, and strongly directed bass lines.

Detail Reminders

1. Avoid voice crossing for now.
2. Avoid consecutive dissonances, except for a weak passing tone followed by a strong passing tone descending.
3. No parallel, contrary, or direct fifths or octaves. No unequal fifths.
4. Nonharmonic tones cannot be used to correct parallels.
5. Doubling: freely double strong scale degrees; generally avoid doubling tendency tones (leading tone, chord sevenths, altered tones, chord thirds); line sometimes takes precedence over doubling.
6. Never choose a note for harmonic reasons only.
7. Stay focused on line. Use typical melodic figurations, including cadence figures; work for motivic unity, shape, pattern, and continuity.
8. Always work from, and be aware of, a structural pitch framework (skeleton), both for shape of line and strength of counterpoint.
9. You are writing *music*, not just "theory exercises." Rhythmic flexibility, coherence and expression are very much to the point.
10. Check all work at a keyboard, or two instruments.
11. Analyze as you work:
    intervals between voices on each beat
    motion relationships
    rhythmic relationships
    harmony, both structural and embellishing
    nonharmonic tones
    all instances of patterning, including LIPs and sequences
12. Always remember the large issues in any music:
    shape
    coherence
    consistency
    pattern
    flow (continuity)

Cumulative Exercises

Play the following examples and locate and discuss all the musical, stylistic, and technical errors in them. There are many errors of line, harmony, rhythm, counterpoint, and style.

PROCESS DEMONSTRATIONS. It will be helpful before proceeding to the exercises to read and play through the following process demonstrations. Stay, in all your waiting, within the range of Bach's keyboards, as found in *The Well-Tempered Clavier* (C→c^3).

Given Figured Bass

1. Work out chord implications of figured bass. Spell the chords.
2. Supply structural pitches, based on the chord tones available, working for strong vertical intervals and a good shape. This is the middleground framework.
3. Fill in between structural pitches, working for regular rhythmic flow, using consistent motivic figures and a strong cadence. This forms the rhythmic/motivic foreground.
4. Check your work, analyzing all chords, nonharmonic tones, vertical intervals, motives, dissonance treatment, scale-degree patterns in the bass, sequences, and LIPs.

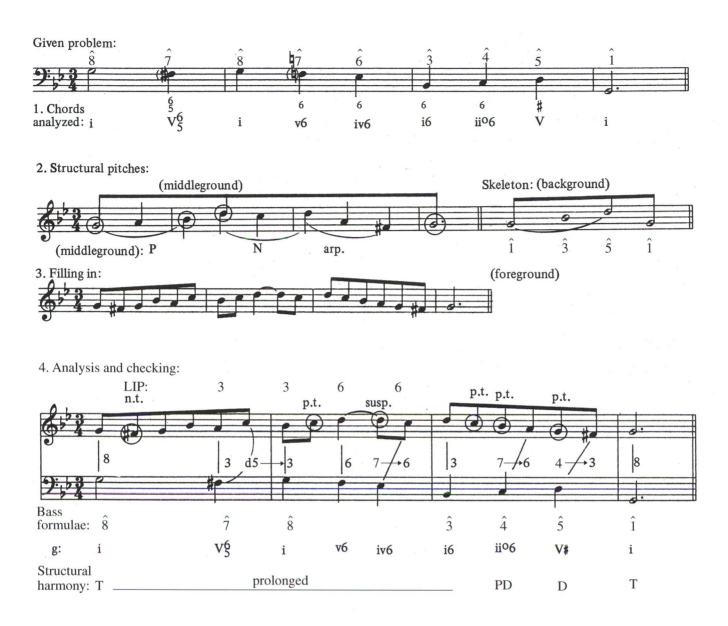

Given Upper Voice

1. Work out the chordal and nonharmonic tone implications and cadence type. Give alternate possible chord choices.
2. Write a bass line resulting from your chord choices, working for typical progressions, strong harmonic intervals, a strong line, typical use of inversions and nonharmonic tones, and a good contrapuntal relationship to the given voice.
3. Check your work, analyzing all chords, nonharmonic tones, and vertical intervals.

Given Problem (Analyzed):

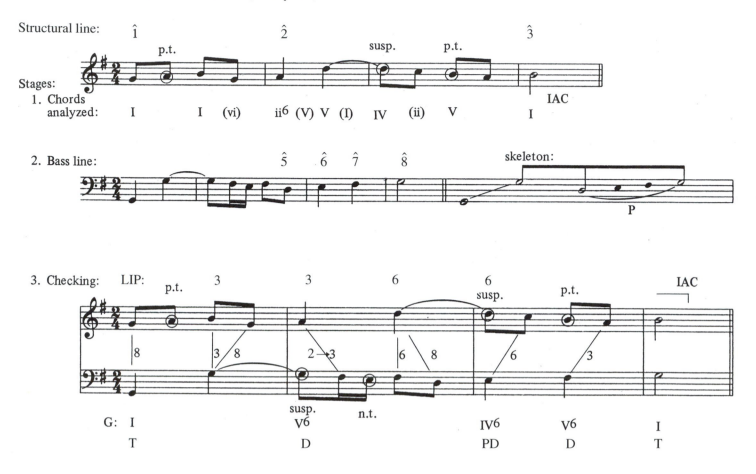

Given Two-Voice Framework

1. Work out the chordal implications, including inversions. Analyze the skeleton, including structural harmony, LIPs, and scale-degree formulas.
2. Articulate the structure, based on these harmonic implications, employing motivic figurations and nonharmonic tones as well as a typical cadence figure. Check your work, analyzing all chords, nonharmonic tones, and vertical intervals.

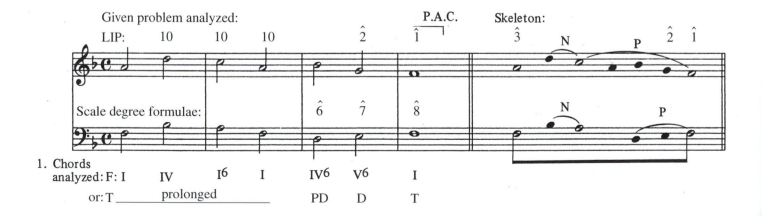

2. Articulation and Checking:

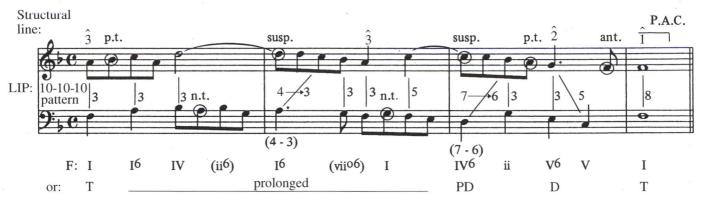

Chord-Phrase Format (Harmonic Framework)
1. Spell the chords and compose a two-voice framework.
2. Articulate the framework in the usual way, and check thoroughly.

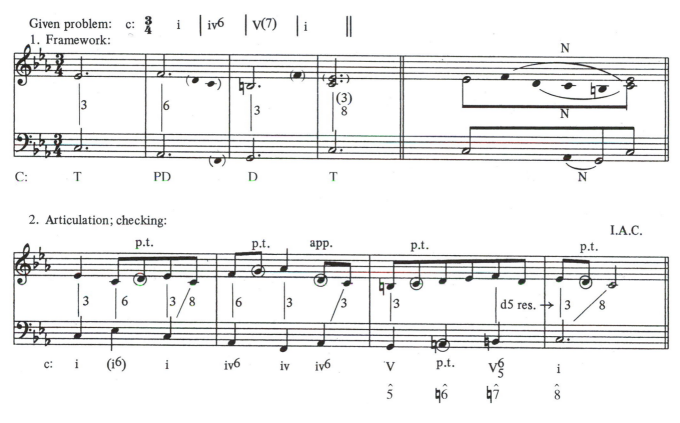

Exercises in Two-Voice Composition

A NOTE ON WRITTEN WORK (TO THE STUDENT). It is wise to follow closely the given exercise at first. If, after both your technique and your feeling for the style become solid (and with the consent of your instructor), you wish to depart slightly from a given format (for instance, substituting a I⁶ for a I, or a ii⁶ for a IV, or changing slightly a given line), feel free to do so. Further, if an exercise seems to be working out well musically and you wish to carry it out longer, by all means do.

Refer constantly to the Essentials and Reminders lists, pp. 64–65. It would be very helpful to photocopy these lists and have them available as you work.

In the following exercises, add voices as indicated, following the working-out processes suggested on pp. 66–69. Play all your work and check your technique with great care. Always work for a musically satisfying and stylistically correct result. Analyze fully, including structural pitches, harmony, nonharmonic tones, motives, cadences, scale-degree formulas, sequences, and LIPs. Many of the most typical scale formulas and LIPs are built into these exercises. These exercises may also be improvised at the keyboard or using other instruments or voices.

Add a new voice above the given voice, mainly in eighth and some sixteenth notes, using a variety of typical nonharmonic tones, including suspensions. Use sequences and LIPs as appropriate.

Note: Some of the following basses are unfigured. You should first determine where inversions are appropriate, based on the scale-degree patterns in the bass, and then work out the harmonic implications.

Again, solutions to these basses may be improvised at the keyboard, or using other instruments.

To the lines below, add new bass lines mainly in quarter and eighth notes. Work for clear harmony, steady harmonic rhythm, strongly directed lines, typical use of inversions and bass scale-degree formulas. Use sequence and LIPs where appropriate. Analyze.

The Craft of Tonal Counterpoint

Articulate these two two-voice frameworks, mainly in eighth notes. Be attentive to motifs, rhythmic continuity, and nonharmonic activity. The voices should be roughly equal in rhythmic activity. Use some suspensions. Analyze.

Exercises 18a and 18b below may be reserved for use in chapter 3.

To exercises 19 and 20 add new bass lines. Review the instruction before exercise 11 first. Analyze fully.

Compose two-voice counterpoint based on the following harmonic models. Analyze fully.

21. D: $\frac{3}{4}$ I |V |vi |ii |V |I |IV |V |

22. a: $\frac{2}{4}$ i |vii°⁶ |i⁶ |iv |V |VI |iv |V |i ||

23. B♭: $\frac{6}{8}$ I |IV |V |I |vi |ii⁶ |V⁷ |I ||

24. b: $\frac{3}{4}$ i |i |iv |V |iv |V |i ||

Continue the given openings for several more measures, ending in a stylistically typical cadence idiom. These may be allowed to modulate, if that seems appropriate.

Moderato

25.

Andante

26.

Gigue

27.

Moderato

28.

Allegro

29.

Adagio

30.

Siciliano
31.

Notes

1. As suggested on p. xiv, the Directed Study materials can be omitted or deferred until a later point in each chapter, at the discretion of the instructor.

2. These can be shown from the beginning of each beat to the next, or from the end of each divided beat to the beginning of the next. Both facets should be explored. In the sample here, they are shown only from the end of each beat into the next beat.

3. Obviously, in 2:1 counterpoint (in which one voice moves twice as fast as the other) there will be constant oblique motion within the beat. This should simply be ignored in favor of analyzing the motion from one beat into the next.

4. Whatever the reasons for the virtually universal proscription of consecutive (parallel) fifths and octaves, the fact is that under these conditions the voices seem to lose their sense of independence. An occasional exception to the prohibition of parallel fifths can be found in Bach, as a result of simultaneous nonharmonic tones. Such parallel motions invariably involve short, unaccented tones.

5. In crossing, the two voices exchange places, the higher voice becoming the lower. In overlapping, one crosses where the other has just been on the preceding beat.

6. Observe, incidentally, the direct fifths (very rare) in m. 7, between beats 1 and 2.

7. There are, of course, questions as to which notes are perceived as nonharmonic. For instance, the d in the lower voice, m. 1, could be heard as a passing tone, within tonic harmony, making the d^2 in the right hand also nonharmonic, though they are consonant with each other. Whether or not a note is heard as belonging to the underlying harmony is largely a function of the length and metric placement of that note, in relationship to the speed of the harmonic rhythm.

8. The conditions under which the P4 becomes a consonant interval (in writing for more than two voices) will be discussed later.

9. The fact that we are focusing on vertical intervals at this point in our study should not make us lose sight of the fact that these intervals arise from the combination of *lines*, which continue to be of primary importance.

10. For practical reasons, this text uses Jean-Philippe Rameau's concept of chordal identity, and of roman-numeral functional analysis. The instructor may wish to discuss at this point Bach's approach to teaching, which stressed a more purely intervallic concept—that of figured bass. In two-voice textures, the underlying harmony is implicit rather than explicit, and results from the intervallic relations between the voices. The use of roman-numeral analysis should not be taken to imply that this music is purely harmonic in orientation, or that harmony must precede line in the compositional process.

11. This text posits for practical reasons the identity of chords in inversion. The instructor may wish to point out that inversions can often be demonstrated to arise from linear motion in the bass. It should also be stressed that root position chords are far more stable and have much stronger structural significance—especially the structural harmonies, T, PD, and D.

12. The larger issue raised implicitly of whether some "chords" exist at all as entities, especially in two-voice music, is more philosophical than practical; this text makes the assumption, for pedagogical reasons, that they do. Many of the "chords" in a tonal work, other than the strongest structural T, D, and PD harmonies, may be understood as arising from line. Such an understanding will be helpful in focusing the student on the principal harmonic goals of a work, as well as on the primacy of line.

13. Some theorists use the term *essential dissonance* to refer to a dissonant note that is a chord member, such as a chord seventh or ninth.

CHAPTER 3

CHROMATICISM IN TWO VOICES

To this point the music with which we have been dealing has been largely diatonic. It is appropriate now to take up the subject of chromaticism, since the music of Bach is more characteristically chromatic than that of his contemporaries.[1]

Before dealing with Bach's specific chromatic usages, a few general observations are in order.

Two factors are involved in correct chromatic *spelling:* direction of resolution and harmonic background. Generally speaking, notes resolve in the direction of their inflection: upward-inflected notes resolve up, and downward-inflected notes resolve down.

Ex. 3–1

Equally important is the tonal/harmonic background. For instance, in example 3-2, while G♭ would be the "correct" spelling for the line, F♯ implies a typical functional chord in the key (a secondary dominant of V), and is therefore the better spelling. When there is any conflict between melodic and harmonic spelling, the latter prevails.

Ex. 3–2

Cross-relation, in which a note in one voice is followed immediately by a chromatically altered version of that note in another voice, is fairly rare in this style. In Bach, a chromatic alteration more usually occurs in the voice that just had the diatonic version of that note (direct chromaticism). Cross-relation is sometimes called *false relation.*[2]

Ex. 3–3

The most typical case occurs when the cross-relation involves the use of the two forms of the melodic minor scale, one form in each voice.

Ex. 3–4

descending melodic minor

ascending melodic minor

Simultaneous cross-relation, in which the two forms occur at the same moment, is even less common, though isolated instances may occur in slow, highly chromatic and expressive movements.

Lines are, as always, highly directed. Aimless, "fussy" chromatic figures, as in example 3-5, are generally avoided, though in highly chromatic works this observation is less strictly applicable.

Ex. 3–5

Weak:

As with all the other musical elements, chromatically altered notes are used purposefully and consistently. That is, they usually function as part of the motivic/thematic fabric, rather than as incidental details. Further, they most often occur within an essentially diatonic structural framework. It is possible to distinguish two basic categories of usage: nonfunctional and functional chromaticism.

Nonfunctional (Nonessential, Decorative, Melodic) Chromaticism

Bach's music makes sparing use of chromatically altered decorative tones, usually restricting their use to brief, unaccented passing and neighboring figures. Dissonances, as we have seen, tend to be brief and diatonic. A few altered decorative tones are to be found in the examples below, and will be pointed out as they occur. Example 1-31 (p. 19) may be reviewed at this time.

Functional (Essential, Harmonic) Chromaticism

Bach's use of chromaticism most often involves functional chords, usually secondary dominants.

Secondary (Borrowed, Applied) Dominants

Bach's harmony is, for its time, rich in secondary dominants, almost always functionally (normally) resolved.[3] These may occur in isolation or as part of a sequential pattern, often involving a circle of fifths.

In example 3-6, mm. 12–17 comprise a sequential series of secondary dominants, of D (V), of A (ii), and of E (vi). Note that each one resolves normally (to the expected chord of resolution), and that the resolutions form a pattern of rising perfect fifths: D–A–E. The logic of these normal resolutions, plus the larger-scale logic of the sequence, make such progressions very strong and predictable. Note also the circle-of-fifths progression in mm. 17–19 below, with successive roots on E–A–D–G–C (G: vi–ii–V–I–IV). Note too that all chromatically raised notes are leading tones of the next chord. Observe the linear-intervallic patterns (10–10 and 6–6), mm. 12–19.

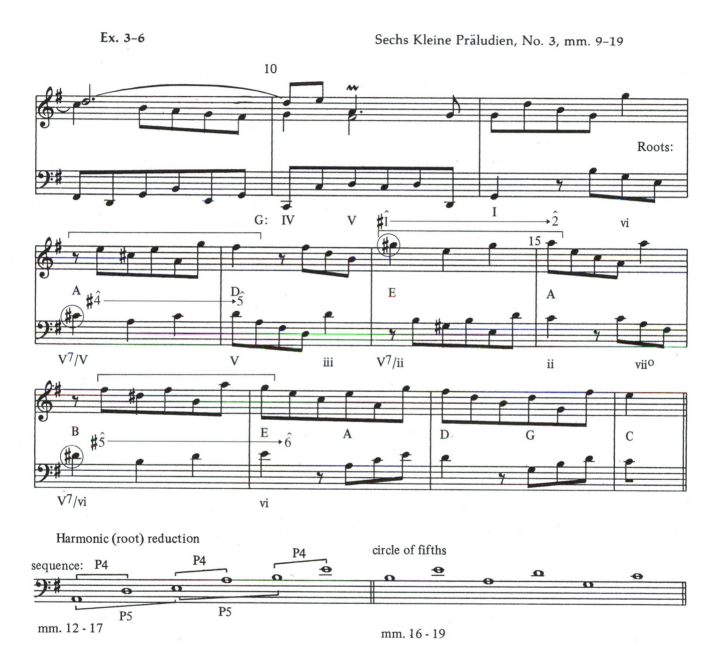

Ex. 3–6   Sechs Kleine Präludien, No. 3, mm. 9–19

Two points should be made regarding the harmonic implications of altered scale degrees:

1. As we noted in example 3-6, a chromatically raised note will usually be the leading tone of the following chord; that is, the third of a V^7 or the root of a vii^{o7}.
2. A chromatically lowered note will most often imply the seventh of a secondary dominant V^7 or vii^{o7}.

Ex. 3–7

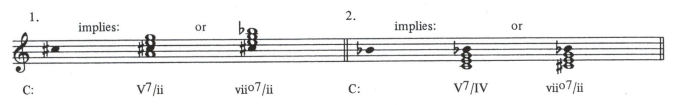

1.   implies: or

C: V⁷/ii   viio⁷/ii

2.   implies: or

C: V⁷/IV   viio⁷/ii

In example 3-8, mm. 14–15, we find a circle-of-fifths sequence involving secondary dominants. It progresses partially around the circle, E–A–D–G–C. Note that the D-minor triad in m. 14 is not a secondary dominant (it could have been V/VI), but a diatonic iv. This diatonic choice strengthens the feeling of key and keeps the harmony from straying too far afield. It is characteristic for Bach thus to retain a sense of the diatonic basis of the harmony, even within a secondary dominant sequence. Note the simplicity of the bass line skeleton, and the 10–10 pattern in mm. 14–15.

Ex. 3–8   Sechs Kleine Präludien, No. 5, mm. 13–17

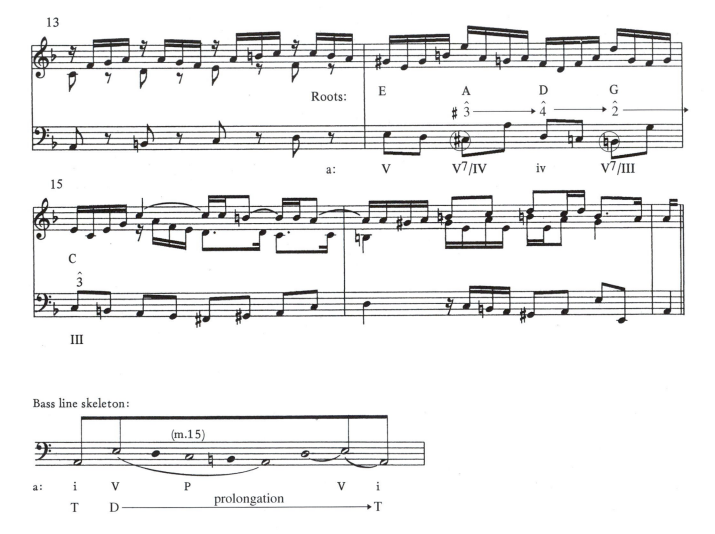

Bass line skeleton:

You will have observed that these passages are developmental music, operate by sequence, and are given harmonic interest by the use of secondary dominants. Example 3-9 also functions on the same basis, following a sequential pattern around the circle of fifths, again with a developmental purpose.[4] In such passages there is normally a very strong structural bass line.

Kleine Präludien (from the Notebook for W. F. Bach), No. 2

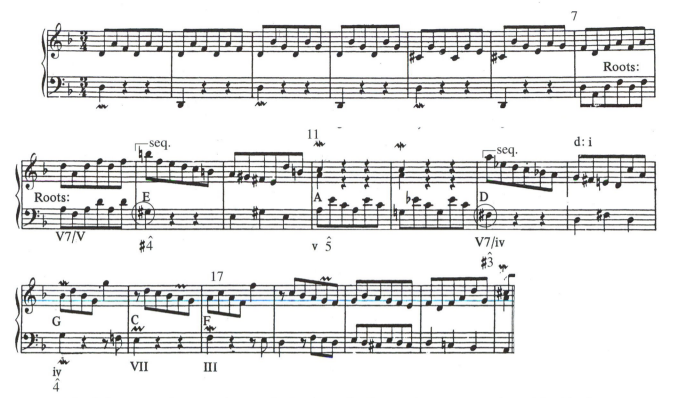

The following reduction of example 3-9 (mm. 6–17) reveals a very simple and highly directional pitch structure. Note the passing motions, as well as the parallel tenths apparent in the skeleton graph.

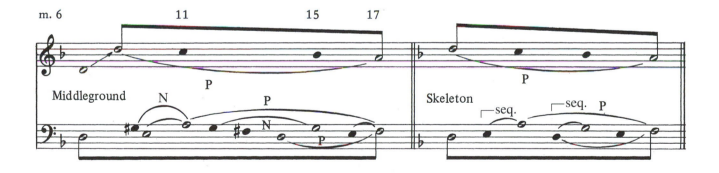

Bach generally prefers secondary dominant seventh chords (V^7) to triads (V and vii°), as they have stronger resolving tendencies. He is especially fond of secondary fully diminished seventh chords (vii°7). In this style, any diatonic major or minor triad may be preceded by any of its secondary dominants, but it should be noted that a minor triad is never preceded by a half diminished vii°7. Progressions around the circle of fifths may involve series of secondary dominants, but more often alternate diatonic triads with secondary dominants. Such passages may progress entirely around the circle, but more commonly will move only four to six steps around, in the interest of avoiding overlong sequences. Such circle sequences often modulate.

HARMONIES RELATED TO CHROMATIC LINES

It is quite common in the music of Bach's time to find highly chromatic passages, especially in minor mode, organized by means of patterned chromatic lines. Such lines most often occur descending in the bass voice, filling in between the tonic and dominant notes. The descending tonic-to-dominant tetrachord (descending perfect fourth filled in by step) has formed an essential gestalt (basic structure) for Western music for several hundred years. Bass lines tend to gravitate between these fundamental tonal "pillars," or primary structural pitches.[5] Chromatic descending lines filling in the tonic-to-dominant tetrachord often involve series of secondary dominants, as can be seen in example 3-10.

Ex. 3-10   Four Duets, No. 1, mm. 1–6

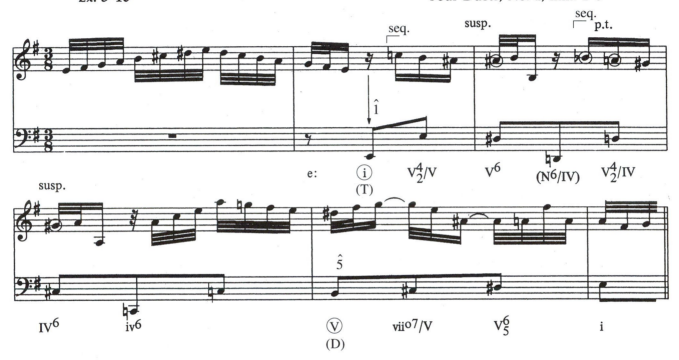

In example 3-10 we find a descending chromatic bass line, e ⟶ B. Several other common harmonizations of these bass notes are given in the reduction below (example 3-11). Observe also the sequence of secondary dominants: V_2^4/V–V^6, V_2^4/IV–IV^6. Such sequences are common.

Ex. 3-11

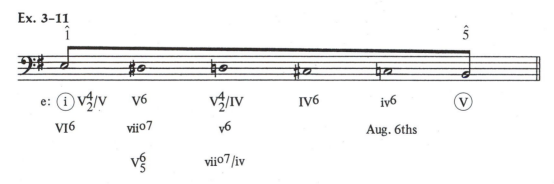

Incidentally, m. 3 of example 3-10, upper voice, will be seen to contain two (rare) chromatic nonharmonic tones, a suspension (a$\sharp^1$) and a passing tone (b$\flat^1$), although the latter may be understood to imply the Neapolitan chord.

In example 3-12, a descending chromatic line, i ⟶ V, is again employed. Here the thin texture causes some ambiguity as to the harmonic implications.

Ex. 3-12   Sinfonia No. 9

Example 3-13 will be seen to ornament the fundamental tetrachord, g ⟶ d.

Ex. 3-13   Two-Part Invention No. 11

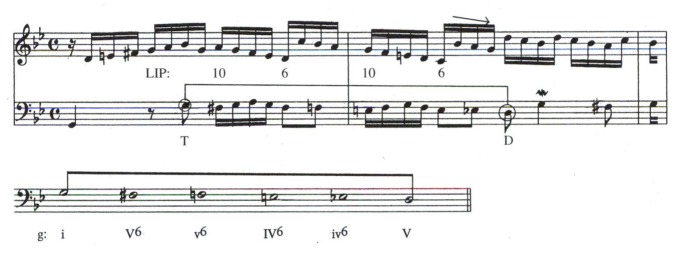

Here again the harmonies are only implied.

Not all chromatic lines are confined to the descending tetrachord. Example 3-14 extends the basic a ⟶ e tetrachord downward, transferring it in m. 2 to the upper voice. This example contains several chromatic nonharmonic tones, built into the highly chromatic nature and expressive affect of the line and resulting in an "out of phase" feeling in the harmony. This is very highly structured music, as seen in the sequential patterning and the LIP.

Ex. 3-14   Well-Tempered Clavier II, Prelude No. 20

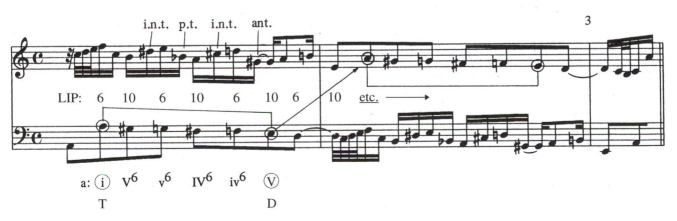

The Neapolitan Triad

Bach uses the Neapolitan chord sparingly, especially so in thin textures. It is a highly charged sonority for this style, typically reserved for moments of expressive tension. It tends to occur toward the ends of phrases, where the most harmonic interest is needed, functioning as a cadential predominant (dominant-preparation) chord. It is used almost exclusively in the minor mode, and in first inversion, followed by a dominant-function chord, or more rarely i⁶ or vii°⁷/V. The following passage shows one of its rare occurrences in a two-voice texture. Note that it is placed approaching a climax, on a weak beat, and is resolved on a dominant chord.

Ex. 3-15   Two-Part Invention No. 13

Augmented-Sixth Chords

Bach employs chords of the augmented sixth even more sparingly than he does the Neapolitan chord. They are more likely to appear in slow homophonic movements than in strict contrapuntal passages, though brief isolated instances such as that shown in example 3-16 may be found. The most typical idioms are German $^6_5$–V and Italian $^6_3$–V.

Ex. 3-16   The Art of Fugue, Fugue IX, mm. 73–78

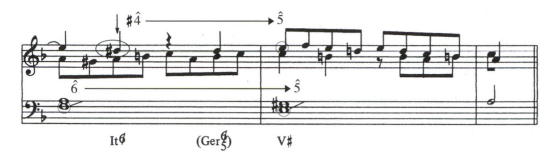

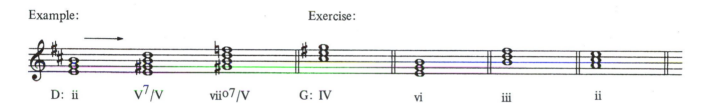

(Note the barely avoided parallel fifths between bass and middle voice in the fourth and fifth measures of the example.)

Exercises

1. Analyze several more chromatic passages from the anthology, as found on p. 324 ff. Discuss nonessential chromaticism, functional chromaticism, harmonic sequence, and the use of structural bass lines.
2. Spell the following chords, from the root up.
   D: V^7/V, $vii°^7/iii$, V^7/IV, $vii°^7/ii$, V/vi, $vii°/vi$;
   d: V^7/iv, V^7/III, V^7/VII, $vii°^7/iv$, $vii°^7/VI$.
3. Substitute for the given diatonic chord two secondary dominant chords with the same function. Consult the chart on p. 283, if necessary.

Example: Exercise:

D: ii V^7/V vii°⁷/V   G: IV   vi   iii   ii

4. Substitute, in the following diatonic sequences, secondary dominants for some of the diatonic chords. Try several versions, with a variety of secondary dominants. Analyze fully, including sequences and LIPs.

A.

B.

C.

The following two exercises may be omitted or reserved for use in chapter 13.

5. Show with roman numerals or figured bass symbols two typical harmonizations of the following chromatic line.

d:

6. Analyze the harmonic implications of the following unfigured bass. Add figures to the bass, including all necessary accidentals. Then write several versions of an upper voice above it, including a few chromatic nonharmonic tones. Use mainly eighth and sixteenth notes. Work in all these exercises for clear shape, limited motivic content, suspensions as appropriate, and clear patterning, through sequence and LIP's. Analyze fully.[6]

Adagio

7. Analyze the harmonic details, structural harmony, and structural pitches of the following figured basses and write out at least three versions of a new voice above each one. At least one version of each should be a compound line. Use eighth notes with a few sixteenths as decoration. Be aware of bass line scale-degree idioms; use sequences and LIPs as appropriate. Analyze fully.

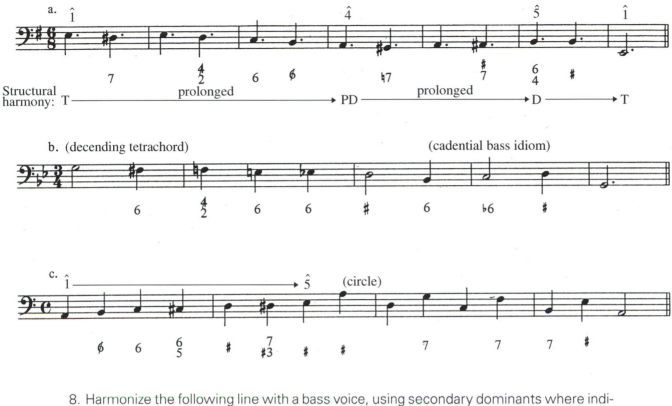

8. Harmonize the following line with a bass voice, using secondary dominants where indicated by "x."

9. Harmonize the following compound line, adding a voice below.

10. Write two-voice counterpoint in the Bach style, based on the following chord-phrase formats. All should be slow and expressive. Analyze fully.

c: $\frac{4}{4}$ i V$^6_5$/iv $\Big|$ iv vii$^{\text{o}7}$/V $\Big|$ V VI $\Big|$ ii$^{\text{o}6}$ V^7 $\Big|$ i $\Big\|$

d: $\frac{3}{4}$ i V$^6_5$ $\Big|$ i vii$^{\text{o}7}$/iv $\Big|$ iv vii$^{\text{o}7}$/V $\Big|$ V i^6 $\Big|$ N^6 V^7 $\Big|$ i $\Big\|$

e: $\frac{6}{8}$ i vii$^{\text{o}7}$ $\Big|$ i V$^4_2$/iv $\Big|$ IV^6 iv^6 $\Big|$ V i^6 $\Big|$ N^6 vii$^{\text{o}7}$/V $\Big|$ V^7 $\Big|$ i $\Big\|$

f: $\frac{4}{4}$ i vii$^{\text{o}7}$ $\Big|$ i V$^4_2$/iv $\Big|$ iv^6 It^6 $\Big|$ V V^7 $\Big|$ i $\Big\|$

Notes

1. Consideration of this chapter may, at the option of the instructor, be postponed until a later time, following chapter 5 or chapter 8.
2. For background on cross-relations, see *The New Grove Dictionary of Music and Musicians*, "False Relations," vol. 6.
3. It is again assumed that the student is conversant with the theory and practice of secondary dominants, the Neapolitan chord, and the augmented-sixth chords. If not, a brief discussion in class should suffice by way of introduction, perhaps with reference to appendix 1 (p. 283). Scale-degree alterations as they relate to secondary dominants should be discussed.
4. Such progressions nearly always move up by fourth (or down by fifth), rarely in the other direction around the circle.
5. Further discussion and examples of this technique are to be found on pp. 171 ff and 260 ff. The term *tetrachord* is used broadly here to include any stepwise filling in of the descending tonic-to-dominant leap, not only the diatonic four-note version. Consideration of this material may be reserved until the discussion of passacaglia and chaconne in chapter 13, or chapter 13 may be taken up in a preliminary way at this time.
6. It is possible to introduce passacaglia at this point (see chapter 13).

CHAPTER 4

COMPOSITION OF BINARY DANCE FORMS

Perform the following movement (example 4-1) in class and discuss it as suggested below.[1]

Directed Study

Analyze the formal aspects of this movement, including the following items:

1. Overall form, showing main sections, cadence points, and phrase and period structure, using a format similar to this one:

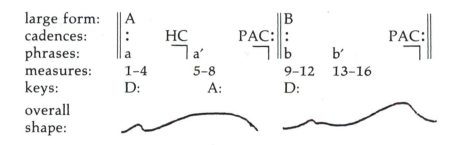

2. Main motivic content and principal devices of motivic manipulation, including repetition, sequence, LIPs, inversion, fragmentation, and so on.
3. Modulations: where, to what key areas, and by what means?
4. Miscellaneous observations: Is there a climactic point, or perhaps a series of them? If so, how are they achieved (by line, texture, harmony, rhythmic activity)? Where are the moments of maximum rhythmic activity in both voices? What cadential figures are used? Prepare a structural-pitch graph of both voices, including structural harmony.

Ex. 4–2   French Suite III, Menuet

b:

Comments on example 4-2

This is a typical menuet, with a steadily flowing triple meter, highly accented on the first beat by means of harmony and line.

The overall form could be graphed as:

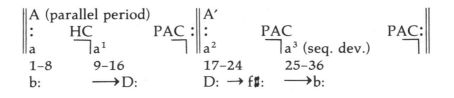

The phrase structure is regular, built on multiples of two measures. For instance, the inner phrase organization of mm. 1–8 could be graphed as:

```
         repetition        sequence
        ┌──────────┐      ┌──────────┐
        a       a¹        b       b¹      c (cadential)
        1-2     3-4       5       6       7-8
```

There is no clear-cut climactic point, though there appears to be a rising curve from m. 24 to m. 30, and again from m. 31 to m. 34, with a quick dropping off at the end.

Motivically, the work is flexible and subtle. The upper voice at the beginning forms a compound line, with the main melodic voice at the bottom of the line. The principal figure appears in the lower voice in mm. 17ff. Other motivic figures are not literally the same but mostly seem to be derived or "spun off" from it. The subsidiary figures include standard bass voice cadential patterns (mm. 16, 23, 26, 28), a few scalar patterns (mm. 7, 8, 17, 18, etc.), and the ♩. ♫ ♩ figures found in the upper voice, mm. 25 and 27. Otherwise, all the material seems clearly related to the triadic outlines set up in mm. 1–2.

Unifying and developmental devices include repetition (mm. 1–4, 9–12, 17–21), sequence (mm. 5–7, 13–15, 25–28, 29–32), and melodic inversion (mm. 29–32, right hand, are a rough inversion of mm. 1–2). Elsewhere these devices are more subtle, one melodic shape merely suggesting another. As usual, the rhythmic aspect of motive seems more important than the purely melodic aspect.

Modulation. The tonal areas are b, D, f♯, and b, outlining a tonic triad, which is typical of Bach's shorter works in the minor mode. The first modulation may be understood to occur in m. 13 by common chord on beat 3, with b:iv becoming D:ii. This modulation was prepared earlier by the harmony in mm. 5–6, as well as by the emphasis on the note d^2 in the upper voice in mm. 1, 2, 4, and 5. The modulation to f♯ occurs around m. 21, beat 1, where D:vi could be heard as becoming f♯:iv.[2] The tonal direction of mm. 25–28 is momentarily obscured by the secondary dominant sequence, but B minor has been clearly reestablished by m. 31, through a prolonged dominant in mm. 28–30.

The lines are strongly directed. This is perhaps most clear in mm. 1–8, where the two voices first prolong tonic harmony, then fall by step in a series of parallel tenths, a very typical gestalt for tonal music.

Ex. 4–3

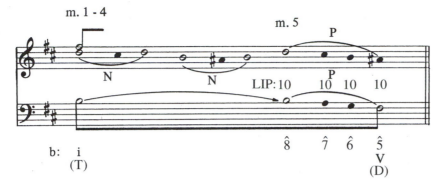

This feeling of linear purpose is especially strengthened by the sequences of mm. 5–7, 25–28, and 29–32. Mm. 24–36 may be heard as having the following shape.

Ex. 4–4

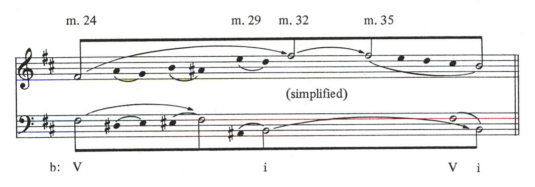

Discussion

The formal models for this chapter are the dance movements of Bach, especially the shorter binary movements from the suites (the French and English Suites, the Suites for solo cello, the Orchestral Suites, and the keyboard Partitas, for instance). Such movements may be in two equal or roughly equal sections (symmetrical binary form), or may have a longer second section (asymmetrical binary form). In the latter, the second section will be more developmental, unstable, and modulatory. There may be an explicit return of the opening music in the tonic key near the end (rounded binary form), or the opening music may merely be hinted at there (incipient rounded binary), as in example 4-1, mm. 29–30. The ending music often rises to a climactic point a few measures from the end. The climax is emphasized by line, harmony, and rhythmic activity. The overall form, then, can be roughly graphed as:

1. Symmetrical   expos./devel.   expos./devel.
   Binary   ‖:A   :‖:A′   :‖

2. Asymmetrical expos.   devel.
   Binary   ‖:A   :‖:A′   (B)   :‖

3. Rounded   expos.   devel.   return
   Binary   ‖:A   :‖:A′   (B)   A   (A²):‖

Within this overall organization, there is usually a regularity of phrase, organized into groups of two and four measures. The first section, especially when relatively short, is often a parallel period (see example 4-2, mm. 1–16), while the second, being more developmental, is less likely to contain periodic structures. Cadences will normally occur every four or eight measures, depending on the length of the movement, though the latter part of the second section will often be more continuous and climactic, with fewer cadences. Developmental processes will include all those we have observed so far, with the usual predeliction for sequence. Some movements are more clearly organized than others around motivic content, as a glance at the two menuets will reveal.

Modulatory schemes are fairly standardized. Movements in minor usually modulate to the relative major at the end of the first section; those in major will usually modulate to the dominant. The following schemes are the most typical:

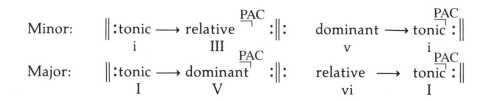

Other possible modulary schemes are:

Minor: ‖:i ⟶ v (or HC in tonic) :‖: iv (or III) ⟶ i :‖

Major: ‖:I ⟶ V (or HC) :‖: ii (or IV) ⟶ I :‖

Any closely related key is available, and is usually emphasized by an authentic cadence. The longer the movement, the more different keys may be tonicized. Modulations will normally be by common chord, though modulations by sequence are possible.

Bach, like other composers, often suggests the new key beforehand by means of harmonic direction, or by melodic emphasis on the upcoming tonic. For instance, in example 4-2 Bach implies the move to D major through the harmonies in mm. 5–6 and by the emphasis on the note d^2 in the upper voice in mm. 1, 2, 4, and 5. It is because of this "setting up" process that good modulations sound so natural and inevitable.

The chart below shows several dance movement types common at the time of Bach, and should be used for reference while doing the written exercises at the end of this chapter. Examples of these dance types are to be found in the anthology.[3]

Dance	Meter	Tempo	Typical Rhythms	Characteristic Details	Page in Anthology
Allemande	$\frac{4}{4}$	Moderate	♪ | ♫♫ ♩	steady six-teenth note flow; quite contrapuntal; motivic imitation	303
Courante	$\frac{3}{2}$ or $\frac{6}{4}$	Moderate	♪ | ♩.♪ ♫♫	♩.♪ or ♫♫ pattern, frequent shift of accent pattern	308
Sarabande	$\frac{3}{4}$ or $\frac{3}{2}$	Slow	| ♫♩ ♩ or ♩.♫ ♩	activity on beat 1, irregular pulse, homophonic, accent on beat 2	305
Menuet	$\frac{3}{4}$	Moderate	♫♫♫	regular flow of eighth notes	301
Gavotte	$\frac{2}{2}$	Moderate-slow	♩♫ | ♩♫♩	stately	309
Bourrée	$\frac{2}{2}$	Fast	♩ | ♩♫♩	often folk-like	
Gigue	$\frac{6}{8}$ or $\frac{12}{8}$	Fast	♪ | ♫♫ ♫♫	may be in any compound meter, including fast $\frac{3}{8}$. Contrapuntal, even fugal. 2 voices.	312

Exercises

1. Analyze selected dance movements, as found in the anthology. Focus on overall form and shape; phrase, cadence, and period structure; motivic content and manipulations; key scheme and modulations. Prepare formal graphs as suggested on p.92. Also prepare structural-pitch graphs.

2. Focus on modulation. Name two chords that could be used as (diatonic) common chords to modulate between each of these pairs of keys: B♭–g; a–C; d–F; e–b; f–c; A–E; E♭–B♭.

3. Compose a short menuet in symmetrical binary form, based on the following two-voice framework. Before you begin, perform and study several Bach menuets, such as those in this chapter and in the anthology (see pages 301 and 304). Analyze fully, including structural pitches and harmony, and all aspects of patterning.

Menuet

4. Compose brief suite movements in two voices, based on these models. Before starting, study several Bach examples of the type of dance you will be writing, to be sure of the character, tempo, harmonic rhythm, accentuation, and typical rhythmic figures of each dance type.

a. Menuet:

$$\|{:}\mathrm{E}\flat{:}|\ \mathrm{I}\ |\ \mathrm{IV}\ |\ \mathrm{I}\ |\ \mathrm{V}\ \overset{\text{HC}}{\rceil}\ \Big[\begin{array}{l}\mathrm{E}\flat{:}\ \mathrm{I}\\ \mathrm{B}\flat{:}\ \mathrm{IV}\end{array}\Big|\ \mathrm{V}\ \mathrm{I}\ \Big|\ \mathrm{IV}\ \mathrm{V}^7\ \Big|\ \mathrm{I}\ \overset{\text{PAC}}{}:\|$$

$$\|{:}(\mathrm{B}\flat{:})\ \mathrm{I}\ |\ \mathrm{V}^7/\mathrm{IV}\ \Big[\begin{array}{l}\mathrm{B}\flat{:}\ \mathrm{IV}\\ \mathrm{E}\flat{:}\ \mathrm{I}\end{array}\ \Big|\ \mathrm{vii}^{\circ7}/\mathrm{ii}\ |\ \mathrm{ii}\ |\ \mathrm{V}^7\ |\ \mathrm{I}\ \mathrm{IV}\ \mathrm{V}^7\ |\ \mathrm{I}\ \overset{\text{PAC}}{\rceil}:\|$$

b. Courante:

$$\begin{array}{cccc}\overset{\text{HC}}{} & \overset{\text{PAC}}{} & \overset{\text{HC}}{} & \overset{\text{PAC}}{}\\ a\ \rceil\ a'\ \rceil & & b\ \rceil\ b'\ \rceil\\ 1\text{--}4 \quad 5\text{--}8 & :\|{:}9\text{--}12 & 13\text{--}16 & :\|\\ c{:}\ \longrightarrow\ \mathrm{E}\flat{:} & \longrightarrow & c{:}\end{array}$$

c. Gavotte:

$$\begin{array}{ccccc} & \text{IAC} & \text{PAC} & \text{PAC} & \text{PAC}\\ a\ \rceil & b\ \rceil & c\ \rceil & c\ \rceil & :\|\\ 1\text{--}4 & 5\text{--}8 & :\|{:}9\text{--}16 & 17\text{--}24\\ g{:}\ \longrightarrow\ \mathrm{B}\flat{:} & \longrightarrow\ d{:} & \longrightarrow\ g{:}\end{array}$$

5. Use the graphs prepared under exercise 1 above, as well as your observations of the music, to compose suite movements based on those models. It is wise at first to stay very close to the model. Analyze your work in detail.

Notes

1. This chapter can be omitted, at the discretion of the instructor, if the imitative forms are to be emphasized in the course. The instructor may wish to point out that some movements in the suites of Bach are homophonic in orientation and should be considered as falling outside the focus of this text.
2. An instructor preferring to speak of "temporary tonicizations of the tonic triad members D and F♯" should feel free to do so, as this text does not wish to require any particular view of modulation.
3. Definitions and further details are to be found in *The New Grove Dictionary of Music and Musicians*, under each suite movement, and in *Gauldin* (see bibliography).

CHAPTER 5

DOUBLE (INVERTIBLE) COUNTERPOINT

Ex. 5–1   Two-Part Invention No. 6

Ex. 5–2   Two-Part Invention No. 9

Directed Study

Play and discuss the excerpts above. Compare position I of each to position II. How does II relate to I? What is it about the vertical (harmonic) intervals used in I that makes II equally successful? Generalize about what you find here in terms of harmonic intervals as well as rhythmic, directional, and motivic relations between the voices.

Discussion

The above excerpts are written to sound equally satisfactory with either of the two voices as the upper, that is, in the versions $_B^A$ and $_A^B$. These passages are written in *double* or *invertible counterpoint*.[1] The technique of double counterpoint is widely used by composers. Without it, it would be far more difficult to compose extended contrapuntal works, as one would constantly have to invent new accompanying material. The use of double counterpoint ensures a consistent thematic content and a contrapuntal relationship not achievable by other means. Composers often invent themes in pairs, with one theme intended to accompany the other at each occurrence. We will study this relationship later (as that of subject and countersubject). The use of double counterpoint also ensures that a theme will not always have to appear in the same voice, but can be freely interchanged between voices. Each voice must be capable of functioning as a convincing bass line and must as always be a satisfying melodic line in itself. In any given work, the two versions (positions) may follow one another immediately, as they do in the music above, or the second (voice-exchanged) version may be placed at some later point in the work, usually transposed to some other key.

Bach employs three types of double counterpoint, which we will examine in order of importance.

DOUBLE COUNTERPOINT AT THE OCTAVE OR FIFTEENTH

By far the most common type of double counterpoint is shown in examples 5-1 and 5-2, where the voices exchange positions, moving by a total of one, two, or three octaves. This is known as double counterpoint "at the octave" or "at the fifteenth." (The number of steps in two octaves adds up to 15, not 16.) It is also sometimes called "natural double counterpoint," in distinction to that at other intervals. In example 5-3, an original pair of voices (a) has been exchanged at the octave (b) and at two octaves or the fifteenth (c). In practice, either voice may be transposed by one or two octaves to cross the other, so that either version of (b) or (c) is possible, depending on considerations of register or shaping of lines.

Ex. 5–3

(a.) original   (b.) voices exchanged at the octave

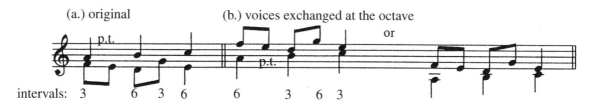

intervals: 3   6   3   6   6   3   6   3

(c.) voices exchanged at the fifteenth

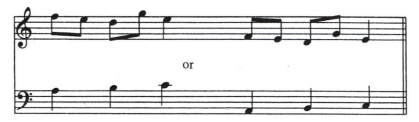

You will observe in example 5-3 that, under conditions of voice exchange at the octave or fifteenth, most of the harmonic intervals retain their character. That is, imperfect consonances remain imperfect (thirds become sixths, and vice versa), dissonances remain dissonant (seconds

---

become sevenths, and vice versa), and the octave and unison exchange, as do diminished and augmented intervals (A4 becomes d5; d7 becomes A2).

In neither position (the original or the exchanged version) are the two voices allowed to cross, as this would obscure the double counterpoint, and the independence of each voice. For this reason it will often be necessary to exchange the voices at the fifteenth (or even at three octaves), rather than the octave. It is also wise to keep the range of each voice within an octave.

Ex. 5-4

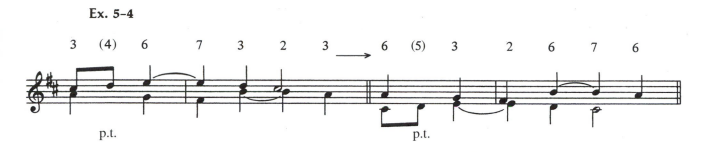

The only interval that takes on a different character is the perfect fifth, which becomes a perfect fourth and thus changes from a consonance to a dissonance. Therefore, in the original version, perfect fifths must be treated *as if they were dissonant*—in other words, in typical nonharmonic tone idioms.

Ex. 5-5

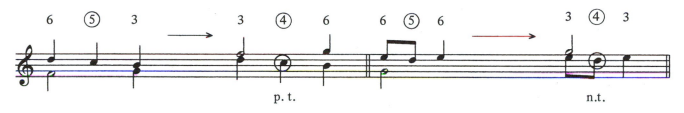

The usual suspensions work well in double counterpoint.

Ex. 5-6

The 7-6 becomes 2-3 (and vice versa); but the 4-3 becomes 5-6 which, while acceptable, is less effective since the perfect fifth is not a dissonant interval.

Below is a table of intervals for double counterpoint at the octave. Observe that each interval-pair adds up to nine.

Original:	1	2	3	4	5	6	7	8
Inverted:	8	7	6	5	4	3	2	1

DOUBLE COUNTERPOINT AT THE TWELFTH

Here the lower voice of the original is transposed up an octave (or two) and the upper voice down a perfect fifth, for a total of twelve steps, as in example 5-7, position II. Or the upper voice may be transposed down an octave (or two) and the lower voice up a perfect fifth for the same intervallic result (example 5-7, position III). Double counterpoint at the twelfth is typically rich in thirds and tenths, since these two imperfect consonances are inversionally complementary at the twelfth. Perfect consonances remain perfect (1→12, 5→8, and the reverse), and most dissonances remain dissonant (2→11, 4→9, and the reverse). The problem interval here is the sixth, which becomes a seventh and must therefore be treated as if it were dissonant. Observe in example 5-7 that the sixths are treated as passing tones in the original position (I) so that they become properly treated dissonances (sevenths) in positions II and III. Also note that the 11-10 (equal to 4-3) suspension at the end becomes a 2-3 suspension, indicating the invertibility of both the 4-3 and the 2-3 suspensions at the twelfth.

As with double counterpoint at the octave, the voices are not allowed to cross each other in either the original or the exchanged positions, and the individual voice ranges are often kept within one octave.

Ex. 5–7

In example 5-8 the voices have exchanged places in the second version, with the upper voice transposed down an octave and the lower voice up a perfect fifth, for a total of twelve steps. Note that each voice sounds equally good as the lower voice, and that each voice has considerable independence of motivic content as well as integrity and shape. The individual lines to be used in double counterpoint must of course display all the features of good linear writing that we have discussed. Here again, thirds and tenths interchange, all dissonances are handled normally in both versions, and the sixths in position I are treated as if they were suspensions (ornamentally resolved on the next beat), so that they become correctly treated sevenths in position II.

Ex. 5-8   Well-Tempered Clavier I, Fugue No. 2, mm. 5–6

In example 5-9 the upper voice has been transposed down an octave, and the lower voice up a fifth (plus two octaves, to maintain registral independence from the other voice, and avoid crossing), for double counterpoint at the twelfth. This example demonstrates well the interchangeability of fifths and octaves.

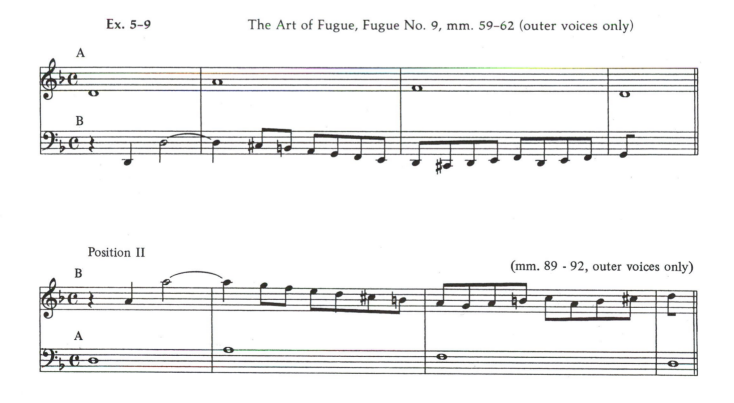

Ex. 5-9   The Art of Fugue, Fugue No. 9, mm. 59–62 (outer voices only)

(mm. 89 - 92, outer voices only)

Here is a table of intervals for double counterpoint at the twelfth. Observe that each interval-pair adds up to thirteen.

Original:	1	2	3	4	5	6	7	8	9	10	11	12
Inverted:	12	11	10	9	8	7	6	5	4	3	2	1

DOUBLE COUNTERPOINT AT THE TENTH

Double counterpoint at the tenth is encountered even less often than that at the twelfth, though there are some instances in Bach. The advantage of this interval of inversion is that consonances remain consonant and dissonances remain dissonant. One limitation is that imperfect consonances become perfect, so that if the original version is as rich in imperfect consonances as is typical in the style, the voice-exchanged version will have too great a proportion of perfect consonances and may thus sound harmonically weak or empty. Furthermore, parallel thirds will become parallel octaves and parallel sixths will become parallel fifths. A preponderance of contrary and oblique motion will be required to avoid such problems. The severe restrictions on the use of thirds and sixths in succession makes the tenth a difficult interval of contrapuntal inversion, and one rarely employed in the literature (and then usually for short passages).

In double counterpoint at the tenth, the lower voice may be transposed up an octave (or two), and the upper down a third (example 5-10, position II), for an interval total of a tenth (or seventeenth). Or the upper voice may be transposed down an octave and the lower up a third (example 5-10, position III). Example 5-10 demonstrates the difficulty of composing workable counterpoint in this technique. Notice how the parallel sixths and thirds become unusable parallel fifths and octaves.

Ex. 5–10

In example 5-11 the upper voice has been transposed down an octave, and the lower up a third, crossing to form invertible counterpoint at the tenth (octave plus third equals tenth). Observe in this excerpt (which has been simplified for demonstration) the preponderance of tenths, fifths, and octaves in position I, which become unisons, sixths, and thirds in the inverted form (position II). Note also the considerable use of contrary and oblique motion, and the complete absence of parallel motion, arising from the limitations of this technique.

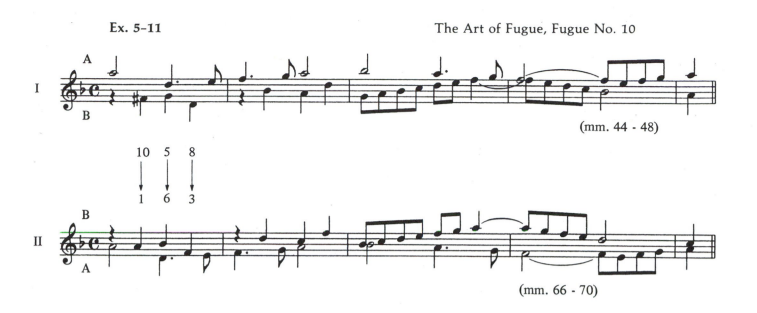

Here is a table of intervals for double counterpoint at the tenth. Observe that each interval-pair adds up to eleven.

Original:	1	2	3	4	5	6	7	8	9	10
Inverted:	10	9	8	7	6	5	4	3	2	1

General Comments

The following four points should be kept in mind when writing double counterpoint.
1. Do not allow the voices in the original position to be separated by more than the interval of inversion, else they will not cross properly in the exchanged version. Adding an octave to the inversion interval of one of the voices will help in avoiding this problem. Thus, double counterpoint at the fifteenth will allow more freedom of range than that at the octave.

Ex. 5-12

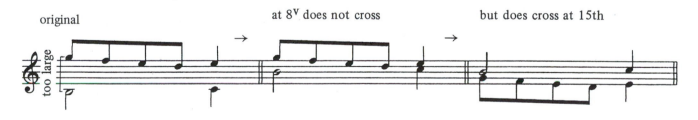

2. Be especially careful of the "problem" intervals, being sure to treat them with care in the original position. These include:

		Original	Inversion
A.	double counterpoint at the octave:	fifth	fourth
B.	double counterpoint at the twelfth:	sixth	seventh
C.	double counterpoint at the tenth:	sixth	fifth
		third	octave

3. In double counterpoint at the twelfth and tenth, because these transpositions produce pitches on scale degrees other than those of the original, the exact size of the *melodic* intervals in each voice may vary somewhat between versions. For example, an M3 in the original may invert as an m3, or vice versa. Compare, for instance, the two versions of voice B in example 5-11, where the melodic intervals have the same number value in each version but have slightly different qualities because of their different positions within the scale.

Ex. 5-13

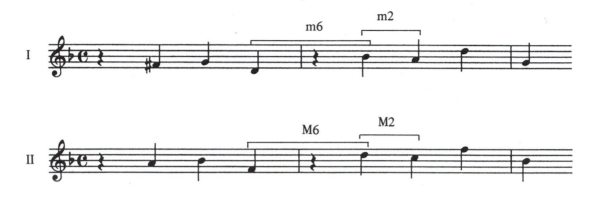

Such minor discrepancies are necessary to preserve tonality and scalar identity. It will also occasionally happen that chromatic alteration (inflection) of one or two notes of the inverted version will be required by harmonic or melodic considerations. See, for instance, the two versions of voice B in example 5-9.

4. A particularly characteristic device for Bach is a sequence in which the two voices alternate two themes, using double counterpoint.

Ex. 5-14   Well-Tempered Clavier I, Fugue No. 10, mm. 15–18

Invertible counterpoint in three voices (triple invertible counterpoint) will be discussed in chapters 9 and 10.

Exercises

1. Will the following example make acceptable counterpoint at the octave? At the fifteenth? Write it out in its voice-exchanged versions to check your answer. Discuss any problem intervals.

2. Will the following example make acceptable double counterpoint at the twelfth? Check by writing out its second version. At the tenth? Mark and discuss problem intervals.

3. Add a new voice in double counterpoint at the octave or fifteenth to these given lines. Check each in its exchanged version. Write out every harmonic interval as a number on the music. Be sure the new voice has clear shape and motivic variety, and that there is no voice crossing.

Above

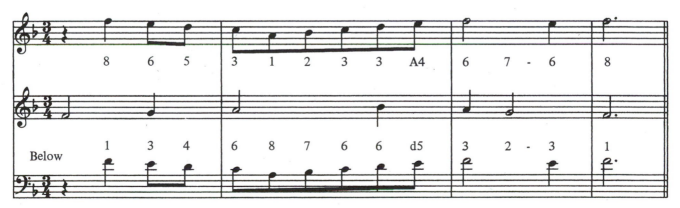

a. (new voice in quarters and eighths)

b. (new voice in halves and quarters)

4. Add a new voice in double counterpoint at the octave or fifteenth, then continue in the same way for a few more measures, breaking off the double counterpoint just before the cadence to allow for a typical PAC figure. Check both versions for harmonic clarity and vertical intervals.

a.

b.

5. Add new voices to the lines given above (in exercises 3 and 4), using double counterpoint at the twelfth and tenth. Analyze the harmonic implications and vertical intervals.

Notes

1. *Double* will be the preferred term here, as *invertible* often seems confusing because of its association with melodic inversion. Invertible counterpoint in three voices will be referred to as "triple invertible counterpoint." For further information on double counterpoint, consult *The New Grove Dictionary of Music and Musicians*, "Invertible Counterpoint," vol. 9.

IMITATION; CANON

Ex. 6–1   Two-Part Invention No. 8

Ex. 6–2   Organ Sonata No. 1, First Movement (manuals only)

Ex. 6-4   Canonic Variations on "Vom Himmel hoch," Variation No. 1

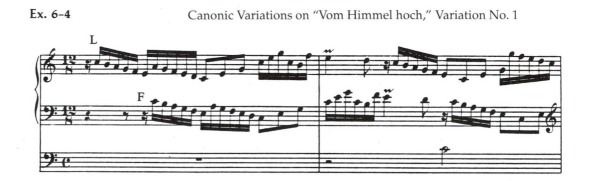

(free bass voice)

IMITATION

Directed Study

Perform and discuss the excerpts above, focusing on the thematic relationship between the voices. They share the same material, by the process we call *imitation*, in which the two voices begin the theme at different times, and often on different pitches. When analyzing imitation, we need to focus in turn on several different aspects of the music:

1. What is the *time interval* of imitation—that is, how many beats or measures after the first voice (the *leader*, shown as L) begins does the second voice (the *follower*, shown as F) enter?

2. What is the *pitch interval* between the first note of the leader and that of the follower? Is the follower above or below the leader?

3. For how long does the imitation continue? Distinguish between slight adjustments of accidentals, used for harmonic variety or modulation (as in example 6-4, m. 3, lower voice, beat 1), and actual changes of note, indicating an end to the initial imitation (in example 6-1, compare m. 7, upper voice, with m. 8, lower voice) and perhaps a shift to a different interval of imitation. If there is change of time or pitch interval, for how long does the imitation continue at this new interval?

4. Above all, what is it about the rhythmic and harmonic/intervallic structure of a given theme that allows it to be imitated successfully at a particular interval? In other words, what allows a given theme to form good counterpoint against itself?

Discussion

Imitation is an ancient and powerful musical device that allows composers to limit radically the amount of musical material required for a work, to integrate the voices thematically with each other, and to ensure equal interest in all voices. First explored in the late medieval period, techniques of imitation had been well developed before Bach, so that he came as the culmination of a long tradition, to which he brought unsurpassed mastery of technique and breadth of conception.

Imitation is the essential technique used in composing canons, inventions, and fugues. Bach also uses the device often in the composition of other forms. The ability to construct themes suitable for imitation, and to understand the ways in which the imitative process can be applied to them, is a prerequisite for the composition of larger imitation-based forms. This may best be accomplished through the analysis and writing of canons.

A brief discussion of the excerpts opening this chapter will be helpful here. We would describe example 6-1 as using "imitation at the octave below, at three beats" (or "at one measure"). This imitation continues strictly, note-by-note, from m. 1 to m. 8, third note, when the lower voice has a c^1 instead of the expected d^1. At this point, the pitch interval of imitation shifts to the ninth below, for harmonic reasons, allowing the music to stay in C major. This imitation ends at the beginning of m. 12, beat 1, lower voice.

Observe the harmonic and rhythmic structure of m. 2 of the theme (the leader). It implies a tonic triad, allowing the first measure of the follower, which implies tonic harmony, to enter against it. Further, its rhythmic content forms good 2:1 counterpoint against the follower, and the overall contours of these two measures provide contrary motion. Likewise, m. 3 of the leader is so constructed as to form solid 2:1 counterpoint (with contrary motion) against m. 2 of the follower, and so on through the passage. Any theme meant to accompany itself (that is, to be treated imitatively) must be thus calculated to serve as the best possible counterpoint against itself, at whatever intervals of imitation are appropriate to its rhythmic and harmonic/intervallic structure. Observe throughout these examples that good themes for imitation are also satisfying as lines (that is, are well-shaped and coherent).

The imitation in example 6-1, mm. 9–11, uses only the diatonic notes of C major, even though this means that the imitation is not exact as to interval quality. For instance, comparing m. 9, upper voice, with m. 10, lower voice (example 6-6), we see that the placement of the whole and half steps is different in the two voices. These subtle differences in interval quality (but usually not in the actual number value of the intervals) are characteristic of imitation in this music, and are needed to allow the music to stay in one key area.

Ex. 6-6

Example 6-2 is an instance of imitation at the fifth above, at two measures. Notice that the first voice is in E♭ major, and the second voice imitates it a fifth higher, using the notes of B♭ major (the a♮² in m. 4). Imitation at the fifth usually implies imitation in the dominant key.

Example 6-3 imitates at the tenth above, at four measures. Imitation of a minor theme at the tenth will automatically produce the relative major key. Notice the b♭¹ in m. 8, last beat, upper voice. This is a typical adjustment-by-accidental for a harmonic reason (a secondary dominant of C).

In example 6-4, the upper voices imitate at the octave at one beat, a very close imitation interval that does not allow the ear to assimilate the theme fully before it is imitated. The imitation continues strictly, except for the f♯, m. 3, beat 1, lower voice, a harmonic adjustment which is needed to preserve the (temporary) feeling of G major.

Example 6-5 imitates at the sixth above, at one beat. The imitation continues strictly (within the diatonic scales of G and D major), right up to the cadence in m. 16. The nonimitative bass voice provides harmonic clarification, motion, and motivic filling-in.

CANON

When imitation is carried out rigorously through an entire piece, or a substantial section of a work, we speak of *canonic imitation*. A self-contained movement or work using strict imitation throughout is a *canon*. These are some important aspects of canonic writing:

1. The theme must be interesting and memorable, with a clear-cut melodic profile and at least one interesting melodic or rhythmic feature.
2. After the follower enters, the leader must continue with a natural-sounding continuation of the opening material, obeying the dictates of good linear writing and sound counterpoint which we have been studying. It will often form double counterpoint against the other voice. Both voices, as they continue, must have clear direction and motivic unity, and interrelate rhythmically in a convincing way.
3. The most common and easy-to-handle time intervals will be one or two measures. The follower usually starts on a beat, weak or strong, comparable to the leader, thus reinforcing the meter. That is, if the leader starts on beat one, the follower is very likely to also. The only exception to this latter point will occur in very close (stretto) imitation.[1] Close stretto tends to obscure the leader; very long time intervals imply a very lengthy continuation.
4. The most common pitch interval for imitation is the octave. The principal difficulty with imitation at this interval is harmonic monotony and static tonality, which is the reason for the adjustments by accidental which we have seen (examples 6-3 and 6-4), allowing for secondary dominants and modulation as the work progresses. The harmonic implications of the theme will determine both the time and the pitch intervals, as will be demonstrated below. A canon at any pitch interval is possible, as long as scalar (accidental) adjustments are used to assure tonal stability and harmonic clarity. Imitation at the unison will cause voice crossing (see example 6-7), and is usually best avoided. The larger the pitch interval, the easier it will be to avoid crossing.

Ex. 6–7   Goldberg Variations, Variation No. 3

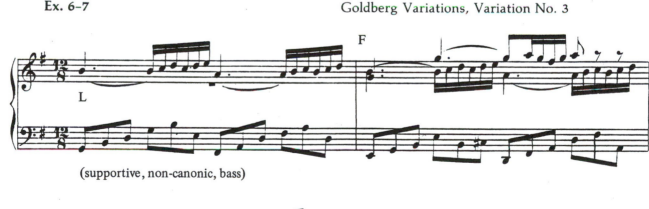

(supportive, non-canonic, bass)

---

5. Canons can end in various ways:
   A. The voices can end together (as in example 6-5), the canon continuing up to the cadence.
   B. The leader can continue to the end, the follower breaking off before the end and continuing with free (nonimitative) material to the cadence. Or the leader may break off, the follower continuing its imitation to the end.
   C. Both can break off before the end, finishing with nonimitative figuration, as in several of the *Goldberg Variations* canons.
   D. The canon can continue indefinitely, if it is so written (using repeat signs or a verbal instruction to that effect). This is an "infinite" or "circular" canon. One of the canons in *A Musical Offering* is of this type.
   E. The voices can simply trail off as each finishes the theme, so that the canon ends with one voice alone. Vocal canons (rounds) often end this way.

The process for composing a canon is straightforward.[2] The following order is recommended, and is shown in example 6-8.

1. Compose the leader up to the point at which the follower enters, keeping in mind harmonic clarity and simplicity, shape, motivic unity, and rhythmic drive.
2. Bring in the follower in an appropriate place in terms of time and pitch interval.
3. Continue the leader against the follower, keeping in mind the precepts of good two-voice counterpoint as regards vertical intervals, clear harmony, idiomatic nonharmonic tones, and rhythmic interplay. This line must represent a smooth, logical continuation of the opening of the leader.
4. Continue the follower exactly as you did the leader in example 3, above. Here, though, you may begin to make subtle adjustments (by accidental only, not note) to accomplish a modulation and/or avoid tonal monotony. See example 6-8, m. 5, lower voice c♮.
5. Meanwhile, the leader will continue with its counterpoint, reinforcing any new tonal direction taken by the follower. The canon may be continued in this way for as long as the materials suggest. Be sure to return to the tonic key before the end.

Modulation can best be accomplished by reinterpreting some *diatonic* note of the theme in a new harmonic/tonal context. Thus, in example 6-8, the d^1 from m. 3, beat, 2, upper voice, is harmonized by a B♭ triad in m. 5, providing a common chord modulation into F major.

Ex. 6-8

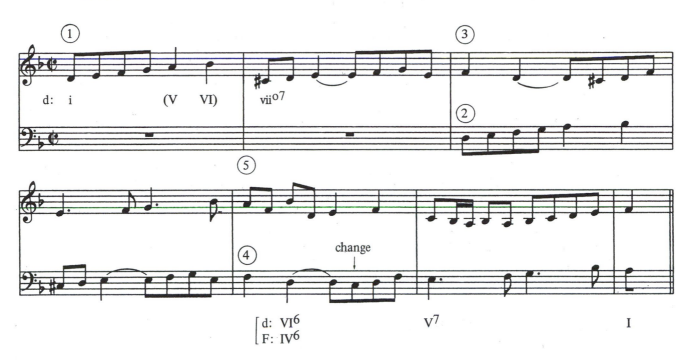

Circled numbers refer to the process suggestions above.

In example 6-9, the harmonic implication of beat two of the leader (marked "X") is ambiguous. It could be understood as implying either a V^7 in G minor, or a V in B♭ major:

In mm. 1, 2, and 3 it is treated as implying V^7 in G minor, and then reinterpreted in m. 4, beat 2, as V in B♭, setting up a new tonality in the following measure.

Ex. 6-9

Example 6-10, a canon at the ninth, is intended to demonstrate that canons at dissonant intervals will imply harmonic changes as the follower enters. Thus, the entrance of the follower in m. 2 causes a harmonic change from tonic to dominant. In the same way, imitation at the unison, third, fifth (in some cases), and octave implies that the follower may come in with tonic harmony, as in example 6-8. This canon demonstrates a brief tonicization of the relative key, with the new scale introduced in mm. 3–4. The circled number again indicates the order of composition of each measure.

Ex. 6–10

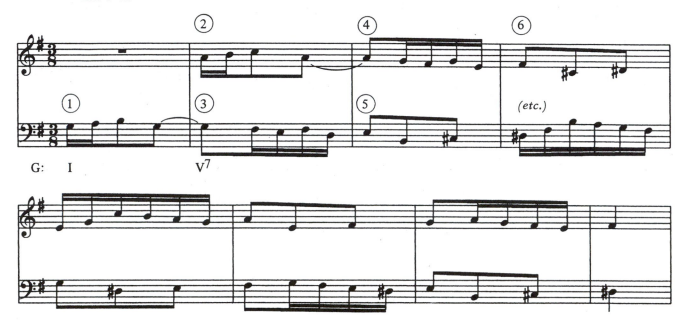

One further point about imitation (it will be covered in more detail under fugue, pp. 188 ff): the imitations we have been studying have mostly been *real* (see examples 6-1, 6-2, 6-4, 6-7, and 6-8)—that is, the melodic intervals are the same number-value for leader and follower. In most typical cases of *tonal* imitation, a tonic-to-dominant leap at or near the beginning of the leader is answered by a dominant-to-tonic leap at the comparable place in the follower, and vice versa. There are other aspects of tonal imitation, but this statement covers most cases. In canons real imitation is preferred. Changes of *accidentals* only, often needed for harmonic (scalar) reasons, do not constitute tonal imitation. See example 6-4, m. 3, beat 1.

Ex. 6–11

Variants in the Imitative Process

While it is not the intention of this text to be exhaustive in its coverage of all possible forms and procedures, still it will be of interest to show examples of several special types of imitation, as these will become useful later as devices for development within larger forms, especially in fugal composition. Any of these devices can be carried out consistently through a work, making it a canon, or one may appear as an incidental contrapuntal detail in the course of a larger work.

In *imitation by melodic inversion (motu contrario,* or *contrary motion),* the follower is a melodic inversion of the leader. Example 6-12 imitates by contrary motion at the fourth below, at three beats. There is a free, supporting bass.

Ex. 6–12   Goldberg Variations, Variation No. 12

(supportive bass line)

Example 6-13 is a canon by contrary motion at the fifth above at two beats, with a free (non-imitative) bass line. In canons at the fifth above (or fourth below) the follower often enters with dominant harmony.

Ex. 6-13   Goldberg Variations, Variation No. 15

(supportive bass line)

A theme intended to be imitated by contrary motion must have a clear melodic profile, so that it will not lose its identity in melodic inversion. Scale passages (compassing a fifth or sixth) and triad or diminished seventh chord outlines tend to characterize such themes, as such shapes are distinctive, and may be inverted without losing their identity. When inverted, they can be used to imply the same harmony as the noninverted form, as shown in example 6-14.

Ex. 6-14

g: i ——————   i —————   g: vii°7 ————   vii°7 ————

"Royal" theme (*Musical Offering*)   *Art of Fugue*, theme

In imitation by *augmentation*, the follower doubles the note values of the leader. In example 6-15 the bottom voice (the pedal part has been omitted here) is a canon by augmentation with the upper voice. The middle voice is not imitative, having the function of filling in the harmony and reinforcing the motivic material.

Ex. 6–15   Canonic Variations on "Vom Himmel hoch," Variation No. 4 (manuals only)

The excerpt below (example 6-16), which Bach describes as a "canone per augmentationem in motu contrario," is for only two voices, with no freely supporting voice.

Ex. 6-16   The Art of Fugue, Canon No. 1

The following fugal exposition (example 6-17) uses augmentation and contrary motion between the lower and upper voices. The middle voice imitates the lower voice by contrary motion but with the same rhythmic values.

Ex. 6-17   The Art of Fugue, Fugue No. 7

Imitation ends

Themes to be imitated by augmentation must be planned very carefully so that the theme will retain its character in augmentation, and create no problems of motion or harmonic rhythm.

In imitation by *diminution* the follower halves the note values of the leader. In the following fugal opening, the upper voice imitates the lowest by diminution and contrary motion, while the middle voice imitates the lowest by diminution only.

Ex. 6-18   The Art of Fugue, Fugue No. 6

In a *double canon*, two themes are treated simultaneously in canon. In example 6-19 the outer voices have a canon at the octave at three beats, using as a theme the Christmas chorale "In dulci jubilo," while the inner voices have a different canon at the octave at three beats.

Ex. 6-19   Chorale Prelude "In dulci jubilo"

In *retrograde canon (crab canon or canon cancrizans)* the follower is a melodic retrograde (backward) version of the leader. Clearly, the listener is unlikely to be aware of such devices when hearing the work.

In a *table canon (Tafelkanon)* the same music is read from opposite sides of a table, so that one player is reading the retrograde inversion of the other player's part, often using a different clef, as specified by the composer). Works of this kind belong to the genre of musical parlor tricks, with which several of the great composers have entertained themselves. The *Musical Offering* contains examples of retrograde and table canons.

Rounds (catches) are vocal canons at the unison or octave, usually very simple in technique and aesthetic. Many of the great composers wrote large numbers of rounds for their own and their friends' amusement, notably Henry Purcell, Wolfgang Amadeus Mozart, and Ludwig van Beethoven. Since Bach did not indulge conspicuously in this pastime, we will not take up the composition of rounds here.[3]

Exercises

1. Briefly define the terms *imitation, canon, stretto, contrary motion, real* and *tonal imitation, augmentation canon, double canon, retrograde canon,* and *round.*
2. Make a step-by-step list of the process for writing a canon.
3. Analyze several examples of strict canonic imitation, as selected from the literature by your instructor. The following are the major collections of canons by Bach:
   * *the Goldberg Variations (Aria mit 30 Veränderungen),* one of Bach's greatest and most beloved works, is a masterful set of variations, in which every third variation is a canon at a successive larger pitch interval, from the unison to the ninth, most of them with a supporting bass voice (taken from the bass of the aria)
   * the four canons from *The Art of Fugue*
   * the *Canonic Variations* on *"Vom Himmel hoch,"* for organ
   * the canons from the *Musical Offering,* technical tours de force
   * *Fourteen Canons* on the first eight notes of the aria ground bass from the *Goldberg Variations,* a newly discovered cycle of canons (published by Bärenreiter as volume V/2 of the *Neue Bach-Ausgabe*)

   The Two-Part Inventions Nos. 2 and 8 are in canon, and there are several chorale preludes using a strict canonic technique. Canon is widely used elsewhere in Bach's music as a device for development.

   As you analyze, be aware of:
   * time and pitch intervals of imitation
   * length of exact imitation (place at which the imitation breaks off)
   * adjustments by accidental for harmonic/modulatory purposes
   * special devices (inversion, augmentation, diminution and so on)

4. Themes for Imitation Practice

Attempt systematically to find every practicable time and pitch interval (both above and below the leader) for imitation of these themes. Try first the unison at each time interval, including close stretto; then try the second at each time interval, then the third, and so on, including the octave and ninth. Slight adjustments of accidental are permitted. Do not attempt imitations by contrary motion, augmentation, or diminution. Those themes beginning with a leap of a fourth or a fifth may be given tonal or real imitations. An octave or fifteenth may be added to the pitch-interval of imitation, as needed, to avoid voice-crossing.

Present only those versions that work well in terms of intervals and harmony.

5. Next, to the themes given in exercise 4, attempt systematically to find every practicable interval for imitation by contrary motion, augmentation, and diminution, and combinations of contrary motion with one of the other devices. Those themes above marked with an X are especially worth trying, but not all the themes are aesthetically suited to all these treatments (for instance, a diminution of h will sound silly). As in exercise 4, adjustments of accidentals, and octave displacement of the follower to avoid voice crossing, may be employed as needed. Every time and pitch interval should be explored. Present only those that prove successful.

6. Continue the following canonic openings for six to twelve more measures. Allow them to modulate if that seems appropriate. End in an authentic cadence, breaking off the canon at the last possible moment.

   The canons should be written in double counterpoint. Be sure, while composing, to keep in mind the necessity for clear shape, motivic consistency, idiomatic harmony and nonharmonic tones, and a sound rhythmic relationship between the voices. Analyze fully.

   A supportive, noncanonic bass voice may be added to exercises f and h. See pp. 181 ff for discussion.

7. Study in detail one of the canons from the *Goldberg Variations* (or one of the *Fourteen Canons* on the Goldberg aria ground bass). Use it as a procedural and harmonic model for a newly composed canon at the same time and pitch intervals.

8. Compose original instrumental two-voice canons at a variety of intervals. Some of these may employ supportive bass lines, as in the *Goldberg Variations*. Read pp.181 ff before writing the bass line.

9. Compose rounds based on texts of your choosing, or as assigned by the instructor. This may also be done as a group assignment for the whole class, working together at the blackboard.

Notes

1. *Stretto* implies imitation at a very close time interval, typically of a theme that was imitated at a longer time interval earlier in the same work. This device will be discussed in detail in chapter 11.

2. A segmental approach is suggested here as a practical and effective way of learning to compose canons. The danger of this process is that the student may lose sight of the shape and continuity of the canonic melody, and these aspects may need periodically to be brought to his or her attention. The aim is to develop the ability to construct a melody that will form good counterpoint against itself. To this end it will be wise to play all the way through each canonic voice of the examples in this chapter and discuss its rhythmic, intervallic, and harmonic construction as these aspects relate to its suitability as a canonic theme.

3. More information on the history and literature of canon may be found in *The New Grove Dictionary of Music and Musicians*, "Canon," vol. 3.

CHAPTER 7

The Two-Voice Invention

The fifteen Two-Part (that is, Two-Voice) Inventions of Bach stand among the very few major collections of two-voice contrapuntal works. Originally intended as keyboard and compositional studies for his son Wilhelm Friedemann Bach (1710–84), the Inventions are a definitive catalog of devices for the making of a great deal out of very little musical material.[1] In some ways, two-voice imitative writing is the most difficult compositional discipline, as one must make the harmony clear and satisfying with a minimal texture, and without the use of any "filler" material. It is perhaps in their works in thinner textures that the technique and imagination of the great composers come through most clearly.

Bach's inventions (his so-called Three-Part Inventions we will call Sinfonias) are the most efficient music: texturally lean, balanced between the voices, and compact. There are no superfluous notes and no purely accompanimental patterns. As with fugue, it is not accurate to speak of "form" in an invention. It is a *procedure* rather than a form, arising out of the principles of imitation and motivic manipulation, as well as certain principles of tonality. Because of this, we will need to be careful not to generalize too much from what we find in any given invention. There are, however, some generalizations one can safely make about all inventions, and that is the purpose of this chapter.

The Exposition: Theme and Countertheme

Below are given the expositions of several inventions. Play them, and discuss them as directed.

Ex. 7–1   Invention No. 1

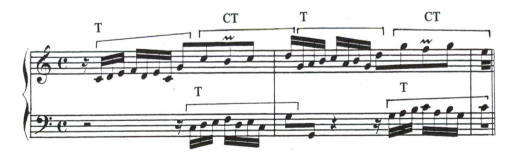

Ex. 7–2   Invention No. 3

Ex. 7–3   Invention No. 4

Ex. 7–4   Invention No. 7

Ex. 7–5   Invention No. 9

Ex. 7–6   Invention No. 13

Directed Study

Analyze these expositions in the following terms:

1. Identify the theme (T) and countertheme (CT). There may or may not be a consistent CT (the counterpoint heard against the T). In what ways is the T-CT relationship an example of good counterpoint?

2. Analyze the imitation intervals (both pitch and time) between the voices. For how long is the imitation carried on strictly?

3. Analyze the harmony and nonharmonic tones. Is the tonic made clear? Is the harmony simple and functional? In what ways is the CT used to clarify the harmonic implications of the T?

4. What motivic ideas seem to comprise each T? Each CT?

5. Based on what you hear and see in these excerpts, what would you say are the characteristics of a good T? A good CT?

6. Graph the form of each exposition. Here as a sample is a graph of No. 1.

T	CT	T	CT
T		T	

Discussion

The first section of an invention, in which the thematic material is presented, is called the *exposition*. It consists of from two to four statements of the theme, often with a countertheme in the other voice.[2] As you have seen, there are various possible layouts for an exposition, in fact even more than appear above. The type of invention we will be concentrating on is typified by Inventions 1, 3, and 4, in which the T is heard first in the upper voice, alone, and imitated immediately by the lower voice at the octave, while the upper voice continues with the (optional) CT.[3] There are several variants of this process, though. For instance, in Invention No. 9 both T and CT appear simultaneously, in double counterpoint, exchanging voices in mm. 5–7. Numbers 5, 6, and 9 are of this type. In several of the inventions the lower voice is used at the opening to establish key and downbeat, though in No. 13 this voice has a version of the fragmentary CT (m. 1, beats 1–2). And two of the inventions, 2 and 8, have extended expositions in canon.

While there are several ways, then, of organizing an exposition, some generalizations can be made.

1. The T is a relatively short musical entity (usually 2–6 beats; never longer than four measures), with all the features of a workable musical theme:
   - clear meter and key
   - clear diatonic, functional harmony (often only I and V)
   - a restricted range (within an octave)
   - restricted and consistent motivic content
   - consistent rhythm (usually all sixteenth notes)
   - memorable shape and motivic detail
   - contrapuntal workability (capable of thematic/contrapuntal manipulation of various kinds).

2. The CT, when there is a consistent one, exhibits all the features of good counterpoint in this style:
   - forms good rhythmic contrast and complement to the T
   - verifies meter
   - clarifies harmonic implications of the T
   - flows naturally out of the end of the T
   - is often written in double counterpoint at the octave against the T.

   There may, as mentioned, be an "extra" note or two in the lower voice beginning m. 1, meant to establish downbeat and key, but this is usually not part of the CT proper, and is found only when the T begins after a rest. The CT is, in any case, far less important than the T to the invention as a whole, and is in many inventions highly variable or fragmentary.

3. The exposition begins with the T in the upper voice, imitated immediately by the lower voice. The imitation is at the octave (except for No. 10, which imitates at the eleventh below, on the dominant). In these imitations, the follower always enters on a beat (weak or strong) comparable to the leader. After the T ends, the upper voice continues smoothly—usually by melodic elision—into the CT, if there is to be one.

---

4. There are several possible formal schemes for the exposition, of which the most common are graphed below.

A.	upper voice:	T	CT		(No. 2)
	lower voice:		T		
	key:	I--------------------			
B.	upper voice:	T	CT	T	(No. 4)
	lower voice:		T	CT	
	key:	I--------------------			
C.	upper voice:	T	CT	T	(CT) (No. 1)
	lower voice:		T	CT	(T)
	key:	I-------------- (V)------------------			
D.	upper voice:	T	CT		(No. 6)
	lower voice:	CT	T	(double counterpoint)	
	key:	I---------------------------			

Inventions with relatively long T's (Invention No. 2, for instance) tend to use a type A exposition. Only with a very short T (two to four beats) will the "extra" entries of types B and C not seem redundant. One way of avoiding the feeling of redundancy inherent in type C is to transpose the T and CT to the dominant, as is done, for example, in Invention No. 1 (m. 2). This will work especially well if the T ends on the dominant note.

Here is an analysis of the exposition of Invention No. 4.

Ex. 7–7

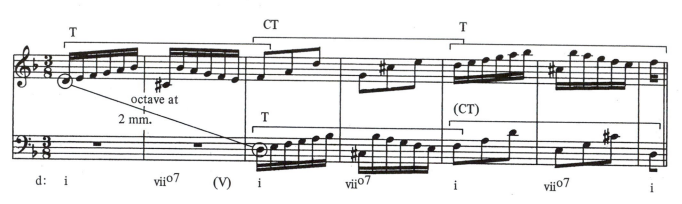

The T is a strongly directed scalar shape, starting on the downbeat on tonic. The harmonies implied are: i | vii°⁷ (or V) | i |, or T | D | T; structurally, the exposition simply prolongs tonic harmony. It closes with a brief IAC on the mediant note (m. 3, beat 1), eliding with the first note of the CT, which comes smoothly out of it. This note of elision or overlap is typical, and very important for covering the "joints" in any imitative work. The CT provides new material, a rising triadic outline, which may also be heard as coming out of the T (every other note of m. 1 presents a D-minor triad outline). Thus, both contrast and unification are inherent in this CT. It also provides a 2:1 rhythmic contrast to the T and reinforces its metric and harmonic implications.

The lower voice imitates the upper at the octave below, at two measures. Observe that m. 6, lower voice, is not exactly the same as m. 4, upper voice, but their shapes and harmonies are the same. The CT is usually far more variable than the T, and clearly subsidiary to it.

The CT in the upper voice then elides into an "extra" statement of the T, mm. 5–6, an octave higher than the first statement. This redundant entry gives the listener one more chance to assimilate the T before the first episode begins, and provides access to a higher register from which to begin the first episode. The exposition, then, can be graphed as:

```
                              IAC
                              ____
              T        CT     T   |
                       T      CT
```

Exercises

1. Analyze and graph several more expositions as suggested on p. 125. Several inventions can be found in the anthology.
2. Compose themes based on these chord formats, based on the observations above:

g: $\frac{4}{4}$ T | D | T

D: $\frac{3}{4}$ T | PD | T D | T

e: $\frac{3}{8}$ T | PD | D | T

A: $\frac{3}{4}$ T | D | T

3. Compose CTs for the following Ts:

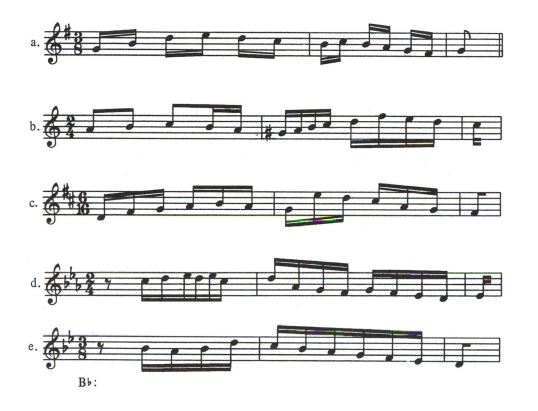

The CT should provide good rhythmic and directional contrast, and metric and harmonic reinforcement of the T. It should form effective double counterpoint at the octave with the T.

4. After the Ts you wrote in exercise 2 have been corrected and approved by the instructor, compose CTs to them.
5. Compose expositions based on the best T–CT pairs done in exercise 4. Work for a smooth elision from the T into the CT (and back, if there is an extra entrance of the T). Try several of the formal schemes suggested on p. 126. Analyze fully. Consult the sample exercise below for process.

Sample Exercise

1. Chord format given:

   e: $\frac{2}{4}$ i | iv   V | i   or: T | PD   D | T

2. T written:

3. CT written, checked against T:

4. Exposition composed:

Points to note are clear harmony, strong vertical intervals (tenths and sixths), typical nonharmonic tones, clear shaping, 2:1 rhythms, T and CT eliding smoothly, motivic material suitable for manipulation later.

THE EPISODE

It is in the *episodes* that a composer's inventiveness and technique are most evident. Bach's inventions are a great compendium of ways in which thematic material can be manipulated and combined.

The purpose of an episode is developmental and modulatory. It subjects the thematic material of the invention to processes of transformation and combination, exploring the developmental potential of the theme. It serves the function of a modulatory passage, leading away from the tonic key that unified the exposition tonally. Tonal works tend to modulate; the ear quickly becomes fatigued with one key area, and it is necessary to settle at least momentarily in subsidiary keys.

The first episode follows smoothly after the exposition, without pause, such that the ear may not realize for the first few beats that an episode has begun, especially as the thematic content of the exposition is continued here. The last beat of the exposition is the first beat of episode I. The first episode will last, depending on the meter and length of the theme, for four to twelve measures, and will end in a strong PAC in the relative key (in minor key inventions) or dominant key (in major key inventions). The first episode is often written in double counterpoint, and may be reused in voice-exchanged form as a later episode. It is usually directed downward by step or third, by sequence.

A variety of processes is used in the episodes, including:

- alteration of the thematic material by melodic inversion, fragmentation, extension, or slight changes of melodic intervals
- repetition
- sequence
- canonic imitation
- stretto imitation
- double counterpoint
- augmentation or diminution
- any combination of the above processes, especially those involving sequence and imitation

Of these devices, the overriding one is sequence, which may be combined with any of the other processes listed. All are to be found in the inventions, although augmentation and diminution are rare, being more commonly found in larger works.

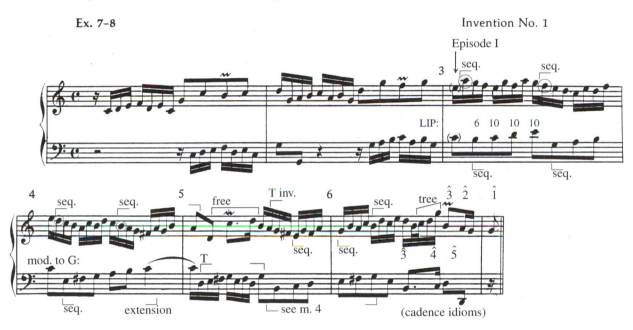

The upper voice in m. 3 has an *inversion* of T, the lower voice an *augmentation* of the first four notes of T. Both are treated by *sequence*, with a two-beat unit, down by thirds. The structure of this invention, on both the local and larger-scale levels, is permeated by thirds. The upper voice iterates the sequence a total of four times, ending in m. 5, beat 1. The lower has a total of three iterations, and an *extension* of the third one, m. 4. The upper voice in m. 5 starts with free material, then continues with the T in inversion; out of the end of this inversion comes, by *fragmentation*, a two-note or four-note sequence unit which drives upward into m. 6, breaking off into a free cadential figure. The lower voice in m. 5 has the T, followed by the same scalar extension out of the end of its sequence that it had in m. 4, and a standard cadential figuration. Incidentally, this episode is written in *double counterpoint* and reappears as the last episode (mm. 19–20) of the invention, in both double counterpoint and melodic inversion.

Take a few moments to make a graphic reduction of this episode. Notice the clearly direct-ed pitch structures, driving toward the new tonic note, G. Observe also the highly consistent LIPs, controlled by the sequences: 6-10 and 10-10.

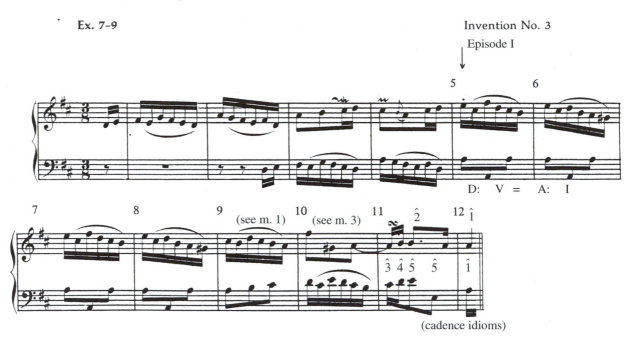

(cadence idioms)

This episode makes use of *repetition* (mm. 5–6 are repeated as mm. 7–8), a device not often employed in this music, as it can easily produce a static effect. It is used here in conjunction with a pedal note in the lower voice, which serves to establish the new key, A major, by reiteration. Note the *imitation* between m. 9, upper voice, and m. 10, lower voice, and note further that the two voices are written in double counterpoint. (The voice-exchanged version is used later.)

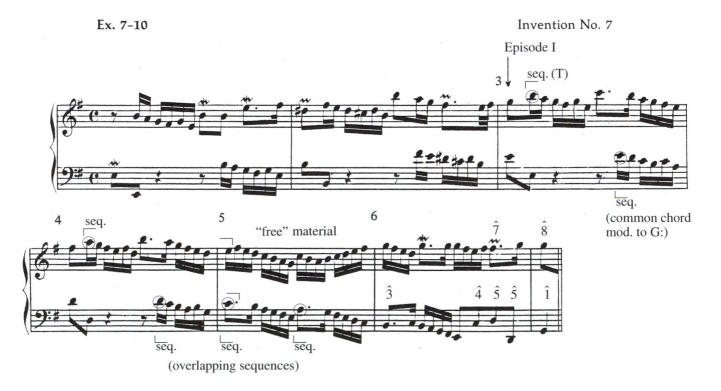

(overlapping sequences)

Here we find again an imitative sequence. A sequence unit based on the T is begun in the upper voice, m. 3, and repeated sequentially in m. 4, transposed down a step. The lower voice imitates the first part of the unit only, treating it sequentially in mm. 3-4, but then picks up the latter part of the unit in m. 5, sequencing it down by thirds. The upper voice in m. 5 has material not strictly related to the theme, but it seems closely related to the sequential material in mm. 3–4, as does the cadential figuration in m. 6. This is well worth mention, for in the inventions material not literally derived from a theme will still seem related to it by shape and/or rhythm.

Ex. 7–11   Invention No. 13

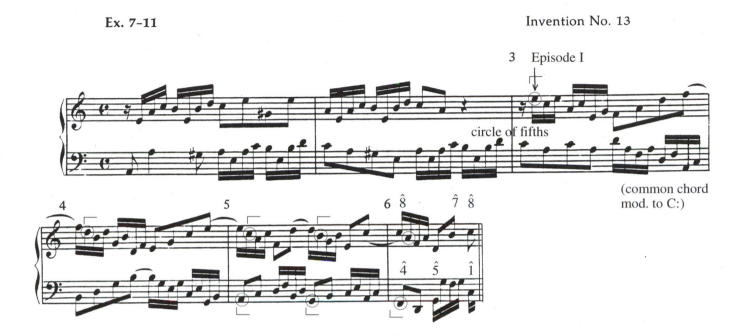

This episode makes use of an idea that, while not exactly that of the main theme, still seems closely related by interval and shape—and, of course, rhythm. This new idea, introduced in m. 3, becomes almost a second theme for this work. Again, both voices are imitative, sequentially organized, and controlled by the circle of fifths. The upper voice has a sequence unit of four beats, transposed down by step in mm. 3–4. In mm. 5–6, it is halved by fragmentation into a two-beat unit, again transposed down by step. The lower voice imitates at two beats, a fifth (twelfth) below, then produces its own fragmentary version of the theme in m. 5, sequentially treated, and cadences in m. 6. The effect of the shortening of the sequential unit in m. 5 is to give a sense of excitement and drive toward the cadence, and a stretto-like effect. Incidentally, you may have noticed that the initial sequences of most works tend to be transposed *down*. Sequences toward the ends of inventions (and fugues), especially a final sequence, will tend to be transposed upward, building toward a climax.

Prepare a linear reduction of this passage and note the clear descending stepwise structures and (slightly hidden) 10-10 pattern.

A more extended stretto is to be found in one of the episodes of Invention No. 14.

Ex. 7–12   Invention No. 14, mm. 12–13

Linear structure: (chain of thirds down)

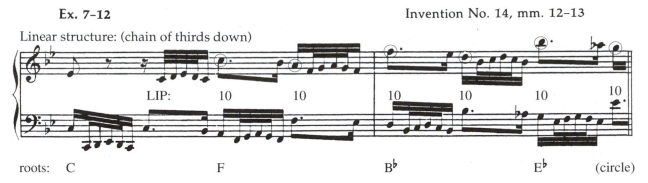

roots: C   F   B♭   E♭   (circle)

This is a stretto at one beat at the fifteenth, progressing partly around the circle of fifths (roots: C–F–B♭–E♭).

For a superb model of extended *canon* as the basis for an invention, see Invention No. 2, on p. 320 of the anthology.

You will have noticed the strong sense of harmonic/linear direction these episodes exhibit as they drive downward from one strong beat to the next and finally into the PAC that ends the first episode. As is typical when sequence is involved, these sections tend to be organized around very highly directed structural pitch schemes, and often operate on the harmonic basis of the circle of fifths. The circle also forms the basis for the sequences in example 7-11 (mm. 3-4, roots: A–D–G–C; mm. 5–6, roots: A–D–G–C–F). The structural pitch lines of example 7-11 are quite clear:

Ex. 7–13

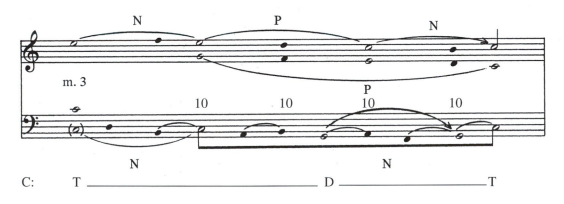

The same essential principles of linear/harmonic organization will be pointed out in the analysis of Invention No. 4, pp. 138–139.

Demonstration of Thematic Manipulation

Here is a series of motivic manipulations and contrapuntal combinations.

Ex. 7–14

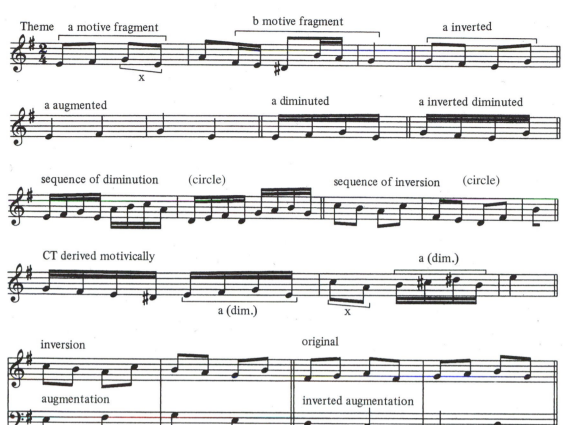

Exercises

1. Analyze several more invention episodes, as found in the anthology on pp. 319 ff. Discuss them in detail, as suggested on pp. 123 ff.
2. Based on your observations of Bach's processes, and on the demonstration above, write a number of motivic manipulations, in one voice only, applied to:
   A. the invention themes on p. 127 and/or
   B. your own newly composed themes, as approved by the instructor, from Exercise 2, p. 127.
   Experiment with inversion, fragmentation, extension, augmentation, and diminution, and treat these transformations sequentially.
3. Write two-voice models of development based on the manipulations written in exercise 2, above, using imitation and sequence.
4. Compose several two-voice invention episodes based on an assigned theme from p. 127, or on an original theme of yours from exercise 5, p. 127, as approved by the instructor. These should flow smoothly from the ends of the expositions composed in that assignment. Analyze fully, including harmony, structural pitches, LIPs, and sequences.

THE INVENTION AS A WHOLE

We have already learned that the invention is not a fixed form. Rather, it is a generalized procedure for writing music. It is possible, though, to draw some general conclusions as to the order of thematic and tonal events in an invention. While an invention, like a fugue, is essentially a continuous work, spun out of the theme by the processes we have been studying, it may at the same time exhibit a sense of section through the placement of strong PACs. In other words, form in imitative works is largely a function of key and cadence, as well as of the alternation of theme and episode.

The only accurate generalization we can make about the overall form of most inventions (and fugues) is that there will be an exposition of the theme, followed by episodes developing the theme and modulating to closely related keys; the episodes will usually alternate with statements of the theme per se (middle entries), and the work will eventually return to the tonic key. Thus, the invention stands as a paradigm or model for the fundamental organizing principle of statement–departure–return. We could graph the formal outlines of an invention as:

Exposition → Episode → Middle Entries/Episodes → Return

It is also possible to refine this formal scheme as shown below. Parentheses indicate thematic or tonal options.

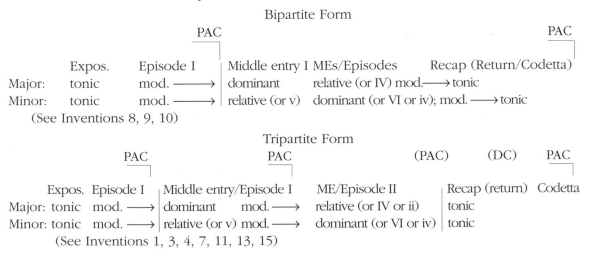

(See Inventions 8, 9, 10)

(See Inventions 1, 3, 4, 7, 11, 13, 15)

There are, as we have noted, several other possible overall schemes. Inventions 5, 12, and 14 are not as sectional as the graphs above suggest. Invention No. 6 is in the form of a binary suite movement (and thus essentially bipartite), written in double counterpoint. Invention No. 2 (being canonic) is also not as obviously sectional as most of the others, as it lacks strong internal cadences.

In the bipartite scheme, the first section is shorter, more stable, and less modulatory (only one modulation) than the second, which has the function of developing and returning. In the tripartite scheme, the three sections may be of roughly equal length, though the last is typically somewhat longer.

Below are several more points regarding the large-scale aspects of an invention.

Cadences

The cadence figures used may or may not relate in an obvious way to the theme. Further, within a given invention they may all be similar melodically, or they may not. For example, in Invention No. 1, the first two cadences resemble each other, but the last is quite different. No two are literally the same, nor is any necessarily drawn from the theme in any obvious way, beyond very general similarities of figure or rhythm. Cadence idioms or formulas, in other words, are usually more style-defining than distinctive to a particular work. Rarely are they an important unifying factor within any given piece.

Ex. 7–15

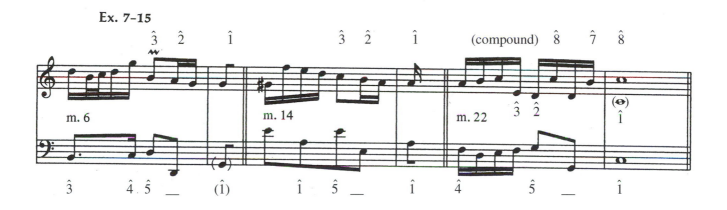

In Invention No. 3, however, all five cadences (mm. 11–12, 23–24, 37–38, 52–53, and 57–58) have the same figuration.

Authentic cadences will be placed quite regularly within a work—in a brief invention about every six to eight measures, in a longer one roughly every twelve to sixteen—since the sections in a larger invention are proportionally longer. There may be a deceptive cadence placed near the end, replacing an expected PAC at or shortly after a climactic point, in the tonic key. Half-cadences are found infrequently in the inventions, and indeed are far less common in Bach's music than authentic cadences.

Episodes

In general, the later episodes will tend to be longer, more complex in technique and more tension-producing, tending more than the earlier ones to such devices as imitation, stretto, and upward-moving sequence. If episode I is written in double counterpoint, it may well reappear as episode III or IV, with the voices in their exchanged positions, and even (as in Invention No. 1) by contrary motion (melodic inversion).

Middle Entries

The theme is likely to return literally, in some closely related key, at least twice in the course of the invention. These returns (middle entries) are distinguished from episodes by the fact that they contain the entire theme (not just fragments and/or manipulations of it), though the ear cannot always distinguish in context between a middle entry and the beginning of an episode. The music immediately following the end of the first episode is usually a middle entry in the dominant or relative key, with the T heard first in the lower voice. For typical middle entries, see Invention No. 1, mm. 7–8; No. 6, after the double bar; No. 8, mm. 12–13; No. 13, mm. 6–7. Middle entries usually contain just two entries of the theme, although one entry is sufficient. The two entries may be imitative at the octave, with the lower voice leading.

Shape; Climax; Ending

The presence of sectional divisions should not make one lose sight of the importance of overall shape and continuity. The sense of linear/harmonic direction given by the structural pitches in the episode is of critical importance to the shaping process, as we have seen. The final section is often climactic, containing rising lines, stretto, faster harmonic rhythm, and/or greater harmonic tension. The final section often includes a clear return of the theme in tonic in one or both voices (see Invention No. 3, mm. 43–44; No. 4, mm. 44–45; No. 5, mm. 27–28). It may also include a coda or cadential extension,[4] following a deceptive cadence (DC), which replaces an expected PAC in tonic (Invention No. 3, mm. 52–53; No. 4, mm. 48–49; No. 7, mm. 21–22). The purpose of the ending section is to release tension in a rapid, dramatic, downward gesture, usually encompassing an octave from tonic to tonic.

Ex. 7–16   Invention No. 7

Ex. 7–17   Invention No. 3

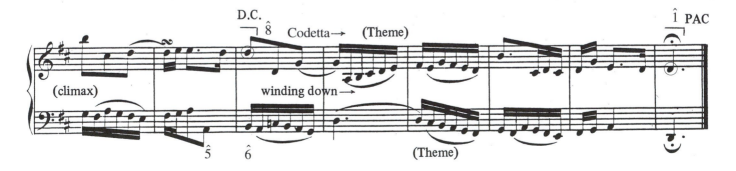

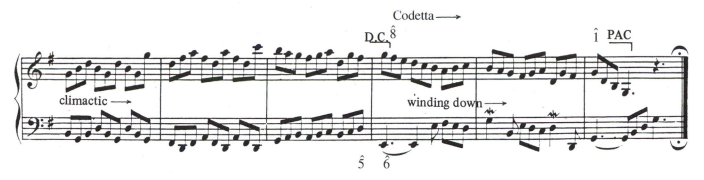

Sectional Elisions

It is important in writing to assure that the sections are elided and continuous. The juncture between the exposition and episode I in particular is accomplished by elision. There are no "dead" or thematically empty beats here, and cadences are immediately followed by important thematic material.

Ex. 7–19   Invention No. 4, mm. 16–20

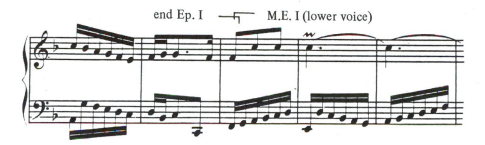

Ex. 7–20   Invention No. 8

(note one-measure overlap)

ANALYSIS OF A COMPLETE INVENTION

The following analysis of Invention No. 4 is not intended to be an exhaustive exploration of this work, but simply suggestive of approaches to the analysis of an invention.

Ex. 7–21

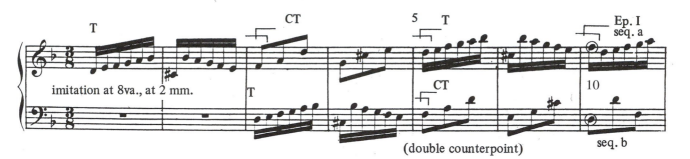

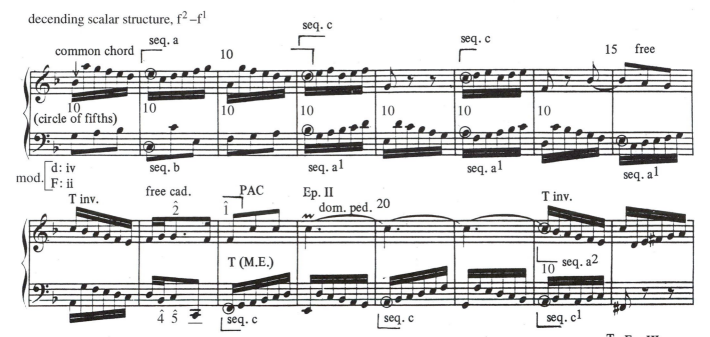

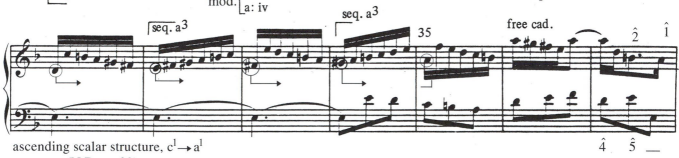

The Craft of Tonal Counterpoint

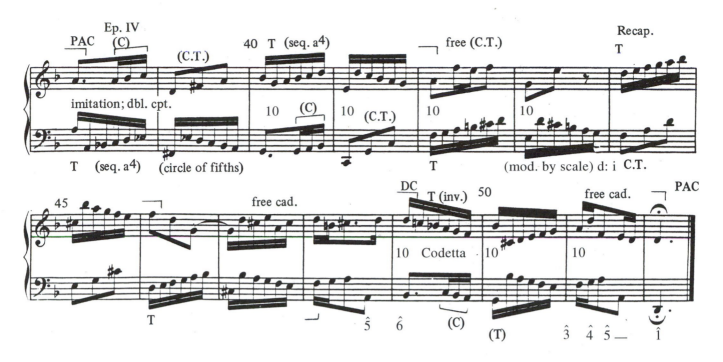

Comments on Invention No. 4

Expos.	Ep. I	PAC	M.E./Ep. II	Ep. III	PAC	Ep. IV	Recap.	DC	Codetta	PAC
mm. 1–7	7–18		18–30	30–38		38–44	44–49		49–52	
d:	F:		F: a:				d:			
length:	18			21				15		

There are climactic moments around mm. 34–37 and 42–45, with textural/harmonic/rhythmic tension concentrated around mm. 46–50, and a rapid tonic octave descent following the DC in m. 49.

A structural-pitch graph of mm. 7–18 follows. Play this reduction and then the music again.

Ex. 7–22

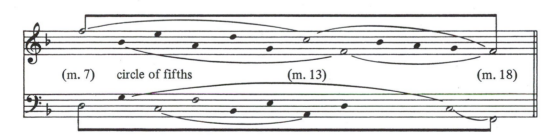

There are several aspects to notice here:

1. The descending scalar passing motions (shown ⌒).
2. The descending octave scale, f²-f¹ upper voice, mm. 7–18, clearly tonicizing F major. These pitches form both a descending tonic scale and a circle of fifths. Note that in a circle of fifths, every second pitch forms a descending scale. This is a fundamental structural pattern for tonal music, including that of Bach.

---

3. The lower voice structural pitches, forming a descending scale in parallel tenths (seventeenths) with the upper voice, also outlining a circle of fifths; this combination of descending tonic-octave scale, circle of fifths, and parallel tenths in the outer voices is a common and very strong linear/harmonic framework for sequential episodes. Compare, for instance, *The Well-Tempered Clavier*, 1, Prelude No. 1, mm. 1–19.

The key areas overall are tonic–relative–dominant–tonic, outlining a tonic triad in D minor (which is also the outline of m. 1). The cadences confirming these keys divide the work into three sections, of eighteen, twenty one, and fifteen measures.

The T undergoes several slight alterations. Its first note is changed to form sequence unit "a" (mm. 7ff. and throughout), and it is inverted in mm. 22–23 and 49–50. This subtle variability of the T after the exposition in this type of invention is quite characteristic.

The cadence figurations are variants of each other, providing another unifying element.

The modulation to F major may be understood to occur by common chord in m. 8; that from F major to A minor in m. 26 also occurs by common chord. The modulation back to D minor occurs around m. 42, and is quite subtle, with both voices sliding down by structural steps F–E–D from m. 42 to m. 46. The tonic scale is reintroduced in m. 42, lower voice.

There is a multitude of wonderful details. To point out just a few:

1. The subtle thematic interrelationships: m. 8, lower voice, which relates to both T (shape) and CT (rhythm); m. 11, upper voice, to T (fragmentation and repetition); the return of this latter figure in m. 38, upper voice, and m. 40, lower voice; the appearance of the T in inversion against itself in m. 50, as a kind of compression of the whole work just before the close.
2. The structural line, upper voice, mm. 30–35, which forms an ascending A minor scale, prefigured in its first measure (m. 30).
3. The two dominant pedals, mm. 19–22 and 29–34.
4. The passage in mm. 38–41, a fine instance of double counterpoint with imitation, with a circle-of-fifths harmonic basis (A–D–G–C).
5. The brief moments of "free" material, mm. 36–37 and 47–48, upper voice. There will usually be one or two brief moments in an invention or fugue that may not demonstrably "belong" to that work (except rhythmically, of course), but in an inexplicable way "feel right." Where these details go, and what they should contain, cannot be taught. It is safe to say, though, that they tend to precede cadences, especially near the end.

Exercises

Note: It is suggested that these exercises be done in the given order, and that each stage of work be checked and approved by the instructor. A good deal of one-on-one work may be required. It is also suggested that all written work fit within the range of Bach's keyboards, or exceed that only slightly.

1. Graph the overall form of several complete inventions from the anthology, as suggested in this chapter. Show:
   • sections, including exposition, episodes, middle entries, recapitulation and codetta (if any)
   • cadences
   • keys
   • exact measures and overall formal proportions
   • climactic points

2. Choose one invention analyzed under exercise 1 above as a detailed model and analyze it again on the music, including the following details:
   - chords, modulations, keys, cadences
   - all entrances of T and CT (if any)
   - all sequences and LIPs
   - structural pitches (circle and/or graph)
   - all transformations of the T
   - all imitations, including stretto (if any)

3. Compose an invention based roughly on the following formal/harmonic plan. It may be based on one of the minor themes composed under exercise 2 on p. 127, or on a newly composed theme. The theme, countertheme, exposition, and sample episode should be approved by the instructor before the entire invention is completed. This scheme need not be followed in every detail, as any formal plan may be altered to fit the implications of a given theme.

	Exposition			*Episode I*	*Middle Entry I*	
				PAC ⌐		
Upper voice:	T	CT	T	Circle of fifth sequen-⌐	CT	T
Lower voice:		T	CT	tial modulation to the relative key.	T	CT
Key:	g:			⟶ B♭:		
Approx. no. of measures:		6 mm.		8 mm.	4 mm.	

Episode II and ME II		*Episode III*	*Return*		*Coda*
	PAC ⌐			DC ⌐	PAC ⌐
Modulation to dominant key		May be a new version of Episode I. Modulation to tonic key.	T CT		
			CT T		
⟶ d:		⟶ g:			
4–6 mm.		6–8 mm.	4 mm.		4 mm.

4. Compose an invention on one of your own themes, following the model constructed under exercise 2 above, including its harmonic language and placement of cadences and sequences, insofar as this format will fit your theme. Particularly recommended as models for a first invention are Inventions 1, 3, 4, or 7, or perhaps 8, 10, or 13.

5. Next, compose an invention on one of your own themes (perhaps one of those written under exercise 5, p. 127, with the episodes written under exercise 4, p. 134). This may be structured along the lines of one of the formal graphs done under exercise 1, p. 140

Notes

1. Bach worked fairly often in the two-voice imitative texture; for instance, Preludes 3, 11, 13, and 20 in *The Well-Tempered Clavier*, book 1 are, in effect, two-voice inventions, as in book 2 are Preludes 2, 6, 8, 10, and 20. The *Four Duets* for keyboard are also imitative. More historical information may be found in *The New Grove Dictionary of Music and Musicians*, "Invention," vol. 9.
2. We are using the terminology *theme/countertheme* in preference to *motif/countermotif*, so that we may reserve the term *motif* for its other usage—that is, as a small fragment or cell of musical "raw material" found within a theme. The term *subject* we shall reserve for the theme of a fugue.
3. It would be possible to take as our model either the extended canonic type or the type opening with extended double counterpoint. The approach typified by Inventions 1, 3, and 4 has been selected as best approximating the conditions found in fugal writing, and thus as the most useful preparation for it.
4. Because of their brevity, these ending sections are sometimes termed *codettas*.

CHAPTER 8

THREE-VOICE COUNTERPOINT I: TEXTURE, RHYTHM, HARMONY

Perform and analyze the following excerpts as suggested on pp. 147 ff. Perform the voices separately, then together. These may be performed on keyboard or on three instruments, or even vocally, as ranges permit.

Ex. 8–1   French Suite III, Gavotte

Ex. 8–2   Well-Tempered Clavier I, Prelude No. 9

5

Ex. 8–6   Goldberg Variations, Variation No. 2

Ex. 8–7   Well-Tempered Clavier I, Prelude No. 24

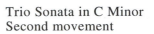

Trio Sonata in C Minor
Second movement

Largo

Ex. 8–11

French Suite I, Allemande

Directed Study

Analyze and discuss the above excerpts, including texture, rhythm, harmony and counterpoint.

TEXTURE. Are the voices equally important and active? Does any voice seem to be harmonic "filler"? Are the voices at times paired with each other? Which pairings seem most common?

Consider spacing. What is the widest interval between adjacent voices? What seem to be the typical spacings? Do you find any voice-crossing? Are the voices always playable by two hands?

What would you say about the range of each voice? Do the voices in general have a wider or narrower range than in two-voice writing?

Do the voices share the same motivic material? Is there any imitation? If there is, analyze it in the usual ways.

RHYTHM. Make a rhythmic chart of several excerpts, as below. Generalize about what you find. Here is a sample, based on example 8-1, mm. 1–3.

Ex. 8–13

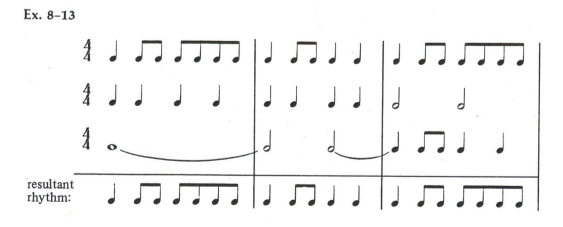

Are there moments when all the voices move in the same values? For how long? Do they ever move together in the fastest available value?

Are the meter and pulse always clear? How is this accomplished?

Investigate the use of rests, ties, and syncopes. What rhythmic and textural functions do they appear to have?

HARMONY AND COUNTERPOINT. Analyze the harmonic intervals in several selected excerpts, between each pair of voices. Are there any new essential intervals? Did you find any linear intervallic patterns in two or all three voices?

What types of chords do you find, in what positions and with what doublings and/or omissions of chord tones? Analyze five or six excerpts in detail.

Does there appear to be any difference in harmonic vocabulary between two- and three-voice counterpoint? If so, what chords are new here?

What nonharmonic tones do you find? Are there any new idioms? Are there examples of simultaneous nonharmonic tones? Consider in detail the use of suspensions, including what the nonsuspending voices do at the points of suspension and resolution. Are there places where two voices suspend simultaneously?

Consider the contrapuntal relations between each pair of voices. Which intervals are used in parallel motion, and for how long? Which are not? Do you find any instances of direct or unequal fifths, or direct octaves? If so, which pairs of voices are involved?

Note what the three voices do, melodically, at cadence points. Write down in musical notation those cadential melodic idioms that appear to be typical, including scale-degree numbers.

GENERALIZATIONS. Based on this sample, what would you say are the principal features of good three-voice counterpoint as regards texture, rhythm, harmony, and any other aspects of contrapuntal relationship? Make a list in class.

Discussion

Three-voice writing is in many ways the ideal texture for counterpoint. There is, compared to two-voice composition, an added richness and explicitness of harmony, more rhythmic variety, and many more possibilities for contrapuntal combination. Composers at the time of Bach show a great fondness for counterpoint in three voices, which can be said to be an even more fundamental texture than four voices. Mastery of three-voice writing leads easily to mastery of four; there are no basic techniques to be learned in thicker textures that cannot be learned as well in three voices. And many four-voice works contain substantial passages of three-voice writing.

There are also some dangers here for the student. One may notice a tendency to think only harmonically, to lose sight of the primacy of line, to let the inner voice degenerate into aimless filler, or the lowest voice into purely harmonic support. New problems of doubling, rhythm, and dissonance treatment may occur. But these problems are overcome with application, and the rewards of mastery of three-voice composition are great.

TEXTURE AND RHYTHM

The excerpts at the beginning of this chapter have been selected to show a variety of possible textures, and rhythmic and motivic distributions. Some feature roughly equal voices, in terms of motivic content and rhythmic activity (examples 8-8, 8-9, 8-12). Five of them pair the upper voices against a rather less active bass (examples 8-2, 8-3, 8-5, 8-6, 8-10). Two exhibit a somewhat predominant upper voice (examples 8-1, 8-4), and one an active bass against paired upper voices (example 8-7). You will have noticed, though, that these textures are likely to change in the course of just a few measures. Flexibility of texture is a characteristic of much three-voice writing in this style. It is possible, through rests, to reduce the texture to two voices for a few beats at a time. Reduction to one voice is very rare. It is also possible to thicken the texture in writing for keyboard, for example, at the end of a movement. Example 8-11 shows a typically free keyboard texture, varying from two to four voices, though it is essentially a three-voice work. This is a good example of *Freistimmigkeit*—literally, "free-voicedness." Your writing, at this stage, should in general be strict about the number of voices employed, limiting textural freedom to an occasional passage in which the texture reduces to one voice (sometimes doubled in octaves), often just before a final cadence; or thickens to four, five, or even six voices at the final cadence.

Both options are shown in example 8-14, from a work that is preponderantly in two-voice texture. All your writing should be playable in two hands, so that the middle voice will always be within an octave of one of the outer voices.

Ex. 8–14   Well-Tempered Clavier I, Prelude No. 3 (end)

Good three-voice counterpoint should possess a feeling of equality between the voices. There will, of course, be moments during which one voice will be subsidiary in activity or interest, though even then there will be some sense of line (see example 8-1, middle voice). The bass voice will at times take the role of harmonic support, by way of pedal point (examples 8-1, 8-2, and 8-3), or of root-outlining movement (example 8-5 and in parts of examples 8-8, 8-9, and 8-10). Pedal point is normally restricted to tonic and dominant notes, and tends to occur at openings, and approaching final cadences, with the purpose of emphasizing and prolonging important harmonic goals. Approaching cadences, the bass will fall into the same harmonic/supportive patterns that we observed in two-voice writing (example 8-1, mm. 7–8; example 8-4, mm. 3–4, 7–8, and 15–16; example 8-6, mm. 3–4, 7–8, and so on).

Rigorous imitation, as in fugue, is a way of ensuring equality of voices. Another is informal motivic imitation, as may be seen in examples 8-3, 8-9, 8-11, and 8-12. This type of casual motivic imitation is much easier to handle technically than rigorous canonic imitation, and is highly recommended as a texture for student work. Observe in example 8-15 the way in which the sixteenth-note scalar figure, in both its original and its inverted forms, is passed among the voices.

Ex. 8–15   Well-Tempered Clavier II, Prelude No. 21

Textures in which two voices are equally active, with the third voice (often the bass) moving in different note values are common, but it is rare to find extended voice pairing unless it characterizes the texture of an entire work, as in example 8-5. Brief upper-voice pairings (that is, trio-sonata texture), such as those found in examples 8-3, 8-6 (see especially mm. 5–7 for a typical texture), 8–7, and 8–9 (mm. 1, 2, and 4) are very common, especially in fugal episodes, where the upper voices may be in canon. The kind of pairing in which two voices, often the upper two, move in parallel thirds or sixths in the same rhythmic values is contrapuntally weak, and should not be continued for long unless one intends a homophonic effect (see example 8-5). In example 8-16, observe that brief homophonic passages (mm. 1–2) may alternate with those that are more contrapuntally distinct (mm. 3–4, 6–8), providing textural variety and effectively bringing the contrapuntal passages into relief.

Ex. 8–16   Trio-Sonata in C Minor, First movement

As regards rhythm, two points can be made here:

1. There are very few passages in which all three voices will move simultaneously in the same values, as this quickly becomes homophonic in effect. It does not occur at all in the examples heading this chapter, and almost never occurs in the shortest available value. Two-voice homophony, as is noted above, is confined to brief passages, unless it characterizes an entire movement.

2. A great variety of rhythmic relationships is available, and the fastest motion is often shared in alternation between two or among all three voices. Here are three rhythmic reductions taken from the excerpts beginning this chapter.

Ex. 8-17

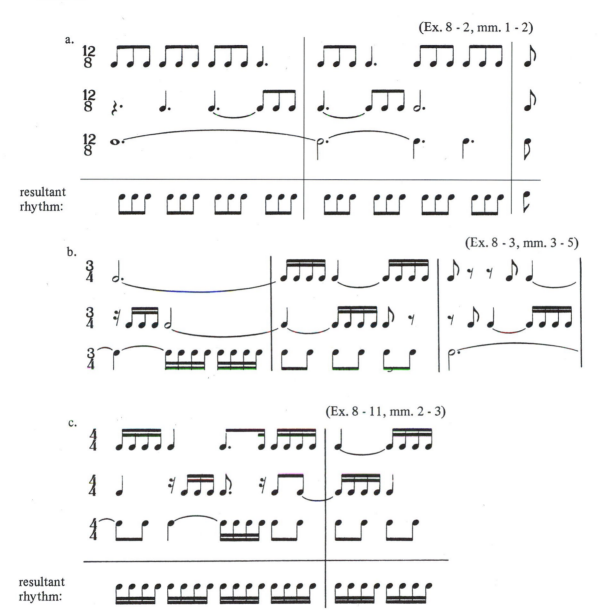

These passages, and others like them, should be studied from this point of view, as they represent an ideal state of rhythmic independence.[1] Be aware in such passages that the shortest note value is passed among the voices, and that on any given beat there will be two or three different durations in the three voices. Note especially the use of short rests and ties to break up the regularity of pulse in each individual line, avoiding the square or plodding rhythm that would result from each voice attacking the beginning of each beat. Groups of eighths or sixteenths often start after a short rest or tie.

Ex. 8–18

These devices give a needed flexibility to the rhythm and should be used freely, as long as the sense of motion is maintained by at least one voice.

In this music the pulse is consistently maintained, and the resultant rhythm (which some theorists call the combined rhythm or macrorhythm) is very regular, as can be seen in example 8-17.

Brief rests can be used freely in a line, longer rests more sparingly. A voice should come to a point of melodic completion before a longer rest. Thus, a long rest should never be preceded by a note requiring resolution. One should not hesitate to employ brief rests. They are the windows and doors of music, letting in air and light.

Ties are normally found in only one voice at a time, though two may tie simultaneously as long as the third voice continues to move steadily. The combination of regular overall momentum (resultant rhythm or macrorhythm) with the individual rhythmic flexibility of each voice is an essential ingredient of all good counterpoint, and should be kept in mind while composing.

Exercises

1. Critique the rhythmic aspects of the error-correction exercise 3 on p. 163.
2. Perform, by conducting and intoning the rhythms on a neutral syllable such as "ta," several three-voice movements from the anthology. Discuss the metric and rhythmic aspects of these works. Is the meter clear from the rhythms only, or is harmonic rhythm also a factor?

RANGE AND SPACING

The individual voices will often be more restricted in three-voice writing than in two, so the use of melodic material involving wide-ranging arpeggiation should be limited. Brief voice crossings or overlaps are acceptable, but are rare. Be aware that crossing the middle and lowest voices will result in the creation of a new bass line, and chord inversions must then be calculated from this new line.[2] While spacings of more than an octave, especially between middle and lowest voice, are found, it is not effective to sustain such passages too long, as this will tend to isolate one of the voices. The spacing ═══ is common, the spacing ═══ less so, as the result quickly becomes muddy, or isolates the upper voice. An even distribution is the ideal texture for counterpoint: ═══

In keyboard writing, the middle voice typically "migrates" between the hands, inhabiting both alto and tenor registers. Be sure your writing is playable in two hands, and conforms to the range of Bach's keyboards (at the discretion of the instructor).

RELATIVE MOTION

The restrictions on parallel motion still hold true for writing in three voices. In all such writing, each of the three voice pairs must be checked in the same way that one checks between the voices in two-voice counterpoint. The following technical details should be kept firmly in mind:

1. Parallel perfect fifths and octaves are not used.
2. Passages of parallel imperfect consonances are found, but for reasons of voice independence should not be allowed to continue too long.
3. Direct octaves and direct and unequal fifths are not usually found between *outer* voices, but an occasional direct or unequal fifth may be used between outer and middle voice. In other words, the *outer* voices behave *exactly* as in two-voice writing.

Ex. 8–19

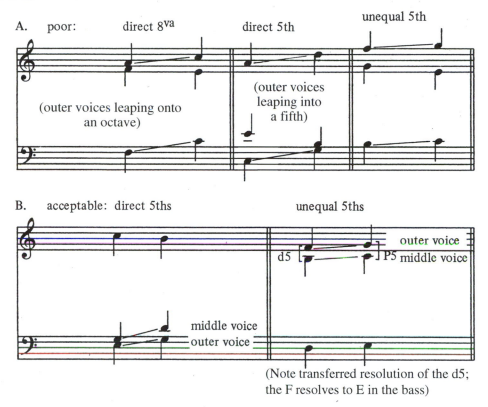

A. poor: direct 8ᵛᵃ   direct 5th   unequal 5th

(outer voices leaping onto an octave)

(outer voices leaping into a fifth)

B. acceptable: direct 5ths   unequal 5ths

d5   P5   outer voice   middle voice

middle voice   outer voice

(Note transferred resolution of the d5; the F resolves to E in the bass)

4. Any mixture of relative motions may be employed, within the above limitations, such as:

but motion by all three voices in the same direction is problematical technically and aesthetically, and should be employed with considerable caution.

Exercises

1. Critique the contrapuntal aspects of exercise 3, p. 163.
2. Critique the exercise below in terms of spacing, rhythm, and counterpoint. There are about twenty errors.

HARMONY

As the harmony at this stage is fuller and the vocabulary slightly richer, a few additional comments on harmony are appropriate.[3]

VOCABULARY. In your analyses of the excerpts beginning this chapter, you will have noticed that, once the nonharmonic tones have been taken into account, the majority of vertical sonorities are major and minor triads in root position or first inversion. The diminished triad is usually found in first inversion (typically in the progressions $vii°^6$–I or $vii°^6$–I^6). Augmented triads, except those occurring momentarily as the result of nonharmonic tone activity, are extremely rare.

Seventh chords are slightly more common in three voices than in two, as it is easier to express them with a greater number of voices. Both dominant (V^7, $vii°^7$) and nondominant sevenths are used (ii^7, etc.), though not as often as are triads. As in two-voice texture, sequences involving either secondary dominant or nondominant sevenths are found, especially in episodic passages.

DOUBLING, VOICING, AND COMPLETENESS. With major and minor triads, the following voicings and doublings are found, in descending order of frequency:

- complete triad
- two roots, one third
- one root, two thirds
- one third, two fifths
- two thirds, one fifth
- three roots (at the end, or briefly on weak beats or weak fractions of beats)

Triads without thirds (root-root-fifth or root-fifth-fifth) are rarely found, and then only briefly, as this sonority lacks harmonic tension and is indeterminate as to quality. The diminished triad is usually complete. Seventh chords are most often used in the following voicings:

- root–third–seventh
- root–fifth–seventh

One cannot successfully omit root or seventh for more than a very brief time, as the chord then changes identity.

It should be reiterated here that the less common voicings and doublings occur mainly on weak beats or parts of beats, and that considerations of line take precedence over doubling. The following chart (example 8-20) thus applies most accurately to sonorities found on strong beats, or the strong half of the beat.

Ex. 8-20

a. Major and Minor Triads

b. Diminished Triad

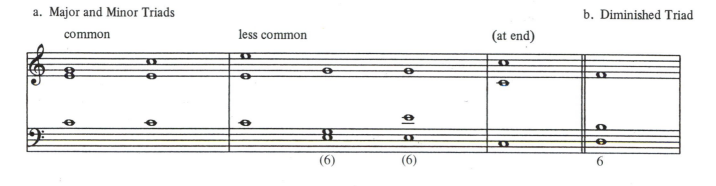

c. Seventh chords (most common voicings)

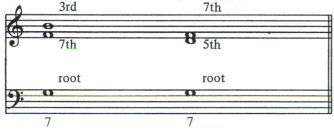

INVERSION. Root-position major and minor triads are employed where harmonic stability is needed (especially at beginnings and ends of phrases).[4] These same sonorities in first inversion are extremely useful for creating mild harmonic tension for forward propulsion, and because of their association with strong, linear bass lines. They are freely used in midphrase. Typical first inversion idioms may be found on p. 56.

Seventh chords may be used in any position, though root position and first inversion are the most common. Again, inversion may be freely used except at authentic cadences, where the root position V^7 (or V) is required.[5] Bear in mind that seventh chords are unstable and require careful resolution of their dissonant intervals and tendency tones (see pp. 50–51 for review of resolution tendencies). Whether Bach heard and understood the chord seventh as a true chord member is debatable. The seventh can almost always be analyzed as a nonharmonic tone, as can the ninth.

To summarize:

Ex. 8–21

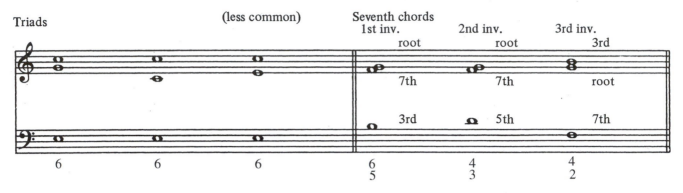

Seventh-chord inversions and doublings are freely interchanged within a chord, due to linear movement, and the aspects of completeness and doubling are therefore quite flexible. This is why the designation D can be very helpful, where dominant sonorities are interchanged in a passage.

Ex. 8–22

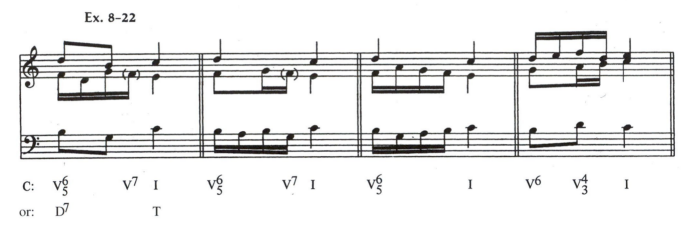

Ninth chords are extremely rare in three-voice writing. The note sounding the ninth can always be understood as nonharmonic.

The perfect fourth between the upper notes of the first inversion major or minor triad is treated as consonant, because of the fact that both these notes are consonant with the bass note. This is the so-called *consonant fourth*. Parallel perfect fourths are possible in writing with more than two voices, in successive first-inversion triads. Such triads normally move by step, most often descending. Bach rarely uses more than three such triads in succession, as the effect tends toward homophony.

Ex. 8–23

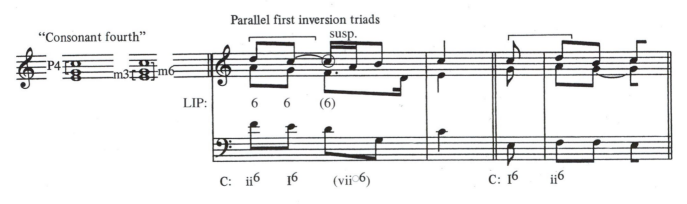

Second inversion of triads is a special case and requires separate commentary.[6] As the perfect fourth is dissonant with the bass, such chords are very unstable and are used in highly restricted ways. The only common usages in the Bach style are these:

1. The cadential [I $\frac{6}{4}$] is normally preceded by I, IV, or ii, is placed on a strong beat (or beat two in a triple meter), and is always resolved on V.

Ex. 8–24

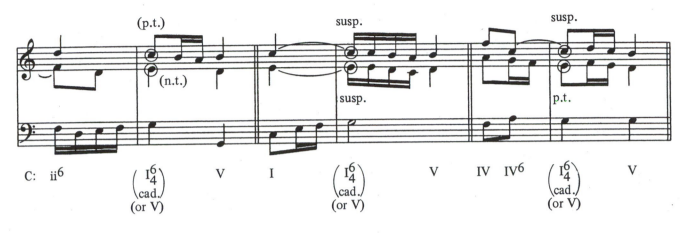

2. The neighboring $\frac{6}{4}$ is placed on a weak beat or part of a beat, coming from and returning to the same root position triad, over a stationary bass note. These are simply the result of simultaneous neighboring motion, and may well be analyzed as such. These are sometimes called "pedal $\frac{6}{4}$'s."
3. The passing $\frac{6}{4}$ is also a brief, weak-beat chord, used with a stepwise bass line to fill in between two different positions of the same chord. Again, the notes involved may simply be analyzed as nonharmonic tones.

Ex. 8–25

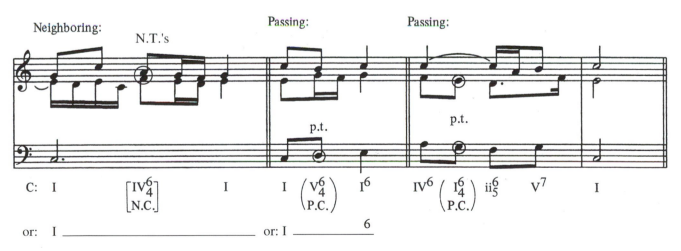

4. The arpeggiated bass line $\frac{6}{4}$ is hardly a true inversion but merely the result of arpeggiation in the bass. Like the neighboring $\frac{6}{4}$, this idiom is fairly rare in the Bach style.

Ex. 8–26

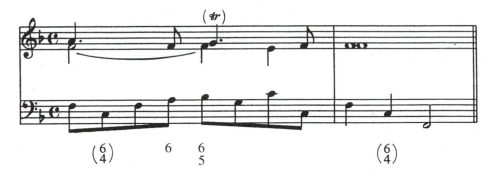

As regards harmonic intervals, there is no new information needed at this stage. With the exception of the "consonant fourth," *each pair of voices* (high-middle, high-low, middle-low) must be calculated in the same terms as in two-voice writing, with attention to incorrect parallelisms or directs, and resolution of dissonant intervals, with especially close attention to the outer voices.

Here, by way of summary to this point, is a harmonic simplification and reduction of example 8-4.

Ex. 8–27

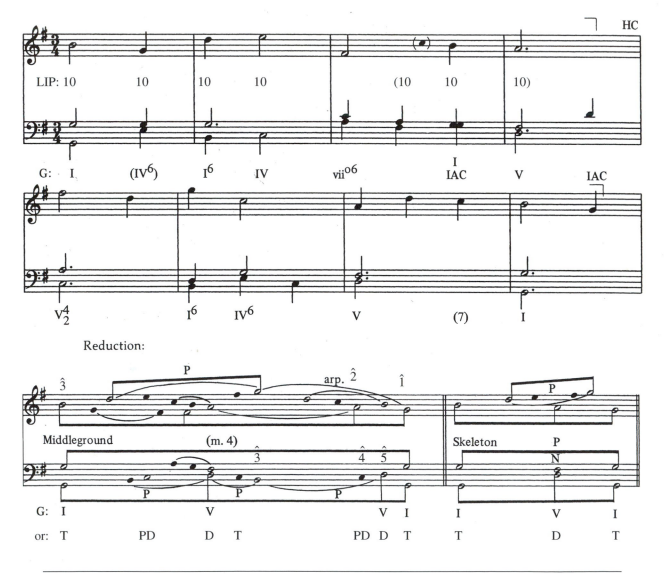

The Craft of Tonal Counterpoint

Exercises

1. Discuss the harmonic problems with exercise 3 on p. 163.
2. Discuss the following exercise in terms of chord choice, doubling, chord completeness, use of inversion, and resolutions. This can also be done by ear, playing the exercise very slowly. There are, as usual, a great many errors of all kinds.

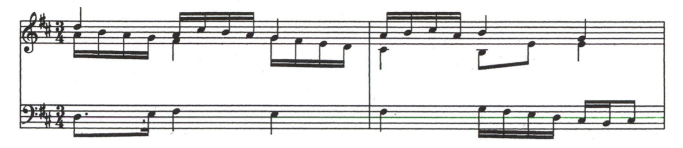

3. Analyze and resolve the following isolated chords. Analyze the dissonant intervals in each sonority, and be sure to resolve them normally. These can also be done as ear-training exercises, with each voice of a chord sung and resolved.

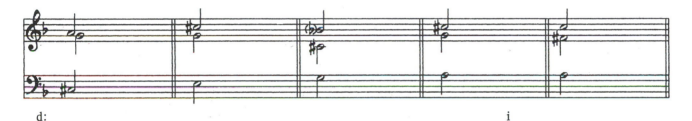

4. Concentrate on $^6_4$ chords. Part-write the following phrases, using quarter notes and three voices only. The specific $^6_4$ chords to be used are given in brackets. After checking the part-writing, articulate these frameworks with faster note values, working for motivic coherence and rhythmic continuity.

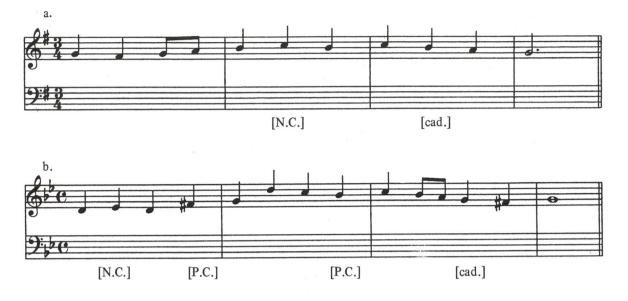

CADENTIAL FIGURES

There are no really new cadential figurations in three voices. In authentic cadences, the two upper voices will most often approach the tonic by step from above and below, and the bass by the usual dominant-to-tonic leap. Or one of the upper voices may step or leap down into the third of the tonic triad. Below are skeletal versions of a few of the common cadential patterns, and typical ornamentations of two of these patterns. The outer voices, in any case, use the same cadential idioms as in two-voice writing.

Ex. 8–28

NONHARMONIC TONES

All the nonharmonic tones employed in the style are, of course, available. They are used carefully so as not to obscure the underlying harmony nor to create harsh effects, which would cause unwanted harmonic tension. As always, the nonharmonic tones in each voice are calculated against the underlying harmony. Two technical points should be made:

1. Simultaneous nonharmonic tones are quite often used in two voices, especially the upper and middle voices.
    A. These tones are usually consonant with each other. As a rule of thumb, the faster-moving voices in any context are usually consonant with each other even when they dissonate against the third voice. See example 8-29, ①.
    B. Conversely, they may be dissonant in respect to each other if each is treated correctly with regard to the third voice. See example 8-29, ②. All dissonances in example 8-29 should be carefully analyzed and discussed.

Ex. 8–29

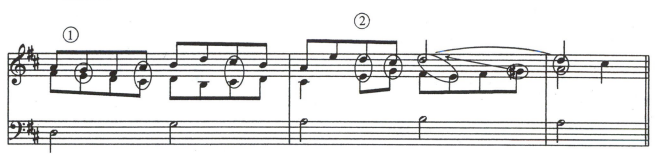

2. There are several new possibilities for suspensions. Upper-voice suspensions are measured against the lowest voice. These include the usual 4-3 and 7-6 types, and the 9-8 is now more effective than in two voices (example 8-30a). In such cases there will be two consonant voices, and one or both may have motion against the suspending voice (example 8-30b). The bass (2-3) suspension is still effective (example 8-30c). The suspension chain can be useful if not carried on too far (example 8-30d), and is particularly typical when accompanied by a change of bass at the point of resolution (example 8-30e). Characteristic in episodic passages is an upper-voice suspension chain in which the upper voices may be in canon (example 8-30f), or an upper-voice chain with a faster-moving bass line (as in example 8-7, or as shown below in example 8-30g). The suspending voices move in parallel thirds or sixths in the double suspension, and each must be correctly treated with regard to the consonant voice (example 8-30h). They can then be combined with the usual ornamentations and change-of-bass idioms. The double suspension is best not overused, as it tends toward homophony. One technical point should be noted here: if the note of resolution is not normally doubled, it should not be present against the suspension (example 8-30i), when the resolution is by half-step.

Exercise 4 on p. 163 may be done at this point.

Ex. 8–30

a.

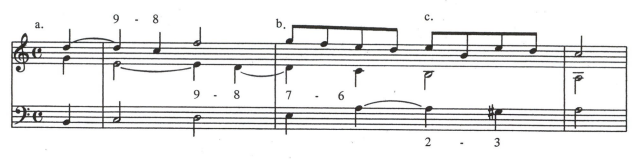

b.

c.

d.

(circle): $\hat{8}$ 7 - 6

e.

$\hat{7}$ $\hat{6}$ $\hat{5}$

(note stepwise descending structure)

f. (Canon)

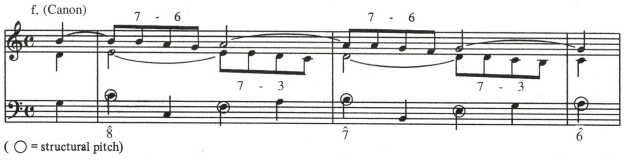

$\hat{8}$ $\hat{7}$ $\hat{6}$

(◯ = structural pitch)

g. (Canon)

(circle)

h.

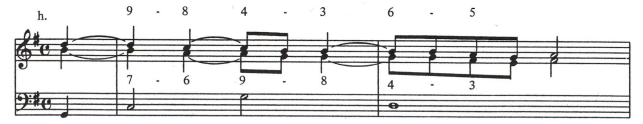

i. poor:

(half-step res.)   (half-step res.)

poor doubling   poor doubling

Cumulative Exercises

In completing the written exercises below, it is advisable to avoid extensive chromaticism, rigorous imitation, stretto, and triple counterpoint, as these will be studied in chapter 9.

1. Perform and analyze nonimitative three-voice works, as selected by your instructor from the anthology, with attention to all aspects of line, rhythm, harmony, and counterpoint. Prepare structural pitch/structural harmony graphs, as directed, paying particular attention to all aspects of patterning, including LIPs and sequences. Discuss historical and performance-practice issues as appropriate.

2. Compose two-measure cadential formulas in three voices as directed below. Write these neatly on one sheet of paper, as they can, after checking, serve as models for your own compositions in this style. Indicate scale degrees in the outer voices.

    g: PAC, IAC   E♭:   PAC, DC
    B♭: PAC, HC   c: PAC, HC
    f: PAC, DC   D: IAC, HC

3. Find the errors of line, harmony, nonharmonic tones, rhythm, and counterpoint in the following example. There are over twenty errors.

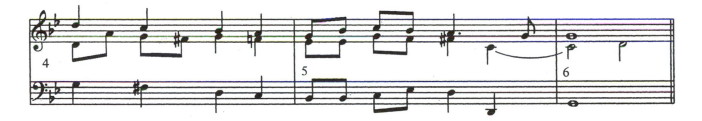

4. Articulate the following exercise by writing or improvisation in three successive versions, first in $\frac{4}{4}$, then converting the exercise to $\frac{6}{8}$ and going through the same process:
    A. Add unornamented suspensions to one or both of the upper voices of this skeletal framework
    B. Ornament the resolutions
    C. Add eighth-note motion in the nonsuspending voice or voices.

5. Add a third voice as indicated to the following exercises, using complementary rhythmic values. Employ suspensions where appropriate. Analyze fully, including harmony and nonharmonic tones. Be especially attentive to flow, motivic coherence, clear harmony, LIPs, and sequences.

A. Add a middle voice.

B. Add an upper voice.

C. Add a bass voice. Be sure to change harmony over barlines.

D. Add a middle voice.

E. Add an upper voice.

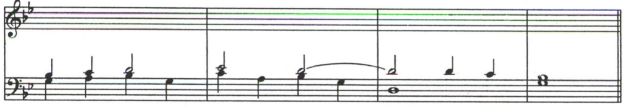

F. Add a bass voice. Work for clear, functional harmony, and clear meter (i.e., harmonic rhythm).

6. Articulate the three-voice frameworks below, using voices of roughly equal activity. Employ mixed note values and a steady eighth-note macrorhythm. Work for motivic unity, clear harmony, and typical nonharmonic tones. Analyze fully.

The instructor may wish to specify textural and tempo models from the anthology—for instance, a suite movement or prelude.

Process Demonstration

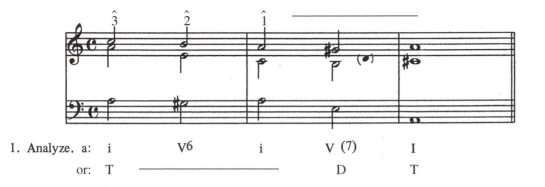

1. Analyze. a: i   V6   i   V (7)   I

     or: T ————————————   D   T

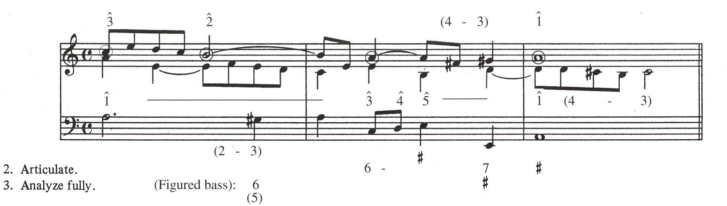

2. Articulate.
3. Analyze fully.   (Figured bass):   6
                                 (5)

A. Cadential frameworks

B. Phrase-length frameworks. Add figured bass first, then analyze structural detail and harmonic detail, then articulate.

7. Compose an eight to twelve measure example of three voice counterpoint based on the following rhythmic model for mm. 1–2. Analyze fully.

8. Compose three-voice counterpoint based on the figured and unfigured basses on pp. 71–72, as assigned by the instructor. Analyze all aspects.

9. Compose examples of three-voice counterpoint based on the chord-phrase formats on p. 74. Analyze.

10. Continue these openings for several more measures, ending on a PAC.

11. Analyze a largely diatonic three-voice nonimitative movement from the anthology. Graph the structural pitches. Analyze the overall formal structure and shape, cadences, and periodic structure, and use this as a model for the composition of a comparable movement in the Bach style. Imitation and triple counterpoint are not required.

12. Instructors who so wish may introduce the chorale prelude at this point, and nonimitative three-voice chorale preludes may be written. See chapter 14.

Notes

1. It is a very good practice to perform such passages, and even entire movements, in class, without pitches, with students intoning the rhythm of individual lines (on a neutral syllable such as "ta") while conducting the meter, thus focusing one's attention on rhythmic independence and interrelationship. It is best if each voice is intoned on a different neutral syllable (as for instance, "ta," "ti," and "too" for the three voices).

2. In music employing double bass or organ pedal with 16' pitch, the tenor may only *appear* to cross the bass.

3. As needed, you may review the material on harmony on p. 283 ff.

4. As suggested earlier, this text assumes the identity of chords in inversion. At the same time, "inversion" can often be understood (and heard) to arise from nonharmonic tone activity in the upper voices or the bass. Such inverted sonorities are of far less structural significance and stability than chords in root position, especially the primary triads (I, IV, V).

5. This is a point at which students weak in theoretical training may need a brief review of the spelling and resolution of seventh chords, which is best accomplished by drill on bass scale-degree idioms and figured bass resolutions (i.e., $\frac{4}{2} \rightarrow 6$, $\frac{6}{5} \rightarrow \frac{5}{3}$, etc.).

6. Again, the choice of whether to analyze $\frac{6}{4}$'s as such, or to understand them as the result of simultaneous nonharmonic activity, is up to the instructor. They are bracketed in the analyses, indicating a sonority of linear origin, or may, when cadential, be shown as $\underset{V}{\frac{6}{4}}$, or simply V with nonharmonic tones in the upper voices.

CHAPTER 9

THREE-VOICE COUNTERPOINT II: CHROMATICISM, TRIPLE COUNTERPOINT, CANON

CHROMATICISM

There are no specific techniques of chromaticism to be learned now that have not been discussed earlier, yet the addition of the third voice provides both a clarifying and a complicating element.[1] The opening of Sinfonia No. 9 is given in example 9-1, with a partial harmonic analysis. Perform and analyze it, with attention to structural lines and harmony, as well as details of harmony and nonharmonic tones. Issues of performance practice and affect may also be discussed, as appropriate.

The application of roman numeral symbols to this music should not be understood to imply that harmonic forces have necessarily generated it, or have more importance than line. The point is that the lines can be understood to imply harmonies that are susceptible of "functional" analysis. The reduction graph in example 9-3 is intended to clarify the linear orientation of the music. It would be wise to make a detailed reduction in class, showing the linear structure of all three voices, which is highly directed and clear.

(non-harmonic tones are circled)

Commentary on Example 9-1

This work, though not perhaps as harmonically problematic as it may at first appear, still has its ambiguities. These are, typically, the result of:

- a thin texture, especially in mm. 1–2 and 5–6
- multiple nonharmonic tones, including many on the beat (appoggiaturas and strong passing tones) and several that are chromatic
- changing key centers
- a complex harmonic vocabulary, including secondary dominants
- a quick harmonic rhythm

PHASE RELATION. In a work as complex as this (due in large part to the use of accented chromatic nonharmonic tones), there will be moments during which the harmony seems out of phase between the voices. The appoggiaturas a♭¹ and b♭¹ in m. 1, middle voice, are the first symptom of this ambiguity. This pattern has been well established by m. 2, though, so that thereafter one tends to hear these appoggiaturas as such (that is, nonharmonic). But the double neighbors (mm. 3–4, lower voice) and the anticipation figure (mm. 5–6) give the effect that the harmony in one voice is arriving at a slightly different time than in the other voices. This sets up a considerable harmonic tension that is extremely effective in giving the music forward impetus and expressive power.

Ex. 9–2

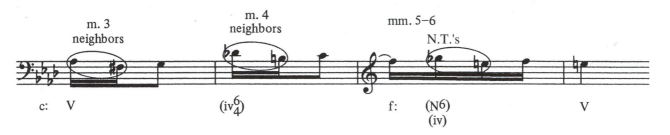

In such contexts as this, when there is multiple nonharmonic activity, including strong and/or chromatic dissonances, there will be questions as to what is harmonic and what is not.

Beyond these surface complexities, however, the underlying harmony and tonal/linear framework are normal and stable. Chromaticism in tonal music normally exists within a predictable and coherent context of *stable key areas* and *bass-line patterns*. Note in example 9-1 that the secondary dominants resolve normally (m. 1: V_2^4/V–V^6; mm. 3–4: $vii^{°7}/iv$–IV_4^6) as do the Neapolitan chords in mm. 5–6 (N^6–V^7).[2] Altered chords, including secondary dominants, the Neapolitan chord, and the rare augmented-sixth chords almost always resolve normally in this style.

Observe, in example 9-3 (a reduction of ex. 9-1, mm. 1–5), the highly directional structural (passing motion) lines, the descending chromatic lines (I→V), and the simplicity of the overall tonal/linear organization. Note especially the typical figured bass sequential (LIP) pattern in mm. 1–2: $_2^4$→6, $_2^4$→6.

Ex. 9–3

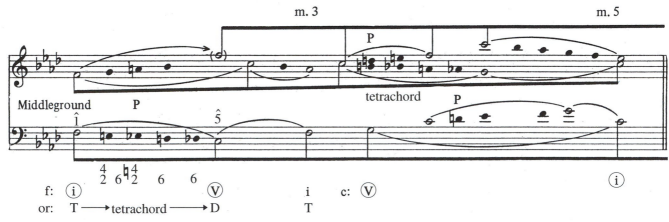

In example 9-4, a canon at the seventh with supportive nonimitative bass, a descending chromatic tetrachord is again to be found.[3]

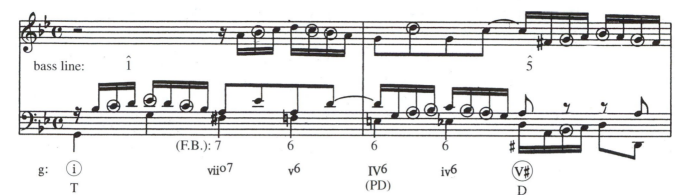

bass line: $\hat{1}$ $\hat{5}$

(F.B.): 7   6   6   6

g: (i)   viiº7   v6   IV6   iv6   (V♯)
    T   (PD)   D

$\hat{1}$ $\hat{5}$ $\hat{1}$

(i) V6   i   V$^4_3$/iv (see commentary) (V♯)i6 ii6 V♯ (i)
T   (PD)   D   (T)

bass-line,
mm. 1 - 3 $\hat{1}$ $\hat{5}$

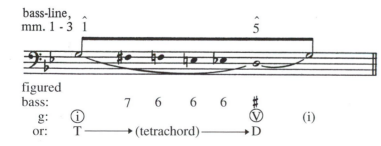

figured
bass: 7   6   6   6   ♯
g: (i)   (V)   (i)
or: T ⟶ (tetrachord) ⟶ D

Commentary on Example 9-4

The thematic surface is filled with accented nonharmonic tones, circled in mm. 1–3, and the harmonic rhythm is fast. The harmony is largely functional, and the only real problem of understanding comes in m. 3, on beats 3 and 4, where there is a temporary shift to the scale of

C minor. This brief passage might be analyzed parenthetically in that key. Better, it can be heard as involving secondary or borrowed chords. Thus, m. 3, beats 3 and 4, could be heard as VI/iv–V⁶/iv–VI/iv–V⁶/V. Or the a♭¹ could be understood as a chromatic passing tone or as part of the N⁶ in G minor (which is perhaps the simplest and most satisfactory interpretation). All of this detail simply prolongs predominant harmony. The point is that this harmony is occasionally ambiguous on the surface, but the underlying chord functions and bass-line patterns are normal. The highly directed individual voices, organized around scale segments, help considerably to give works such as this their shape and momentum, especially when the harmony becomes ambiguous. The more complex the harmony, the more directional the lines typically become, so that we may say that, while great art may be intricate, it is rarely complicated.[4]

Ex. 9-5   Goldberg Variations, Variation No. 25

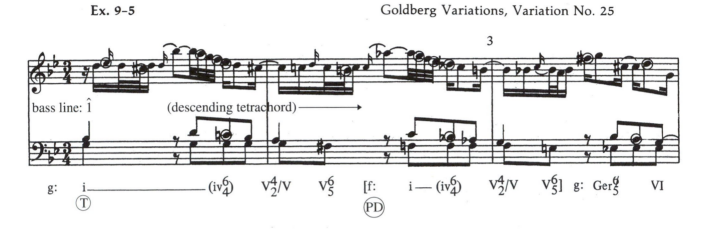

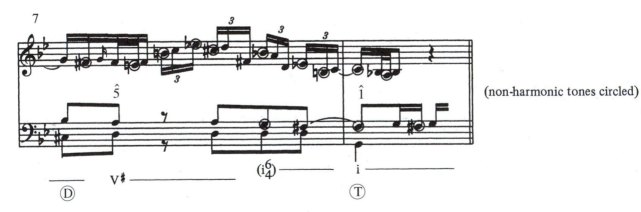

(non-harmonic tones circled)

Example 9-5 also exhibits a descending chromatic tetrachord bass, chromatic accented non-harmonic tones, issues of phase relation, and some altered chords (including an augmented-sixth sonority in m. 3 and secondary dominants in mm. 5 and 6, all normally resolved). It contains a brief parenthetical tonicization of a distantly related key (F minor), by way of sequence (mm. 2–3). This excursion toward F minor can also be understood as embellishing C minor, and analyzed with secondary chords in that key. In any case, it has a strong pre-dominant feeling. It is also one of the most affectingly beautiful passages in all of Bach's music. Here is a reduction of the bass line in mm. 1–8:

Ex. 9–6

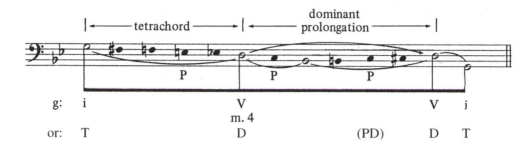

The most typical harmonizations of the chromatic tetrachord are reviewed below:

Ex. 9–7

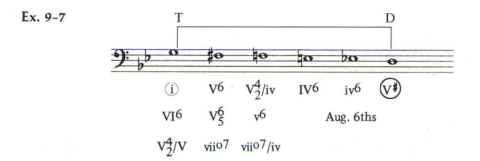

CROSS-RELATION

The matter of cross-relation occasionally arises in chromatic passages in Bach and should be dealt with briefly again. Cross-relation almost always results from the use in proximity of the two different forms of the melodic minor scale in two different voices.

Ex. 9–8   Chorale Prelude "Christ lag in Todesbanden"

On beat 2 the b♭ in the alto voice descends to a, and the B♮ in the tenor ascends to c♯, their normal resolving tendencies within the key of D minor. The two pitches are heard in very close proximity, creating a cross-relation. Simultaneous cross-relation, in which both pitches are heard at the same time, is very rare in Bach.

Ex. 9–9

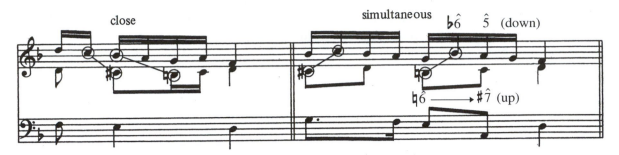

Note in such passages that the cross-relation is brief, that at least one note of the relation is nonharmonic (usually a passing tone or neighbor), and that both resolve normally.

Exercises

1. Analyze the portions of examples 9-1 and 9-4 that have not yet been analyzed. Distinguish between structural and embellishing harmony, and prepare detailed linear reduction graphs. Also discuss those parts that have been analyzed in the text, and discuss alternative analyses if any seem possible.

2. Analyze chromatic passages from the anthology, including their keys, cadences, chords, and nonharmonic tones. Include a reduction of the structural pitches, especially in the bass line, and identify structural harmonies.

3. Articulate the frameworks below, using mixed note values and three roughly equal voices. Work for flow and motivic coherence. Analyze in detail. Provide figured bass symbols, and note the structural harmonies.
   The instructor may wish, in exercises 3–5, to specify instrumentation and texture. Any of these exercises may follow a specific model from the anthology, such as a sinfonia, prelude, or suite movement. They may also be used for improvisation at the keyboard.

a.

b.

4. Work out the figured and unfigured basses below in three voices. Analyze the harmonic implications first. The upper voices should be equally active, in mixed note values. Work for motivic unity through informal (motivic) imitation. Analyze fully, including any instances of patterning.

---

a.

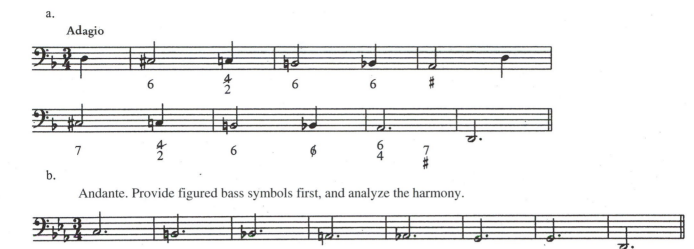

b.

Andante. Provide figured bass symbols first, and analyze the harmony.

5. Alter the following framework with secondary dominants, then articulate. Analyze.

6. Continue this passage for four to eight measures, ending in a PAC in E minor or G major. Analyze fully.

7. Use exercises 7, 8, 9, and 10 on pp. 87–88 as the basis for three-voice elaborations.
8. Chapter 13 may be taken up at this point, and passacaglias based on the chromatic tetrachord may be studied and composed.

TRIPLE (TRIPLE INVERTIBLE) COUNTERPOINT

It will prove helpful, when beginning work in fugue, to be in command of triple counterpoint. The type of three-voice fugue that uses two consistent countersubjects is conceived in terms of a triple-invertible model, and the construction of such a model will ensure the solidity of the exposition and middle entries of the fugue.

In triple counterpoint, the musical effectiveness of the result should be unaffected by the relative positions of the voices. Thus, three contrapuntal lines, A, B, and C, should sound equally good in all six possible positions:

A	A	B	B	C	C
B	C	A	C	A	B
C	B	C	A	B	A

It is unlikely that all six positions will be exploited in any given fugue, but their availability will make its composition a good deal simpler. Fugal episodes are also often written in triple counterpoint (just as invention episodes are often written in double), and are therefore capable of being reused later in the fugue. It is common to find double counterpoint plus one free (non-invertible) voice in fugue expositions and episodes.

The following example is from a prelude rather than a fugue, but the principle is exactly the same.

Ex. 9–9a   Well-Tempered Clavier I, Prelude No. 19 (mm. 1–6)

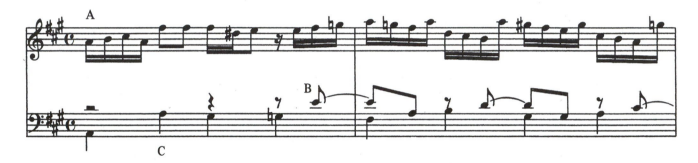

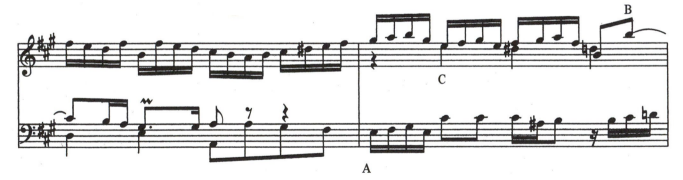

Other examples may be found in *The Well-Tempered Clavier* I, Fugues 2, 4, and 21, and *The Well-Tempered Clavier* II, Fugue No. 17. Sinfonia No. 9, partially analyzed on pp. 171 ff, is also written in triple counterpoint.

The principal difficulty of triple counterpoint at the octave (the only practicable variety) is the problem of the perfect fourth and thus of the $^6_4$ chord. The solutions are: careful doubling of tones in all major and minor triads to avoid complete triads (and thus the perfect fifth which, inverted at the octave, becomes the perfect fourth); the judicious use of brief rests in one voice to avoid a complete triad on the strong part of a beat; the treatment of the note potentially caus- ing the problem as a nonharmonic tone (as in double counterpoint); and the avoidance of those two (of the possible six) positions in which the offending interval occurs (in which case we have what might be called *semi-invertible counterpoint*).

In the demonstration below, the three voices work adequately as triple counterpoint in every arrangement except with line B as the bass in ③, as this position creates unusable $^6_4$ chords.

Ex. 9–10

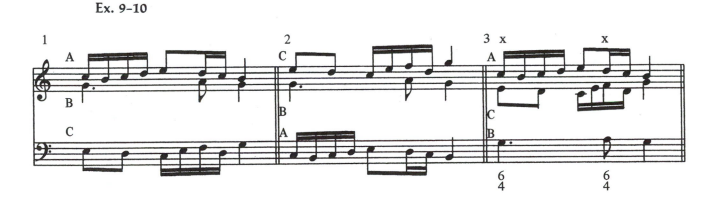

Thus, one of the solutions suggested above would have to be employed to make the com- position workable. In the following two solutions (example 9-11), note the doublings (two roots, one third), which avoid the complete-triad problem, and observe the use of rests.

Ex. 9–11

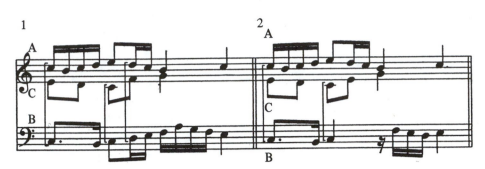

Of course, as in all good three-voice counterpoint, the voices must be successful as lines, their rhythm must be complementary, and the resultant harmony must make sense. Again, it is important to avoid all essential perfect fifths and fourths, treating these intervals as nonharmonic tones. The voices should be restricted to an octave or less in range, to minimize crossings.

Exercises

1. Critique the example below as triple counterpoint. Where are the potential problems? Suggest simple solutions.

2. Add a third voice in triple counterpoint to the results of exercises 3, 4, and 5 on pp. 105–106. One of the original two voices may have to be adjusted slightly to allow the counterpoint to be fully invertible. Write out all six positions to check for interval problems.

3. Add a voice to the following two-voice examples, making triple counterpoint. Check the result in all six positions.

a. (Add a middle voice.)

b. (Add a bass voice.)

4. Use the formats below for composition of passages in triple counterpoint.

a. c: $\frac{4}{4}$ i iv |i vii°⁷ |i |

b. A: $\frac{3}{4}$ I |IV |V⁷ |I |

c. A♭: $\frac{2}{4}$ I |I⁶ |IV |V⁷ |I |

d. g: $\frac{9}{8}$ i vii°⁷ |i VI |iv V⁷ |i |

ACCOMPANIED TWO-VOICE CANON

A very useful texture is the upper-voice canon with supporting bass line. This texture characterizes most of the canons in the *Goldberg Variations*, as well as many fugal episodes. The canonic excerpts from the *Goldberg Variations* that have been studied thus far may at this point be performed and analyzed again.

The Canonic Variations for organ on *Vom Himmel hoch* are also a compendium of canonic techniques. This set is organized as follows[5]:

- Variation I—canon at the octave between the two upper voices, with the chorale melody in the bass (pedal voice) in long notes
- Variation II—canon at the fifth between the upper voices; bass as in Variation I
- Variation III—canon at the seventh between the lower voices; upper voice has a free obbligato
- Variation IV—in four voices; canon by augmentation at the octave between tenor and soprano voices; alto is free, though motivic; bass as in Variations I and II
- Variation V—"L'altra sorte del Canone al rovescio"; a series of canons at a variety of intervals, between varying pairs of voices; the voices not involved in the canon at any particular time have supporting material; this movement is *Freistimmig*, and includes stretto treatment of the phrases of the chorale melody

Following is the first section of Variation No. 9 from the *Goldberg Variations*, a canon at the third below at four beats, with a supporting bass voice.

Ex. 9–12   Goldberg Variations, Variation No. 9

Three-Voice Counterpoint II: Chromaticism, Triple Counterpoint, Canon   **181**

Play the upper voices as a pair, and note the intervallic or rhythmic weaknesses, if any. Then add the bass and observe how it fills in the harmony, provides complementary rhythmic activity, and, in mm. 6–8, drives toward the cadence.

A canon at the third (or sixth or octave) normally involves tonic harmony (or vi) at the point where the follower enters. Therefore the leader often implies dominant harmony immediately before, as is the case in example 9-12. While the canonic voices are quite satisfying as a pair, the addition of the bass improves the effect markedly. For instance:

- m. 2, beat 2—the bass supplies a missing chord third in the I
- m. 2, beat 4—the bass supplies a third for the iii^6, then a secondary dominant effect (V$^6_5$/vi)
- m. 3, beat 3—the bass supplies the missing chord-third
- m. 8—the bass supplies some much-needed activity, as the upper voices might have been insufficiently interesting by themselves
- throughout—the bass reinforces and clarifies the motivic structure

It can be seen from this brief example that the presence of a free, supportive bass allows intervallic and rhythmic effects that in an unaccompanied canon would be weak. The bass in this example shares informally in the motivic material of the upper voices, resulting in a texture of three more or less equal voices. The bass in other accompanied canons may be less integral with the canon than in example 9-12, moving either in faster or slower note values than the canonic voices.

Fugal episodes often contain briefer examples of upper-voice canons with noncanonic bass. Example 9-13 is a three-voice episode from a four-voice fugue.

Play the canonic voices, then add the bass and discuss its effect on the musical result. Also analyze the sequential aspect of the music and the underlying harmonic and linear structures. Prepare a reduction of the lines, noting the descending stepwise structure in the upper voices, clarified by the sequence and typically associated with the circle-of-fifths pattern. Note also the large-scale 7-10, 7-10 LIPs in mm. 46–52.

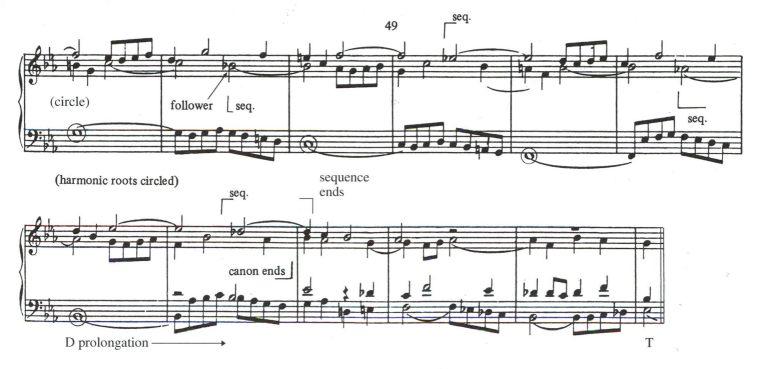

This is a canon at the fifth below, at two measures (eight beats), with noncanonic bass. The bass has the function of filling in and clarifying the harmony, providing rhythmic impetus and reinforcing the motivic content. This passage is also sequentially organized; there is a long sequence unit of four measures, starting in the top voice in m. 45, beat 3, and heard again starting in m. 49, beat 3, transposed down by step. Since the middle voice is canonic, it is automatically also sequential. The harmony is organized around the circle of fifths, with chord roots clarified by the long notes in the bass (G–C–F–B♭), driving toward the upcoming return of the tonic (E♭). This passage is highly typical of one type of fugal episode, being

- developmental
- modulatory
- sequential as concerns lines, harmony and LIPs
- canonic
- constructed on the circle of fifths

The episode below, mm. 22-24, has the same characteristics.

In mm. 22–24 we find a canon between the upper voices (the first two notes of the leader, b[1] and c[2], have been left off but are supplied by the middle voice from the end of m. 21 into the beginning of m. 22). The canon is at the fifth below at two beats, with nonimitative bass. It is also a sequence, with a four-beat unit, transposed down by step, built on the circle of fifths (made explicit in the circled chord roots in the bass, C–F–B♭–E♭–A♭). Since this is sequential, there is automatically an associated LIP, in this case a series of alternating 8-10 and 10-8 patterns between the bass and the upper voices. From these last two examples we can readily see that a canon at the fifth below (or fourth above) is ideally suited to circle-of-fifths sequences.

Exercises

1. Perform and analyze in detail some of the canons from the *Goldberg Variations*, as found in the anthology, pp. 339 ff. Time permitting, it would be possible at this point to take up chapter 13, in which the *Goldberg Variations* are discussed.

2. Continue as strict canons several of the exercises from chapter 6, and add a noncanonic bass voice, filling in the harmony and rhythm and sharing in the motivic content.

3. To one of the canons composed in chapter 6, exercise 7 (p. 122), add a free bass voice.

4. Write upper-voice canons over the basses given below. Keep the imitation going as long as possible, breaking off just before the cadence. Try every possible pitch interval of imitation (unison to octave), using the time intervals of one and two measures only. You may attempt a canon by contrary motion over either or both of these basses, modifying the bass slightly if necessary. It is quite permissible to modify the follower slightly by the use of accidentals, in the interests of harmonic variety and function.

5. Continue the following canonic sequential episodes for a few more measures, leading up to a PAC. These may be allowed to modulate. Analyze fully.

6. Construct canonic sequences with free basses, on the following motives. These may be used in their given forms or modified (for instance by melodic inversion). Continue each smoothly after the sequence ends, closing with a PAC. Analyze fully.

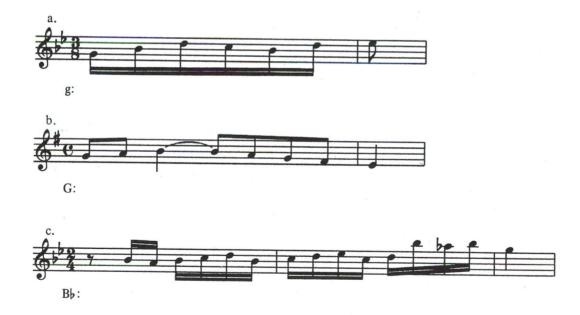

7. Construct canonic sequences with free bass on the following formats. Break off the sequence smoothly and continue briefly to a cadence of any type. These may modulate. Analyze fully.

a. A : $\frac{12}{8}$ vi |ii |V |I
b. f: $\frac{3}{4}$ i |iv |VII |III |VI |ii° | V
c. F: $\frac{4}{4}$ I   V |vi   iii |IV   I |V

Canon in Three Voices

As Bach rarely uses canon in three voices as a developmental device, we will not dwell long on it. It is an interesting discipline, however, to attempt extended instrumental canonic composition in three voices, and a few exercises are therefore provided below. Canonic entrances may be made at the unison or octave, as in example 9-15, under ①, or at the fifth (or fourth below). Or the first follower may imitate by contrary motion at the octave or fifth, as in ②. The third voice may enter at the same time interval relative to the second as the second did to the first, or it may enter a measure or two later, as in ③. As with two-voice canons at the unison and octave, there are potential problems of harmonic stasis, so that accidentals implying secondary dominants and/or modulation should be introduced in the followers. Slight adjustments of accidentals, or even an occasional change of note in the follower, are admissible. As always in composing a canon, one works a beat or two at a time, adjusting leader and followers as needed.

Ex. 9–15

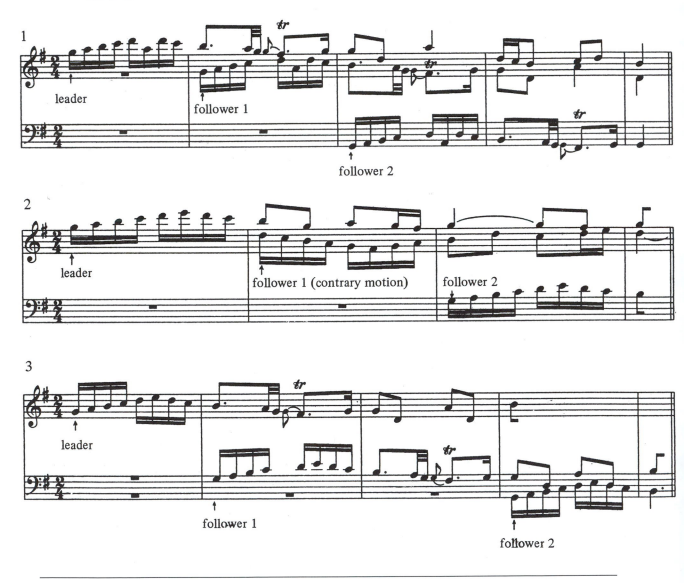

Exercises

Continue the canonic openings below in three voices. You may attempt to imitate the shorter ones, especially Nos. 1 and 4, by contrary motion; No. 2 is specifically to be imitated in this way, as indicated. Continue these for at least eight more measures, breaking off the canon smoothly just before a cadence. The symbol ↓ indicates the entrance of follower 1. Analyze the imitation and the harmony, including nonharmonic tones.

e:

Notes

1. It may be useful at this time to review pp. 77 ff. and pp. 283 ff.
2. Neapolitan chords may alternatively be heard as iv, with chromatic neighbors.
3. It may be useful now for the class to analyze the aria from the *Goldberg Variations*, to be found in the anthology (p. 336), while focusing on the bass line and harmony.
4. For this useful distinction I am indebted to the Rev. Webster Kitchell.
5. There are inconsistencies in the ordering of the canons between the manuscript and the earliest printed versions.

CHAPTER 10

FUGUE I

The composition of fugues in three and four voices is the goal of most studies in tonal counterpoint. In the fugue one applies all the techniques one has learned to a complete and coherent musical entity employing various devices of exposition and development. In composing fugues, we will need to learn very little beyond what we already know of contrapuntal techniques, and will concentrate on building larger structures with these techniques. Composing fugues is an excellent way to learn the essentials of musical organization. All the fundamentals of musical structure are here: statement (exposition), departure (contrast, development, manipulation), and return; large-scale tonal organization; balance, proportion, and shape; and the musical expression of such basic aesthetic dualities as unity/variety, continuity/articulation, departure/arrival, and tension/release. Fugue is a confirmation that in music it is *process*, not "form," that matters most.

The fugues of Bach are indisputably the greatest body of fugal writing. For him, writing fugues is a natural way of composing. We never sense that in his work the fugal process is a hindrance or limitation; it is simply an appropriate means of musical expression. His fugues show a tremendous variety of character and mood. They can seem solemn, jolly, introspective, or dramatic; in fact, the whole range of musical expression is contained in them. They also exhibit a great variety of lengths, textures, processes and shapes, as we will discover.

Directed Study

Perform and listen to the three-voice fugues from the anthology and others by Bach which you may already know. Be aware of the extent to which these are *monothematic* works, arising out of and permeated by the thematic material from the exposition (the opening section). Note, too, that each fugue has its own character and mood based on the nature of the subject (the theme). Be aware of the seamlessness and flow of the music, and its sense of overall shape. It would be useful at this time to investigate the history, development, and literature of fugue.[1]

THE SUBJECT

The main theme of a fugue is called the *subject*. It is analogous to the theme of an invention. Following are several fugue subjects from Bach. Play or sing these in class, and discuss them as suggested below.

Ex. 10–1

Well-Tempered Clavier I, Fugue No. 1

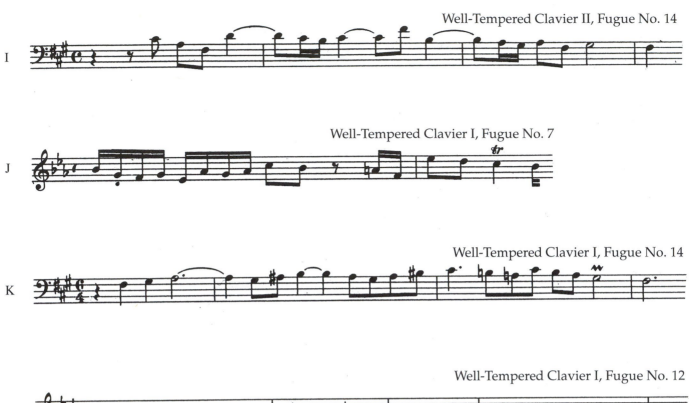

Well-Tempered Clavier II, Fugue No. 14

I

Well-Tempered Clavier I, Fugue No. 7

J

Well-Tempered Clavier I, Fugue No. 14

K

Well-Tempered Clavier I, Fugue No. 12

L

Directed Study

Fugue subjects, like invention themes, come in a variety of lengths and types, but all possess some of the same characteristics. Consider each subject in these terms:

1. Is the tonic key clearly emphasized at the opening? On what scale degree does it begin and end? Does it appear to modulate?
2. How long is it?
3. Is there any feeling of cadence at the end? What type of cadence?
4. Are there one or two (or more) distinctive rhythmic or melodic ideas?
5. Is the implicit harmony clear and functional? Is the harmonic rhythm fairly steady?
6. Does it have an overall shape? Can you distinguish a clear structural-pitch line in terms of specific scale degrees?
7. Does it appear to be in two sections?
8. Does it contain sequences?
9. Where is the first note placed metrically?
10. Try each subject in inversion, augmentation, and diminution. Which sound good in which versions?

Discussion

A good fugue subject will exhibit the features of a good invention theme, just as a fugue is in many ways no more than an elaborate invention. There is, in fact, no clear distinction to be made between an invention theme and a subject (which we will call S) other than to say that most subjects are longer; are more complex in rhythmic, melodic, and harmonic structure; may modulate; may be sequential; and may be in two distinct sections. Subjects vary greatly in length, from one to eight measures or even more (in some organ fugues). Most are two to four measures, and we will concentrate on these.

The following features characterize most fugue subjects:

1. The tonic key and chord are clearly established at or near the beginning. Important tonic triad notes are emphasized; weak scale degrees, especially the leading tone, are not. Most subjects begin on scale degree one or five, and end on one, three, or five. Some begin on the leading tone, but only as a short anacrusis. Each comes to a cadential point at the end, either an IAC or PAC implication, or very occasionally an HC. The harmony is usually diatonic, except with a chromatic S (see H, K, and L in example 10-1), when secondary dominants may be implied. The harmonic rhythm is quite regular, and the harmonic progression is functional and strong.

2. The cadence is placed, as always, on a strong beat.

3. There will be one or two, or even three, distinctive features that will enable the subject to be heard clearly in complex passages, and that will suggest to the experienced composer specific manipulations and contrapuntal combinations. Some subjects are specifically designed to work in stretto, inversion, augmentation, or dimunition.

4. As with any good line, the shape will be clear, and there may well be a clear structural-pitch line (see especially A, F, G, I, and K in example 10-1). The structural-pitch line often falls from $\hat{5}$ to $\hat{3}$ (as in $\hat{5}\,\hat{4}\,\hat{3}$ or $\hat{5}\,\hat{6}\,\hat{4}\,\hat{3}$). Many subjects in minor feature a diminished-seventh outline or leap, from $\hat{7}$ (the leading tone) up to $\hat{6}$, or $\hat{6}$ down to $\hat{7}$.

5. Many longer subjects are in two distinct sections, a "head" and a "tail" (see E, H, and perhaps G and J in example 10-1). These may modulate to the dominant, and often contain several distinct motivic ideas.

6. The range will normally be kept within an octave, with the usual tonal framework formed by tonic triad notes. The more voices, the narrower the range of the subject, avoiding crossings and other complications.

7. Subjects may begin on a strong beat, or after a brief rest. In the latter case, the meter may not be fully clear for several beats, or even until the entrance of the second voice.

8. A good subject will have a strong sense of character and individuality. In Bach each fugue is *sui generis*, a thing in itself, in terms of subject material, overall structure, and expression (affect).

Exercises

1. Perform and analyze additional fugue subjects from the anthology, as suggested by the instructor, focusing on the subject and its recurrences through the fugue.
2. Critique the following subjects, in stylistic and technical terms.

3. Compose subjects based on these melodic frameworks. Use some eighth and six-teenth notes, and work for a clearcut character, harmonic clarity, motivic interest, and coherence. Analyze the implied harmony and nonharmonic tones carefully.

4. Compose subjects based on these chord formats. Consider the use of brief sequences. At least one should be in two sections (head and tail).

   a. d: $\frac{4}{4}$ i   iv | i   vii°7 | i

   b. C: $\frac{4}{4}$ I IV I V7/V | V V7/V V | (modulating)

   c. e: $\frac{4}{2}$ i   vii°7 | i iv | V7 i |

   d. G: $\frac{3}{8}$ I | V | V7 | I |

   e. g: $\frac{2}{4}$ i | iv | vii°7 | i

5. Compose your own subjects, two to four measures long. Choose a variety of meters, tempi, and harmonic frameworks. Use both major and minor modes. Be sure each is clearly shaped. Analyze the structural pitches, motifs, and harmony and nonharmonic tones.

THE ANSWER

In the exposition (the opening section) of a fugue, the second voice enters imitating the S at the fifth above (or fourth below) in the dominant key. This version of the subject is called the *answer* or *response*.[2] Fugal imitation is virtually always at the dominant level (as distinct from imitation in inventions), the answer using the scale and (to an extent) the harmony of the dominant key. This can be handled analytically as music momentarily in the dominant key, or as secondary dominants in the main key; the first approach is recommended here. At the time of Bach, imita-tion at the fifth had become standard practice in fugal composition; it emphasizes the tonic-dom-inant tonal "pillars" of a work, and provides tonal variety in the exposition.

Below (example 10-2) are the answers to several of the subjects given on pp. 188–190. Play the subject (S) and then the corresponding answer (A). You will note that one imitates literally at the fifth, but that in the others there are slight intervallic adjustments. Can you determine the pattern by which these adjustments are made? What is the key of each A? Are the harmonies in each key correspondingly the same for both S and A?

Ex. 10–2

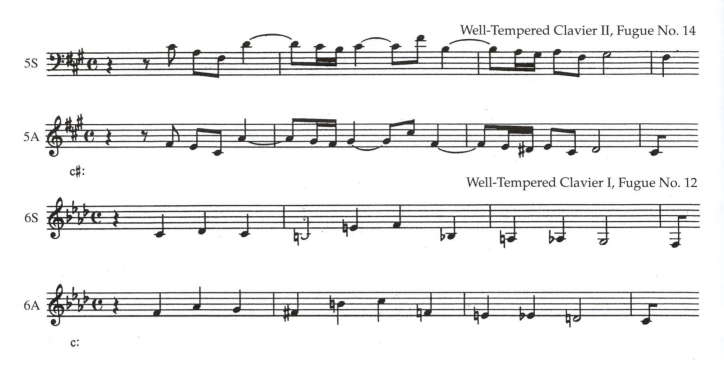

Well-Tempered Clavier II, Fugue No. 14

5S

5A

c#:

Well-Tempered Clavier I, Fugue No. 12

6S

6A

c:

Discussion

In example 10-2, number one, the answer literally transposes the subject up a fifth. The notes of the A are all notes of the scale of the dominant key. This literally transposed response is called a *real answer*. Observe that each scale degree of the S is answered by the corresponding scale degree (in the dominant key) in the A.

Ex. 10–3

An S normally receives a real A if there is no strong dominant note at or near its beginning, and if it does not modulate. Note in S number one that both these conditions are met. There is a dominant note (g[1]) in the S, but it is very short and weak, and not at the beginning; nor does this S modulate.

You will have observed that in the other A's there were adjusted notes, such that not all the notes of the answer imitated the S at the fifth. These adjusted responses we call *tonal answers*. You also noticed that the adjustments involved the tonic or dominant notes of the subject, that is, those scale degrees in the *tonic key*.

Ex. 10–4

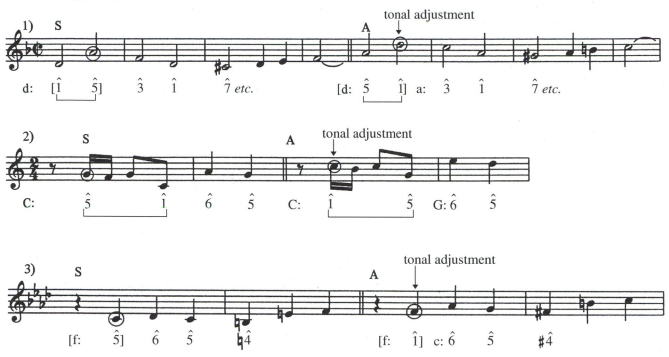

Briefly put, in a tonal A a strong dominant pitch *at or near the head of the S* is answered by the tonic pitch *in the tonic key* at the corresponding point in the A and, because the A is at the fifth, tonic notes are automatically answered by dominant (again, thinking in the *original key*).

After the tonal adjustment has been made, the A *continues as if it had been real.* The readjustment to a real A is made as soon as possible after the tonally adjusted note or notes.

Ex. 10–5

The reasons for the tonal A are to be found in the nature of tonality itself, that is, the necessity for keeping within the tonal framework to preserve the integrity of the tonic key and to avoid modulating endlessly around the circle of fifths. When making the tonal adjustment, it is crucial to think in terms of scale degrees in the *tonic key*.

Ex. 10–6

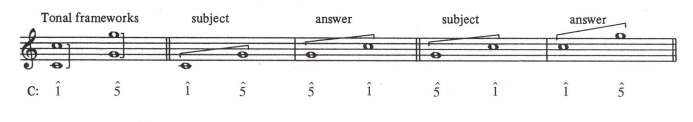

A tonal A will fit harmonically with the end of the S when it enters in the exposition, and will not require a modulatory link after the S (as will be discussed later). That is, the tonal answer enters with tonic harmony in the first key.

Ex. 10-7

A few details concerning the answer should be discussed briefly here.

A subject head built around scale degrees 1–5, 5–1, or around a tonic triad outline normally requires a tonal A.

Ex. 10-8

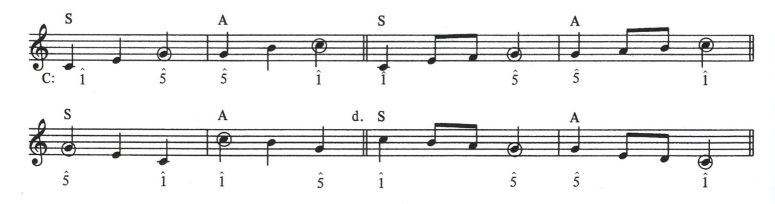

A prominent leading tone at or near the head of the S is usually answered by the mediant note. Below, the music analyzed in the S as implying dominant harmony is answered by that implying tonic in the A, an extension of the principle of the tonal A to several notes.

Ex. 10-9

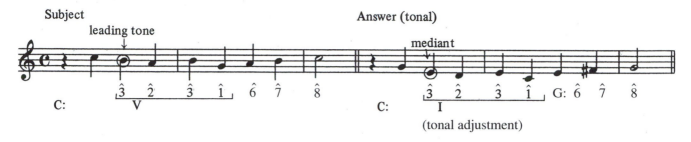

One consideration in making the tonal A is that it preserves the identity and integrity of the S as much as possible and create no awkwardness of line or harmony. Strong scale degrees (especially tonic and dominant) in the S should, if possible, be answered by the corresponding strong degrees in the A. Tendency tones should also be answered by tendency tones when possible, as in example 10-10 (except in the situation explained in example 10-9). After the tonal adjustment, the A should imply the same set of harmonies (in the dominant key, of course) that the S does.

Ex. 10-10

In some cases Bach obviously felt so strongly about the identity of the S that he gave a real A to an S that would normally have required a tonal one. A well-known instance is found in the G-minor organ fugue (example 10-11).

Ex. 10–11

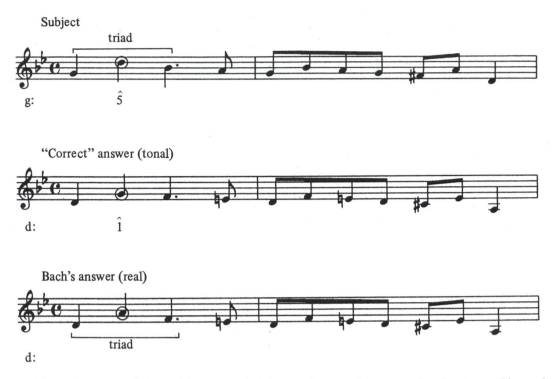

Subject

triad

g: $\hat{5}$

"Correct" answer (tonal)

d: $\hat{1}$

Bach's answer (real)

triad

d:

The other type of S requiring a tonal A is one that modulates to the dominant (the only modulation possible for an S). Such an S must modulate clearly to require a tonal A. Modulating S's are often broken down into two sections, and the adjustment often occurs at the break. Example 10-12 gives the answer Bach made to S no. 10 in example 10-1.

Ex. 10–12
Well-Tempered Clavier I, Fugue No. 7

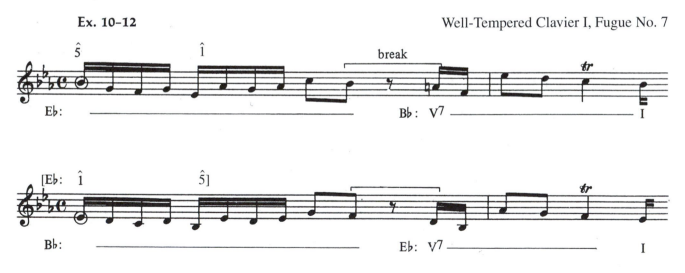

$\hat{5}$ $\hat{1}$ break *tr*

E♭: B♭: V7 I

[E♭: $\hat{1}$ $\hat{5}$] *tr*

B♭: E♭: V7 I

There are two adjustments here: the usual exchange of dominant for tonic at the very beginning, and the adjustment after the rest, transposing the music that was in the dominant key (B♭) in the S to tonic key (E♭) in the A. The brief rest has the function of obscuring or smoothing over this adjustment. There may alternatively be a large leap at the point of adjustment, for the same reason. The situation can be graphed thus:

S: I (music in tonic) → V (music in dominant)

A: V (music in dominant) → I (music in tonic)

This can be understood as another extension of the tonic-for-dominant exchange that characterizes the tonal A.

One more detail deserves mention. In fugues in minor, the A is in the dominant minor key, as can be seen in the A's given on pp. 193–194 and elsewhere. If the S ends on the mediant note, the last note of the A may be its mediant note (in the dominant minor key), or may be raised to become the leading tone in tonic and thus return efficiently, if somewhat abruptly, to the tonic key.

Ex. 10–13

To summarize:

1. The S is answered at the fifth above (or fourth below), in the dominant key.
2. If the S has a prominent dominant note at or near its beginning, it normally requires a tonal A, in which that dominant note is answered by the tonic note; after this adjustment, the A returns as early as possible to its real A form.
3. A modulating S also requires a tonal A.

It would be possible to spend a great deal more time on what Sir Donald Francis Tovey called the "vexatious minutiae" of the answer,[3] but the above discussion covers the vast majority of cases one is likely to encounter. For those wishing a more encyclopedic view, the sources cited on p. 210 are more than adequate.

Exercises

1. Investigate the answers to the fugues in the anthology, including those in more than three voices. Write out each S with the A below it for comparison and discuss any tonal adjustments. Analyze both harmonically.
2. Write answers to the following subjects. Compare and discuss in class. Some should be worked out together at the board. Where variant answers seem feasible, these should be discussed. All except the last eight are by Bach.

E.

F.

G.

H.

I.

J.

K.

L.

M.

3. Write A's to the S's you wrote in exercises 3, 4, and 5, on p. 192.

THE EXPOSITION

Link; Countersubject(s); Bridge

The exposition has the purpose of setting out all the thematic material for the fugue.[4] Most fugues are *monothematic* compositions, having as their premise the drawing of an entire work out of its initial materials. Thus, the clarity and conviction of the exposition are crucial to the success of the fugue. This will necessitate not only the invention of a memorable subject but also the

---

construction of convincing counterpoints in the other voices and of suitable linking and bridging material.

It would be appropriate to discuss first the layout of a three-voice exposition. The order of voice entries with S and A is fairly standardized, with Bach's two favorite successions being:

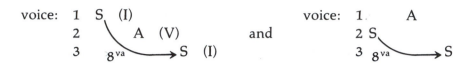

The second entry is always the A, on the dominant; the third entry is nearly always the S (on tonic) and is an octave away from the first entry. Further, in the exposition each following voice comes in on the same beat of the measure, or a comparable beat (strong or weak) as did the first voice; in triple meters, this will mean the *same* beat. In quadruple meters, if the first voice enters on beat 1, the second or third may enter on 1 or 3; if the first entry is on 2, subsequent entries will be on 2 or 4. In Bach, beats 1 and 3 appear to have virtually equal weight and accentuation.

There are other possible orders of entry (such as 3, 2, 1 or 2, 3, 1) but they are rarely used by Bach. The effect of the bass coming in last in the exposition seems to have been highly prized. In any case, the first two entries are always in adjacent voices.

There may be an extra entry at the end of the exposition. This will usually be the A (but see *The Well-Tempered Clavier* I, Fugue No. 6, voice 1, mm. 8–9) and is often found in the voice that began the exposition:

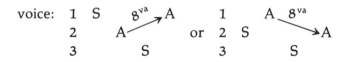

In these cases, the redundant A will usually be an octave from the second entry, just as the two entrances of the S are an octave apart (see *The Well-Tempered Clavier* I, Fugue No. 21, voice 1, mm. 13–17). In few cases does any voice have two successive entries of the S or A, as this would place too much thematic weight on this voice (for exceptions, see *The Well-Tempered Clavier* I, Fugue No. 8, voice 3, mm. 12–14; *The Well-Tempered Clavier* I, Fugue No. 19, voice 3, mm. 6–7).

With very short subjects, there will often be an effect of stretto in the exposition (see *The Well-Tempered Clavier* I, Fugue No. 22; *The Well-Tempered Clavier* II, Fugue No. 3).

Before going into the other details of the exposition, let us look at an entire exposition.

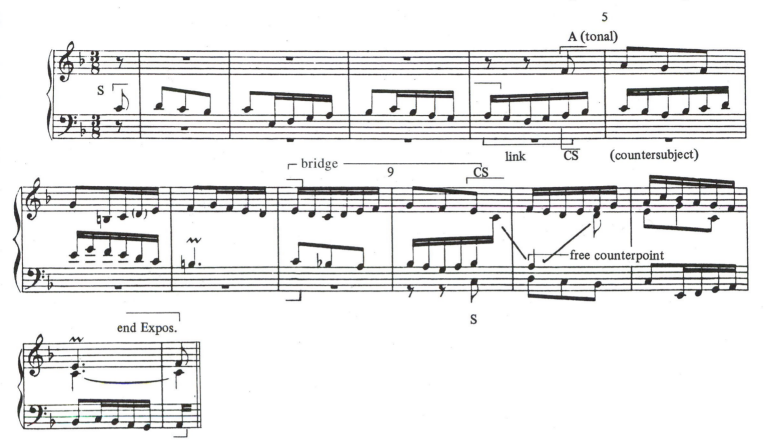

Directed Study

Play each voice through and note that it is a living, organic line, not just a succession of discrete events (subject, link, countersubject, and so on). Then play the three voices together.

The exposition in example 10-15 can be graphed as follows:

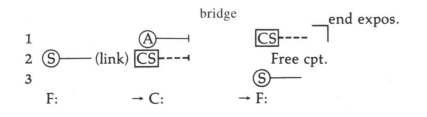

The *countersubject* (or CS—which should perhaps be called the *counteranswer*, as it initially accompanies the answer) is heard against the A in the voice that just completed the S (voice 2, mm. 5–8).[5] It is in double counterpoint with the A, as can be verified in mm. 10–13. The brief link joining S and CS does not occur in all fugues, as we will see later. A consistent CS is not always found; if this line were not to accompany the S or A later in the fugue, it would not be a true CS and would be understood as a free counterpoint. Likewise, the material in the voice that just completed the CS (voice 2, mm. 10–13), if used consistently later, will be called CS2; if not, it is understood as free counterpoint. Following the end of the A there is often a brief two-voice *bridge* (sometimes termed a *codetta*), no longer than the subject and often briefer, remodulating to tonic so that the third voice can enter with the S. The exposition ends when the last voice to enter has completed the S, which in example 10-15 occurs in m. 13.

Ex. 10-16

Well-Tempered Clavier I, Fugue No. 2

Play the voices of example 10-16 individually, especially voices 1 and 2, to be aware of their continuity, shape and integrity as lines; then play all the voices together. Why does the A need to be tonal? What change of note would be required to make it real? What motivic material is used in the bridge? How is the bridge organized? Do you hear structural pitches in the S? In the bridge? How do these pitches relate to each other?

This exposition is organized similarly to that of the F-major fugue in example 10-15. It may be graphed as follows:

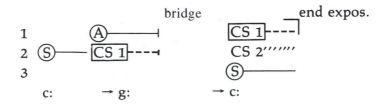

The Craft of Tonal Counterpoint

There is no link here, as CS1 begins immediately following the end of S. The tonal adjustment in the A allows it to enter with the tonic harmony that completes the subject, and thus a modulation to the dominant (which is often one purpose of the link) is not needed before the A can begin.[6] There is a two-measure sequential bridge, developing material from the S (voice 1, mm. 5–6) and the CS (voice 2, by melodic inversion), and remodulating to tonic. The S in voice 3, mm. 7–9, is accompanied by CS1 in voice 1 and CS2 in voice 2. These are quite consistent CSs throughout the fugue, which is written in double and triple counterpoint. These measures may be understood as the model for this fugue, and may well have been composed first. An exposition in triple counterpoint will ensure that the fugue is relatively easy to compose and tight in construction.

The Link

One of the reasons for the tonal A is that it may allow the A to begin with tonic harmony. This happens in the two expositions above. Fugue No. 1 from *The Well-Tempered Clavier* I has a real answer that allows the same treatment.

Ex. 10–17   Well-Tempered Clavier I, Fugue No. 1

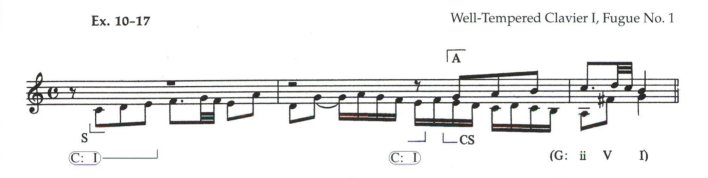

Note here that the first clear sense of dominant key is not reached until m. 3, with the f♯[1]. In such cases, the brief modulatory link following the S and eliding into the CS is not needed.[7] These links come out of the end of the S in a natural, almost imperceptible way, so that the ear may be unsure when the S has ended and when the link gives way to the CS. In fact, what initially appears to be a link may later be revealed to be part of the CS. Such smoothness of connection and flexibility of thematic function are important characteristics of a good fugue. A short link is sometimes used even if it is not needed to effect a modulation to the dominant, simply to get the line to the note on which the CS starts (see example 10-15, voice 2, mm. 4–5). The link, if needed, must be constructed with care so as not to sound artificial or awkward. Links can be found in many fugues, for instance *The Well-Tempered Clavier* I, Fugues Nos. 3 and 7; *The Well-Tempered Clavier* II, Fugues Nos. 12 and 15. Subjects beginning on scale degrees 1 or 5 and ending on 3 often require a link, as will a modulatory S (example 10-18).

Ex. 10–18   Well-Tempered Clavier I, Fugue No. 7

The Countersubject

Directed Study

Study the CS1 in *The Well-Tempered Clavier* I, Fugue No. 2 (example 10–16). Play it by itself, then with the A, mm. 3–5. In what ways does this relationship exhibit the features of good two-voice counterpoint? Think about all aspects: shape, relative motion, motif, harmonic intervals, rhythm, harmony. Next, investigate the CS-to-A relationship as found in the three- and four-voice fugues in the anthology, as directed by the instructor.

Discussion

The CS-to-S (CS-to-A) relationship must exhibit the features of good two-voice counterpoint. The majority of the three-voice fugues in *The Well-Tempered Clavier* have at least one quite consistent CS. The four-voice fugues less typically use consistent countermaterial. Notice in both expositions above (examples 10-15 and 10-16) that the CS is a well-shaped, motivically consistent line which complements the rhythm and shape of the A and is in double counterpoint with it (the intervals are all imperfect consonances or properly treated dissonances). A good CS has these features:

1. It is the rhythmic complement of the A (and S).
2. It uses at least one motivic figure not found in the S, which may provide material for later development in the episodes.
3. It is in double counterpoint with the A.
4. It provides confirmation and clarification of the meter and harmony implied by the S.
5. It has its own identity as a line.
6. It flows in a natural way out of the end of the S or link, and in turn flows into the bridge.

The CS will have to be slightly adjusted to fit with both the S and the A if the A has been tonally adjusted, as shown in example 10-19.

Ex. 10–19   Well-Tempered Clavier I, Fugue No. 11

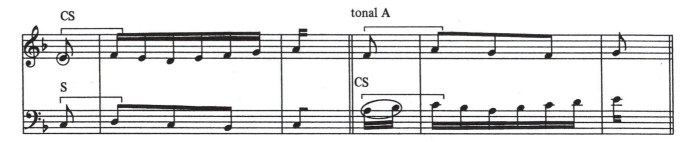

The Second Countersubject

If the exposition is in triple counterpoint, there will have to be a consistent second CS. This line (CS2) will often be somewhat less active than the S or CS, although its rhythm will complement theirs.[8] It may, as in the C-minor fugue above, be simply another version of CS1 (see example 10-16, mm. 7–9, voice 2), or it may be more distinctive. Often one finds longer note values and/or brief rests in CS2.

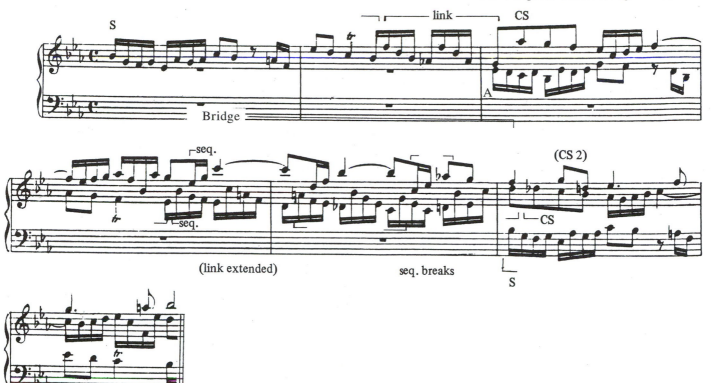

Directed Study

In the exposition in example 10-20, play the CS first by itself, then together with the A (mm. 3–4); note how successfully their rhythms "dovetail." Then play mm. 6–7, first playing CS2 by itself, then combined with the other two voices. Note its simplicity and the fact that it does not complicate the harmony or rhythm but fills out and clarifies, while providing a complement.

The Bridge

Directed Study

Analyze the bridges of the three fugue expositions above (examples 10-15, 10-16, and 10-20). What materials do they use? How long are they? Are they sequential? What LIPs do you find? Are there clear structural-pitch patterns? What appears to be their harmonic and thematic purpose? Play each exposition through, first one voice at a time, then together.

Discussion

The purpose of the bridge is:

- to provide an efficient modulation back to the tonic key, so that the third voice can enter with the S
- to provide an additional measure or so before the third entry to avoid excessive predictability and regularity in the entries
- to provide preliminary confirmation and development of motifs, often by fragmentation and sequence

If the S ends on V or modulates to the dominant, the A will then end on I, so that there will be no necessity for a bridge remodulating to tonic; yet Bach often provides one anyway as a

---

brief episodic relief before the third entry. One probable reason why Bach needed a bridge in the E♭ fugue (example 10-20) is that if he had brought the third entry in as early as possible (m. 4, beat 3), a $^6_4$ chord would have resulted.

A brief discussion of the three bridges will be helpful.

In the fugue in F major (example 10-15) a two-measure bridge (half as long as the S) is provided, written in double counterpoint, modulating from C major back to F. The upcoming key is introduced as early as possible (m. 8, voice 2, B♭). The material in both voices is taken from both the S (m. 1) and the CS or link (mm. 4–5, voice 2).

The fugue in C minor (example 10-16) has a somewhat more elaborate bridge, as long as the S (two measures). It is sequential, in two-beat units transposed up by step. The material is taken from the S (by fragmentation) and CS (by fragmentation and inversion). The structural pitches in voice 1 (e♭², f², g²) are related to the main structural pitches of the S (g¹, f¹, e♭¹). Note also the structural parallel tenths and sixths between voices.

Ex. 10–21

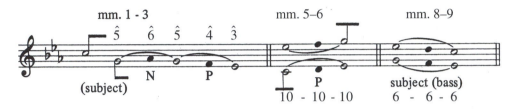

The structural pitches in this fugue are easy to hear, and function both on a surface thematic level and on deeper structural levels (which we will investigate later).

In the fugue in E♭ (example 10-20) we find a six-beat bridge (as long as the S), organized sequentially. As E♭ major has already been reached in m. 3, this codetta does not have the function of returning to tonic, but is used to provide relief and to allow the third voice to enter on beat one. Voice 2 develops sequentially the material of the link. Note again the strong structural lines, and observe how voice 2 in mm. 4–5 drives downward, setting up the entrance of the S (B♭) in m. 6.

Ex. 10–22

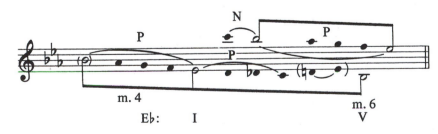

Exercises

1. Perform and analyze several more fugue expositions from the anthology, or from other Bach fugues you know, focusing on the link (if any), the CS (or free counterpoints to the S and A), and the bridge. Note that there may or may not be consistent CS material, and that the CS may be slightly altered without losing its identity.
2. To selected subjects below add a link (if needed), A, and one CS in double counterpoint in the other upper voice. Do not add a bridge or the third voice yet.

A.

(voice 2)

B.

(voice 2)

C.

(voice 1)

D.

(voice 1)

3. Add a link, as needed, and CS to several of the subjects answered in exercises 2 and 3 on pp. 199–201, as selected by the instructor.

4. Next, add a two- or four-measure bridge to selected examples written under exercises 2 and 3 above, designed to lead into the entrance of the third voice. This should develop S and/or CS material, possibly using fragmentation and sequence, modulate back to tonic, and bring the voice that just finished the A to the first pitch of the CS.

5. Bring in voice 3 with the S and construct a second CS in triple counterpoint with the other two voices, in the voice that just had CS1, as in example 10-16.

Your exposition thus will be organized around one of the following schemes, depending on which voice entered first:

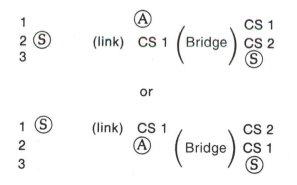

You should compose at least four expositions, two major and two minor. At least one should be on a subject of your own composition, as approved by the instructor.

Notes

1. In *The New Grove Dictionary of Music and Musicians*, "Fugue" (vol. 7), an excellent introduction to the history and development of fugue. The books by Horsley, Mann, and Oldroyd, listed in the bibliography, will be of particular interest.
2. Theoretical and historical questions raised by the fugal answer are beyond the modest scope of this text to treat exhaustively. Among the several books dealing in detail with these questions are those by Horsley, Mann, and Naldin, (see bibliography). See also *The New Grove Dictionary of Music and Muscicians*, "Answer" (vol. 1).
3. Tovey, quoted in Oldroyd, (see bibliography).
4. This is not true for the double fugue, which will be discussed later.
5. The countersubject is considered in more detail on pp. 206 ff.
6. An alternative view might understand CS1 as beginning on beat 3 of m. 3, with beats 1 and 2 as a link.
7. Some English writers on fugue term the link or bridge a *codetta*.
8. This set of relationships is clearly defined in such fugues as *The Well-Tempered Clavier* I, Fugue No.2, and the fugue from the *Passacaglia and Fugue in C Minor*.

CHAPTER 11

FUGUE II

OVERALL STRUCTURE

The overall scheme of a Bach fugue, after the exposition, is variable. As with the invention, the exposition is fairly standardized, but the rest of the fugue, being largely developmental, may exhibit any number of different layouts. All we can accurately say about the plan of a Bach fugue is that there will be an exposition, followed by episodes and/or middle entries and/or strettos and/or other manipulations of the main thematic material, modulating through two or more closely related keys, and returning to the tonic key. Still, it is useful to generalize about the order of events in most fugues, with particular emphasis on the fugues in *The Well-Tempered Clavier*.

The overall structure of most fugues is clarified by the placement of strong internal cadences. Many shorter fugues have one clear internal cadence, placed roughly midway through the fugue, dividing it into two balanced sections, similar to a two-section invention. Other fugues have three fairly clear sections, with two strong internal cadences, comparable to the three-section invention. *Tonal* events may not always coincide with *thematic* events, unlike most homophonic forms, in which tonality and theme are indivisible. Since most fugues are monothematic, thematic contrast cannot be used to clarify form; thus, the difficulty of deciding on the "form" of a fugue. Another problem for the analyst and performer is that internal cadences in the Bach style are often obscured or covered by motion, so that their potential for defining form may be weakened.

Even with these issues of definition, fugues are somewhat sectional. The sections may be defined by:

- cadences
- textural and/or registral changes
- modulations
- clear entrances of the subject or answer
- the distinctive use of such devices as stretto, inversion, and pedal point

By generalizing, it is possible to come up with two typical schemes, similar to the layout of an invention. In the tables below, ME stands for *middle entry*, any entrance of the S or A after the end of the exposition.

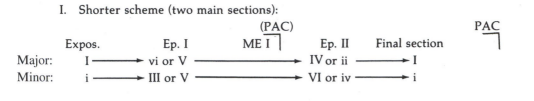

I. Shorter scheme (two main sections):

			(PAC) ME I		Final section	PAC
	Expos.	Ep. I		Ep. II		
Major:	I ⟶	vi or V ⟶		IV or ii ⟶	I	
Minor:	i ⟶	III or V ⟶		VI or iv ⟶	i	

II. Longer scheme (three main sections):

	Expos.	Ep. I ME I (PAC)	Ep. II ME II (PAC)	Ep. III M.E. III Ep. IV Final Section PAC
Major:	I ⟶	vi or V ⟶	V or vi ⟶	IV or ii ⟶ I
Minor:	i ⟶	III or v ⟶	v or III ⟶	VI or iv ⟶ i (I)

These outlines are for the general guidance of the student and should not be taken rigidly as implying that a fugue must exhibit one of these patterns of events. Further, a good fugue is almost a seamless musical entity, and the sections will not be as distinct as the charts above may suggest. The key schemes given are also to be understood generally, as any closely related key is available to Bach, at any time. There are even some fugues that never clearly modulate. The cadences are also variable, but there will normally be at least one strong internal cadence in a fugue (usually in the relative or dominant key), as a point of textural and harmonic arrival or relaxation, as well as tonal and formal clarification.

It is best that the first few fugues one composes be based on specific procedural/schematic models drawn from Bach. This modeling procedure will be set out in the exercises concluding this chapter.

The Episode

Directed Study

Examples 11-1, 11-3, and 11-4 give three episodes, with middle entries, from fugues by Bach. Play and discuss them as suggested here.

1. Compare these episodes to the expositions from which they are drawn on pp. 204, 203, and 207. From what principal thematic material—subject (S) or countersubject (CS)—are the motifs taken? By what processes are the motifs altered? By what processes are they developed? Is there any new motivic material?

2. Discuss the overlappings between episode and middle entry. Is it always clear exactly where a sequence starts? Where it ends? Where an episode starts and ends? Do episodes and middle entries (see pp. 216 ff for discussion) ever overlap?

3. Analyze these passages harmonically and in terms of structural pitches, especially in the bass voice. What patterns of linear and harmonic organization do you find? Any LIPs? Sequences?

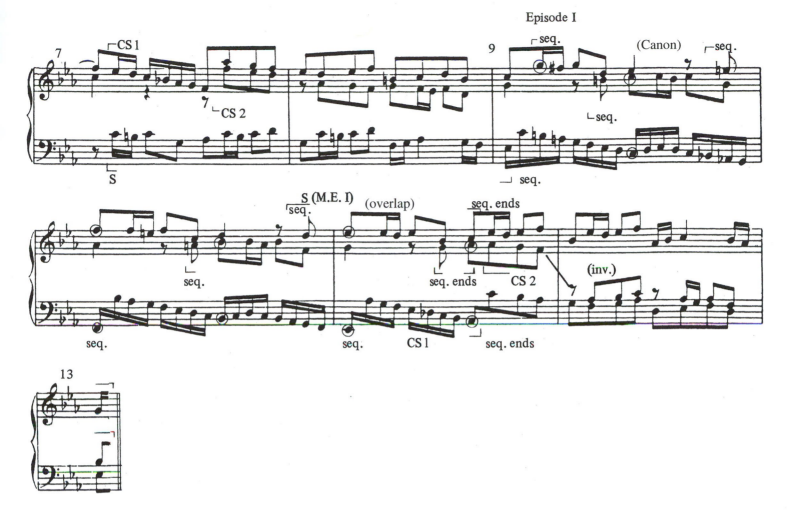

Comments on Example 11-1

The fugue in C minor—*The Well-Tempered Clavier* I, Fugue No. 2—is often selected as a first fugue for study, as it is very tightly constructed as concerns theme and motif, and very clear in organization. It is an excellent model for one's first fugue. The episodic passage following the end of the exposition in m. 9, beat 1, is characteristic in its organization. The upper two voices are in canon at the fifth at two beats (though the first two notes in voice 1 are missing), and form a four-beat sequential unit moving down by step. The material is taken from the first five notes of the S. Voice 3 also has a four-beat sequence unit, based on the head of the CS1. Note especially m. 11, voice 1, where the third iteration of the sequence unit is at the same time the beginning of the first middle entry. Such interlockings or overlaps of material (and of sections) are a fascinating feature of Bach's fugues. Such subtlety requires great skill and imagination; it is something to strive for in one's own writing. This episode is organized around the circle of fifths in mm. 9–11 (C–F–B♭–E♭–A♭). The circle is "designed into" the S, as its initial harmonies, I–IV, can be used to initiate a circle-of-fifths progression, and indeed do so. Any S with this initial progression has, of course, this useful property. By constructing the sequence unit in voice 1 out of the head of the S, Bach was able to elide smoothly into the first middle entry (m. 11), and the fact that the unit in voice 3 is built on CS1 allows it to interlock with CS1 in m. 11. A reduction of mm. 9–11 is shown in example 11-2.

Ex. 11-2

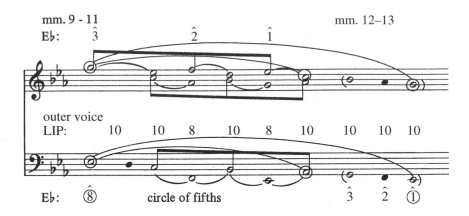

Play the reduction in example 11-2 and then play again the episode based on this strong and simple model. Note the descending scalar shapes outlining perfect fifths and the tonic (Eb) octave, and the descending filled-in third (Eb, F, G) an important thematic and structural line in this fugue. This underlying simplicity of middleground shape is essential as an underpinning to the foreground intricacy of works like this. Lacking such a simple structure, the music would not be likely to cohere in a convincing, shapely way. In writing your own episodes, be aware of the necessity for such directional pitch structures, controlled by sequential patterns of harmony, line and LIPs. Note the "nested" LIPs in example 11-2: the outer voices form a 10-8 pattern, the middle and bass voices form an 8-10 pattern (in alternation with the outer voice pattern), and the upper two voices a 3-6 pattern.

Next, play and study example 11-3, with particular attention to all aspects of patterning.

Ex. 11-3   Well-Tempered Clavier I, Fugue No. 11

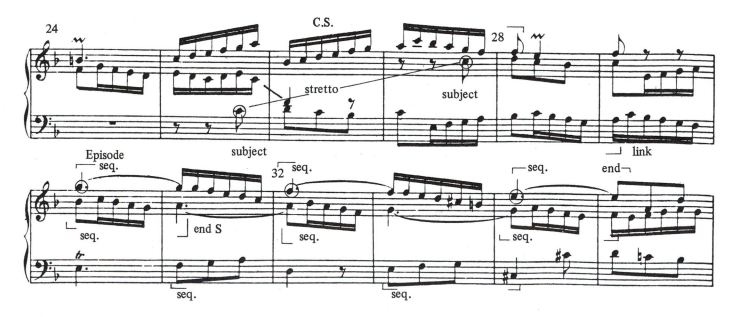

Comments on Example 11-3

This passage has a pair of voices in stretto (voice 1, m. 25, and voice 2, m. 27; stretto will be taken up in detail on pp. 223 ff.) Voice 2 completes the subject in m. 31, overlapping one measure with the beginning of the episode. Voice 1, mm. 30–34, has a two-measure sequential unit, transposed down by step, taken from the sixteenth-note scale figures in the S. Voice 2, mm. 30–35, also has a two-measure unit, transposed down by step and imitating voice 1 (though not literally in canon with it). Voice 3 has a unit derived from the eighth-note scale figure from the S (m. 1), also transposed down by step. It is hard to know exactly where the sequence in voice 3 begins; it could be understood as starting in m. 30 or m. 31. Observe the outer-voice descending scalar pattern in the episode and the 10-10 pattern formed between these voices. Note too the 7-6 pattern between the upper voices (mm. 31–34) and the 5-3 pattern between the middle and bass voices. In sequential writing in three voices, there will of course normally be an interlocking pattern of three LIPs happening simultaneously.

Ex. 11-4   Well-Tempered Clavier I, Fugue No. 7

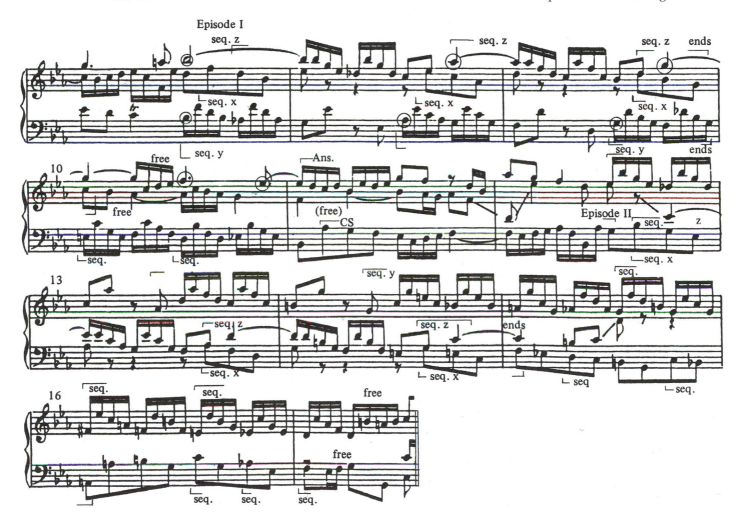

Comments on Example 11-4

This wonderful passage would require too much space to analyze exhaustively here. It will amply repay close inspection, as time permits. Note, though, the dovetailing of episodic material into and out of the answer (A) and the CS; the imitation between sequence units y and z; the ways in which the voices exchange sequence units x, y, and z (compare mm. 7–10 with mm.

12–15); the way in which Bach connects the end of a preceding sequence into the following sequence (voice 3, mm. 9–10; voice 1, mm. 14–17). The linear structure is clear, as the following reductions indicate. Play these reductions and then the comparable passages in the music. Observe the 10-10 pattern and associated LIPs, the lines organized around falling perfect fifths and octaves, and the passing, neighboring, and dominant-to-tonic linear motions.

Ex. 11–5A

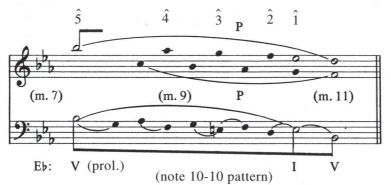

Ex. 11–5B

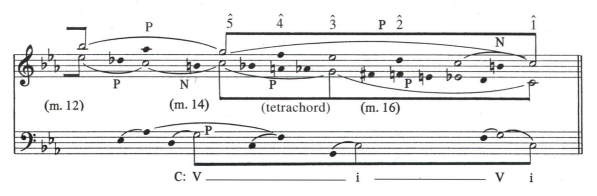

The circle-of-fifths harmony is somewhat hidden. Here is a reduction of chord roots in mm. 7–10 and 11–15.

Ex. 11–6

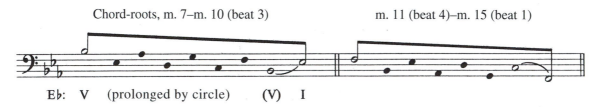

Discussion

Episodes usually operate sequentially on highly directed structural-pitch frameworks, in a way that expositions and middle entries may not. These inner lines, as we have observed before, often descend by step through a perfect fifth or octave, setting up the upcoming tonic, while the harmony typically moves fully or partly around the circle of fifths. All the prominent motivic material derives from the S and/or CS, most often by processes of fragmentation and/or inversion, and may be treated imitatively, either between the upper voices (examples 11-1 and 11-3) or between any pair of voices (example 11-4). The upper voice canon with supporting bass is an effective texture. Three-voice canon is difficult to sustain and is rare as an episodic device. Nonrigorous imitation (example 11-3, mm. 30–34, upper voices), in which two voices share the same material but not in strict canon, is common.

A well-constructed episode overlaps with the end of the preceding and the beginning of the following music. And the first note or two of the first sequence unit may be omitted, due to this overlapping. These interlockings are very important to an effective episode. One voice may break out of the end of a sequence only to begin another immediately, as we saw in example 11-4, mm. 9–10, voice 3 (lowest voice). This latter passage is particularly characteristic: the ending two-beat figure of a four-beat unit is used as the basis of the following two-beat unit. This halving of the length of the subsequent sequence unit drives the music forward effectively toward the cadence. The opposite, a doubling of the length of the unit, is almost never found.

Episodes vary in length according to the length of the fugue and of the S. Four measures is a common length in the three-voice fugues. The longer episodes, when examined, turn out to be two episodes joined smoothly in the middle, or containing one middle entry, as in example 11-4, which can be graphed as follows:

Ep. 1	ME	Ep. 2
7-11	11-12	12-17

Further, episode 2 is broken into two sequential passages, mm. 12–14 and 15–17.

Episode 1 is usually simpler in its texture and devices, and shorter, than later episodes, though it may use stretto if the S is so designed. It may end with a PAC (as in an invention) or, more often, it may elide into the first ME. It is usually better on aesthetic grounds to avoid the cadence here. This episode will normally be followed by the first ME unless there is to be a *counterexposition* (which is discussed on pp. 219 ff). Later episodes tend to be more complex in texture and technique, often including the use of two-voice canon or three-voice stretto. If there are three episodes, Episode 3 may be the contrapuntal inversion of Episode 1, assuming the former had been written in triple counterpoint. It should be pointed out here that a few fugues lack any episodes, specifically those with an S designed to be treated in stretto, the so-called stretto fugue (for instance, *The Well-Tempered Clavier* I, Fugue No. 1). Some stretto fugues, though, do contain episodes, as may be seen in *The Well-Tempered Clavier* I, Fugue No. 3.

MIDDLE ENTRIES

Any entry of S or A after the exposition is a *middle entry* (ME), including, by some definitions, those that are a part of the final section of the fugue, following the return of the tonic key. To be a true ME it must contain at least one complete version of the S or A, in any closely related key. The presence of the complete S distinguishes an ME from an episode, which is based on thematic fragments. The first ME, which usually follows Episode 1, includes one or two entries of the S (or A). This first ME may be in any closely related key, though it is most often in the dominant or relative key.

The later MEs may be somewhat longer, with two or three entries of S or A, and are in a key different from ME1. When the fugue is in a major key, these entries will often be in subdominant, relative, or supertonic key; when minor, in subdominant, submediant, or relative key. These key schemes are by no means rigid. The later MEs often contain stretto, if the S is so designed. If the exposition is in triple counterpoint, the MEs may, in total or in part, be voice-exchanged versions of it, though it is unlikely that any ME will be as long as the exposition. *The Well-Tempered Clavier* I, Fugue No. 2, uses such a scheme.

Demonstration of Episodes

Ex. 11-7

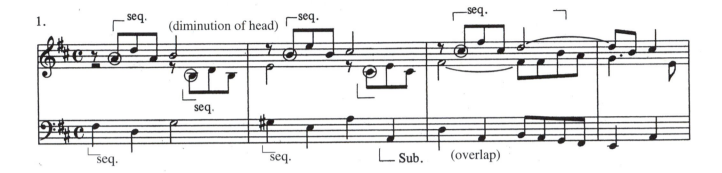

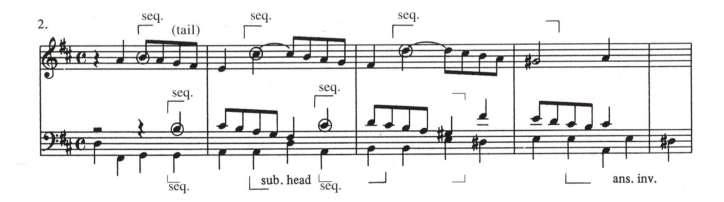

Episode 1 in example 11-7 is based on a diminution of the head of the S. It is in informal imitation between the upper voices, and in sequence, rising by step with a strong structural-pitch line (upper voice: A–B–C#–D). The S is brought in by overlap in m. 2, voice 3, beat 4.

Episode 2 is based on the tail of the S, again in informal stretto imitation between the upper voices, in a sequence rising by step. The bass has the head of the S (mm. 2–3), and then overlaps at the end of the episode, bringing in the answer by inversion.

Exercises

1. Perform and study several more fugue episodes and middle entries, as selected from the anthology. It is important to analyze a number of episodes before attempting to write your own. Note all aspects of linear and harmonic patterning.
2. To the expositions composed in exercise 5, chapter 10 (p. 209), add episodes and one or two middle entries. Be careful to let the first episode flow smoothly out of the end of the exposition and into the first ME. Attempt to use overlap to obscure the "joints" between these sections. Play each line as you write it, being attentive to its overall integrity, continuity, and shape. Analyze fully, including motivic content, harmony, struc-

tural pitches, sequences and LIPs. Reference back to the layout graphs on p. 212 may be helpful at this point.

The Counterexposition

Some fugues contain a *counterexposition* (CE). This is a section, usually following Episode 1, that presents the S and A *in the original keys* (tonic and dominant), normally with the same counterpoints as in the first exposition. The main difference is that the order of voice entries is not the same as in the first. Following are some fugues with CEs:

1. *The Well-Tempered Clavier* I, Fugue No. 11, mm. 17–29. In the first exposition the order of entries is 2–1–3; in the CE it is 1–2–3. See example 11-8.

Ex. 11-8

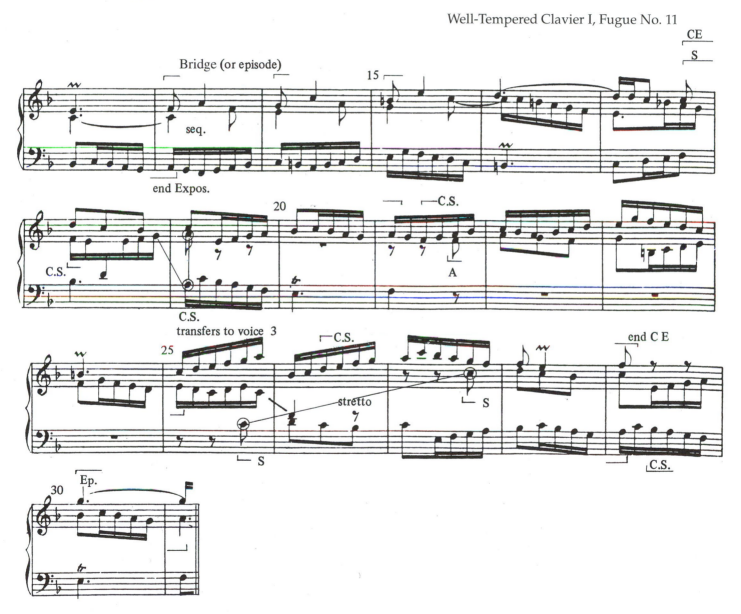

Well-Tempered Clavier I, Fugue No. 11

2. *The Well-Tempered Clavier* I, Fugue No. 1, mm. 7–10 (or perhaps m. 12). As this is a stretto-fugue, the CE is by stretto and sounds episodic.

3. *The Well-Tempered Clavier* II, Fugue No. 9, mm. 9–12. This is again a CE by stretto. Whether such sections, because of their developmental nature, should be thought of as CEs or episodes is an open question. In one view, the presence of the complete (not fragmentary) S would identify this as a CE.

4. *The Well-Tempered Clavier* II, Fugue No. 17, mm. 13–24. In the first exposition, the order of entries is 2–1–3–4; in the CE it is 4–2–3–1.

In any case, none of these CEs is a literal repetition of the original exposition, and each involves a new order of entries, adjusted counterpoints, and a change of texture. All remain in tonic (and dominant) key.

In a few other fugues, mostly stretto fugues (see pp. 223 ff), the lack of clear modulations keeps the S in tonic and dominant through most of the work, in what may appear to be a series of CEs. See, for example, *The Well-Tempered Clavier* II, Fugue No. 1.

AUGMENTATION AND DIMINUTION

Not all themes work equally well in augmentation or diminution. Simple, slow-moving S's are capable of diminution. Here is the S of *The Well-Tempered Clavier* II, Fugue No. 9.

Ex. 11–9

This is in the *stile antico* (old manner), a restrained, somewhat vocal style dating back to the Renaissance *ricercar*,[1] historically one of the forerunners of the fugue. It is used in diminution toward the end of the fugue, in stretto, achieving a climactic effect through increased rhythmic activity and drive (probably the principle reason for using diminution).

Ex. 11–10

Well-Tempered Clavier II, Fugue No. 9 (four voices)

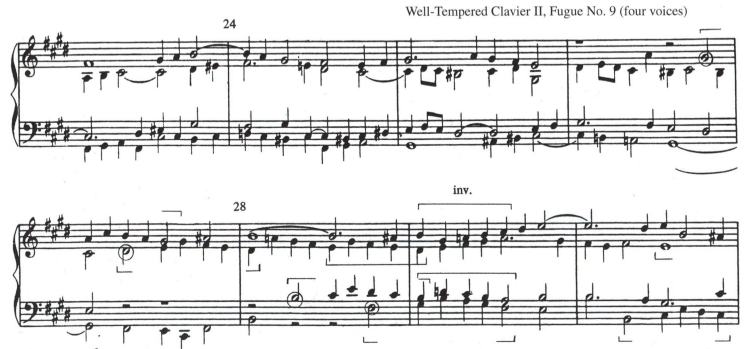

Observe in example 11-10 how the four-note scalar figures (a diminution of notes 3–6 of the S) in quarter notes come to dominate the texture, building to a textural and harmonic climax, mm. 32–33. The use of melodic inversion in conjunction with diminution is particularly noteworthy, as is the appearance of the S in its original form in the middle of the passage (mm. 30–32, voice 2).

Augmentation is normally reserved for an impressive broadening effect at the climax or near the end of a fugue. Only relatively short, simple subjects are suitable for this treatment. It is used in example 11-11 to lead into the end of *The Well-Tempered Clavier* I, Fugue No. 8, accompanied by the S in its original note values. Its first note has been altered from $d\flat^2$ to $e\flat^2$ (making it resemble the A), to fit with the underlying harmony. Note also how the motivic material from the S permeates the texture (compare this to *The Well-Tempered Clavier* II, Fugue No. 9, in example 11-10).

Ex. 11–11   Well-Tempered Clavier I, Fugue No. 8

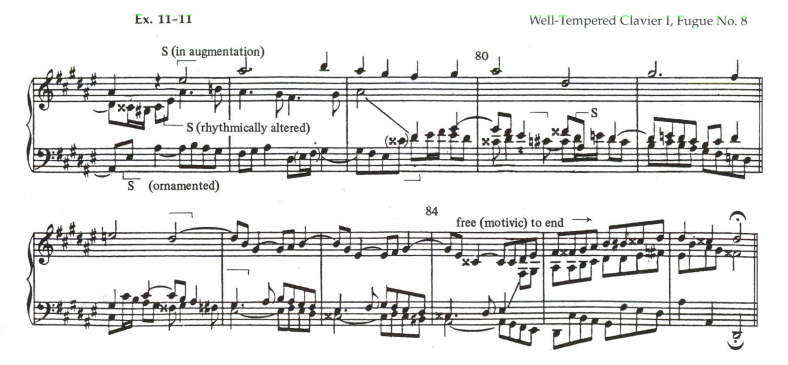

Diminution and augmentation are normally found in 2:1 (1:2) or 4:1 (1:4) note-value ratios.

INVERSION

Melodic inversion is widely used in the fugues of Bach as a device for thematic transformation. Some subjects invert readily and may be designed to work in stretto by inversion (contrary motion). As remarked earlier, an S built around triad and/or scalar outlines will often be found to be workable in inversion. *The Art of Fugue* has such a subject; several of its expositions are by contrary motion. The expositions of Fugues 5 and 6 are given in the anthology. Following is the exposition of No. 7. It should be analyzed in detail in class. Note the occasional changes of accidental in the S, made to fit the underlying harmony.

Ex. 11–12   The Art of Fugue, Fugue No. 7 (four voices)

STRETTO

Stretto imitation has been discussed earlier (see p. 122 fn), but now it comes into its own as a fugal device. Stretto is imitation at a close time interval, such that each successive entry overlaps the preceding. Here are some passages in stretto, to be performed and discussed. Analyze them in detail, noting the time and pitch intervals of imitation, the length for which the stretto is allowed to continue, any instances in which a voice is cut off before it has finished the complete subject (or answer),[2] and any instances of stretto by contrary motion (melodic inversion). Analyze the interval characteristics and harmonic implications of each S to determine what makes it suitable for stretto treatment. Brief subjects beginning with the leap of a fourth or fifth (*The Well-Tempered Clavier* I, Fugue No. 8), or a scale passage (*The Well-Tempered Clavier* I, Fugue No. 1), are particularly suited to stretto. Be aware of the tension-producing, climactic function of such passages.

Ex. 11–13   Well-Tempered Clavier I, Fugue No. 6

(stretto at one beat)

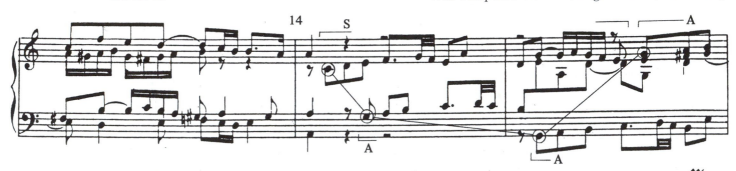

Where the A is real, there is no dependable way of distinguishing S from A in such passages.
For other examples of stretto, see the anthology. These stretto passages should be located, played, and analyzed.

Comments on Stretto

Subjects have to be specifically designed to be effective in stretto. A subject you intend to use in stretto should, before you begin any other work on the fugue, be imitated at a variety of close time intervals to test its suitability for stretto.

Following is a demonstration of stretto, using the subject from p. 218.

Ex. 11–16

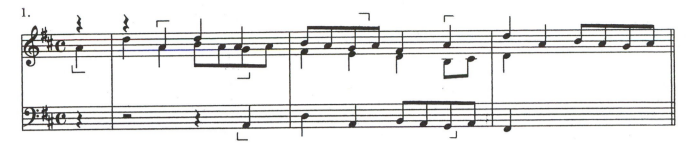

1.

2.

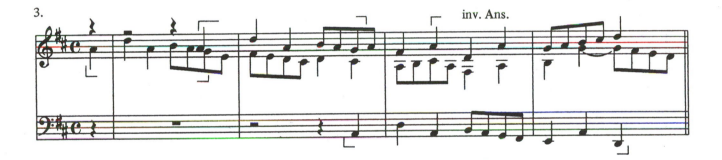

3.

At ① there is a stretto at two beats at the unison and octave. There is a slight adjustment after note 6 of the S for harmonic reasons. This S has a head and a tail, a feature of many subjects suitable for stretto. The head and tail must form good counterpoint against each other. Note that the head leaps a fourth (or fifth) in quarter notes, while the tail is a scalar figure in eighths.

At ② there is a stretto at two beats at the fifth and octave. Again the S is not carried out the whole way, just enough to establish its identity.

At ③ there is a stretto at four beats at the unison and octave, with the last entrance (voice 1, mm. 3–4) an inversion of the answer.

Stretto is an effect often reserved for the latter sections of a fugue, because of its intensifying, climactic effect. It can work especially well in combination with dominant pedal to create tension near the end. The closer stretto intervals are usually reserved for these final, climactic sections.

Generally, only short and rather simple S's are suitable for stretto. Those featuring a leap of a fourth or fifth at the head, with a scalar tail, are often effective. The head and tail should complement each other contrapuntally. Incidentally, the distinction between the S and the A often breaks down in episodic passages, especially strettos, particularly if the A is real (see example 11-15). Likewise, the distinction between ME and episode becomes vague under conditions of stretto, as an ME by stretto may sound episodic.

In a stretto it is not necessary to use the entire S. The more complex the texture, the more an incomplete S will be hidden (see especially the passage from *The Well-Tempered Clavier* I, Fugue No. 8, in example 11-14). The first voice to enter in a stretto, though, generally completes the S (or A). At times only the head is given intact. Stretto passages are not lengthy, unless the entire fugue is based on stretto (a so-called *stretto fugue*). Often only two of the voices are in stretto, especially in earlier episodes; later strettos usually involve all the voices.

A voice may enter on any beat in a stretto passage, especially in the case of stretto at one beat (see examples 11-14 and 11-15). Further, the time interval may change at any point in the passage (though for reasons of forward momentum it will usually shorten rather than lengthen), as may the pitch interval (though once this is established, it will tend to stay the same). Stretto at the fourth, fifth, and octave are the most common. Stretto by contrary motion is not hard to achieve with a simple, suitable S (see the stretto demonstration, p. 225; *The Well-Tempered Clavier* I, Fugue No. 6, in example 11-13; and the exposition from *The Art of Fugue* given on p. 222).

A *stretto fugue* uses an S designed to be workable in stretto at a variety of intervals, and it uses this device throughout, with the shorter time intervals typically coming toward the end. Stretto fugues include *The Well-Tempered Clavier* I, Fugues Nos. 1 and 22; *The Well-Tempered Clavier* II, Fugues Nos. 3 and 5; as well as several fugues from *The Art of Fugue*, in which stretto is combined with a number of other devices.

The following excerpt (from *The Well-Tempered Clavier* II, Fugue No. 2) shows strettos by contrary motion and augmentation. It should be analyzed with care, as it contains several adjustments of the S and A, including slight changes of rhythm, pitch, or accidental, and one instance of filling-in. Such adjustments are permissible as long as they are well covered by other activity, and do not substantially alter the S.

Ex. 11–17

Well-Tempered Clavier II, Fugue No. 2

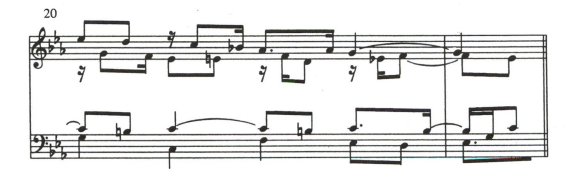

Exercises

1. Perform and analyze any of the strettos from the anthology that have not yet been analyzed. Note the time and pitch intervals used, the length of the S at each entrance, and any adjustments to the S. What is the function of and material in the non-stretto voices?
2. Try the shorter subjects on pp. 199 ff and 209 in stretto, as suggested in the demonstration on p. 225. Remember that slight adjustments are permitted as long as the head is intact, that time and pitch intervals may vary, and that S and A may be used interchangeably. Try every possible pitch interval, up to the octave, at one, two, three, and four beats. Attempt both two-voice stretto with a nonimitative third voice, and three-voice stretto. Try stretto by contrary motion.
3. At what other imitative intervals, in stretto, can you make the demonstration subject (p. 225) work? Try both three-voice stretto and two-voice stretto with a free third voice. Keep these going for four to eight measures. Slight adjustments to the S and A are permissible, as is stretto imitation by contrary motion.

Exercises 1 and 2 on pp. 238 ff may be done at this time.

Pedal Point

Pedal point may occur anywhere in a fugue, but it is most often used toward the end, settling the tonality and providing, like augmentation, a broadening effect.[3] A dominant pedal of one of the subsidiary keys (especially the relative) may be used earlier in a fugue (see *The Well-Tempered Clavier* I, Fugue No. 11, mm. 36–40, voice 3, a dominant pedal of the relative minor). The only commonly used pedal notes are tonic and dominant, and they nearly always occur in the lowest voice. A dominant pedal may occur near the end, over which one may hear the subject, often in stretto, or episodic material. This is typically balanced by tonic pedal at the end, which will give a coda-like effect, especially if the S is heard over it, as is the case in example 11-18. Note the textural thickening at the end and the typical Picardy third in the final chord.

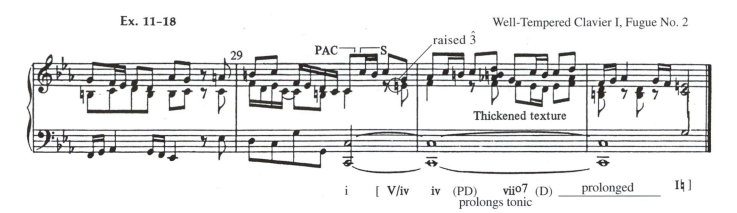

The ending shown in example 11-19 is a coda based on tonic pedal with final stretto entries of the S over it. Note the E♮ at the end of m. 29, not a Picardy third but implying a secondary dominant of iv. Such a move toward predominant harmony is characteristic, nearing the ends of works of most tonal composers. The tonic pedal is arrived at—in this case, as above—through a PAC. Bach must have felt that an ending at this point (m. 24) would have been abrupt, and a coda was needed to stabilize the tonic harmony through prolongation. In fugues in major keys, the introduction of lowered-$\hat{7}$ (the subtonic note) pushes the harmony toward subdominant, nearing the end; this is the function of the B♭'s in mm. 24–26. In fugues in minor keys, the analogous note is raised-$\hat{3}$, as in example 11-18, m. 29.

Ex. 11–19   Well-Tempered Clavier I, Fugue No. 1

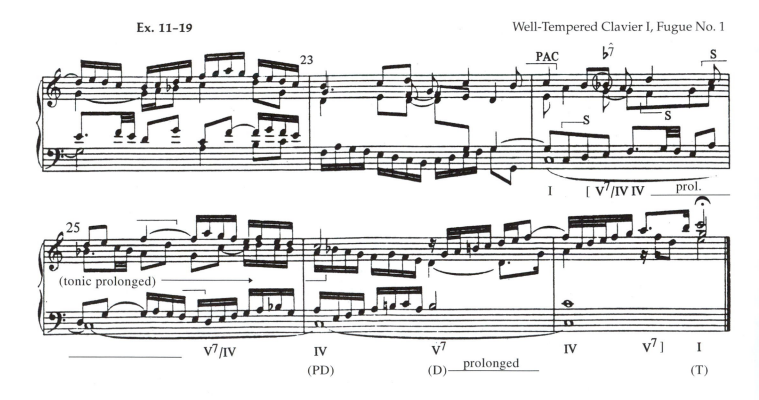

The final section of the fugue in example 11-20 also contains a final version of the S, with a textural climax and a brief dominant pedal, which serves simply to slow the harmonic rhythm at the cadence. The bass line presents a very strong cadential formula in the last three measures ($\hat{1}$, $\hat{4}$, $\hat{5}$, and $\hat{1}$), giving a solid harmonic underpinning to the end.

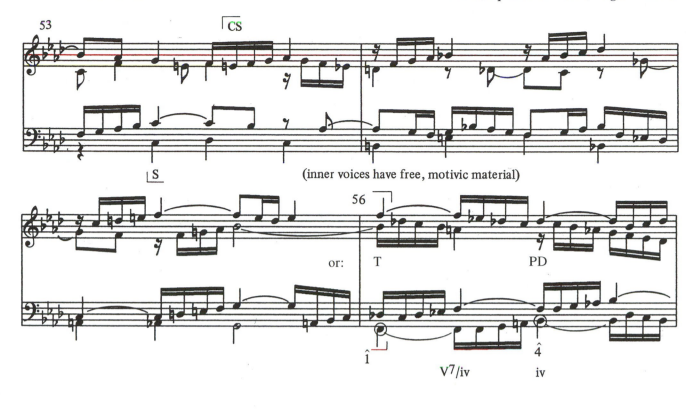

(inner voices have free, motivic material)

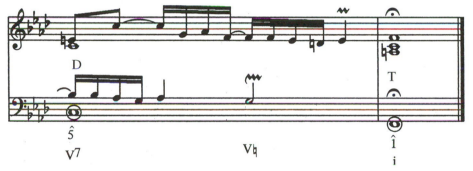

You will have noticed the harmony heard over the tonic pedals in examples 11-18 and 11-19. In each case it progresses from tonic to a secondary dominant of the subdominant, to subdominant, to dominant, to tonic—in effect, a prolongation of the strongest authentic cadence harmonic formula in this style, with a broadening of the harmonic rhythm that leads strongly to the ending. This is a typical harmonic gesture at the end of a fugue. The movement toward IV (iv in minor) and, in general, the subdominant side of the circle of fifths characterizes the endings of many tonal works, just as movement toward the dominant side tends to typify the opening section. Observe also how the raised mediant degree in the V^7/iv prepares the ear for the Picardy third at the end.

One final example of pedal point is given below.

Ex. 11–21   Well-Tempered Clavier I, Fugue No. 4 (five voices)

The ending of the great five-voice fugue in C♯ minor, *The Well-Tempered Clavier* 1, Fugue No. 4 (example 11-21), exhibits the same harmonic framework of iv–V–I that we have seen earlier. The subdominant occurs in m. 104; the dominant is prolonged in mm. 105–111 through pedal and harmonic elaboration, with the S entering in voice 1, mm. 107–109; tonic is prolonged in the usual way at the end, with the motion toward subdominant (V⁷/iv–iv–I), for a plagal cadence. The tonic note arrives in the outer voices in m. 112, not with the expected perfect authentic cadence (PAC) but with a very surprising and dissonant deceptive cadence (DC), mixing implications of tonic and subdominant harmony (again, an issue of phase relationship).

Harmony over the dominant pedal essentially prolongs V^7 and may also involve tonic and subdominant triads. The use of the DC to resolve the dominant pedal, while dramatically effective, is rarely seen in Bach. The dominant pedal, incidentally, is normally approached through subdominant harmony (see examples 11-20 and 11-21), including secondary dominants of V (see example 11-21, m. 109), and is most often resolved by a PAC.

THE ENDING SECTION

Though there is a great variety of ways to organize the last section of a fugue, a few generalizations are possible.

There will be a return to tonic harmony somewhere after the halfway point, often two-thirds to three-quarters of the way through the fugue. If this return to tonic is accompanied by a statement of the S (and CS material, if any), then there is what some writers on fugue would term a *recapitulation*.[4] *The Well-Tempered Clavier* I, Fugue No. 2 (example 11-22), has a clear recapitulation in mm. 20–22.

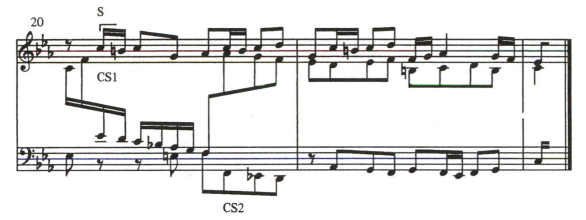

It is typical that the S does not occur in the voice that began the fugue (voice 2), but in another voice (voice 1), for variety. This fugue is written in triple counterpoint throughout, and the order of voices used here, CS 1, has not yet been heard in the fugue, so that this is not a literal recapitulation. Nor will one often find a repetition of the entire exposition at this point, as this would seem redundant. Many fugues return to tonic without an unambiguous return to the S, and thus lack a recapitulation.

The final section will probably contain a thickening of the texture through increased rhythmic activity, and an intensification of the harmony. It may well involve two- or three-voice stretto, especially in fugues rich in stretto (see *The Well-Tempered Clavier* I, Fugue No. 16, mm. 28–30; *The Well-Tempered Clavier* II, Fugue No. 5, mm. 43–end).

Pedal points, as discussed above, may well be employed. Tonic pedal at the end is common; dominant pedal preceding it is somewhat less so. If the tonic pedal is prolonged for four measures or so, it will have the effect of a coda, especially if introduced by a strong cadence (PAC or DC) and if the S is heard over it. A final stretto over tonic pedal is also a possibility. It is very important that this coda be fully integrated with the rest of the fugue, in terms of motivic material, texture, and harmonic vocabulary; it may otherwise feel "tacked on," and thus ineffective.

There may be a final very close stretto, perhaps with an improvisatory, toccata-like flourish just before the final cadence, as in example 11-23.

Ex. 11–23　　　　　　　　　　　　　　　　　Well-Tempered Clavier II, Fugue No. 2

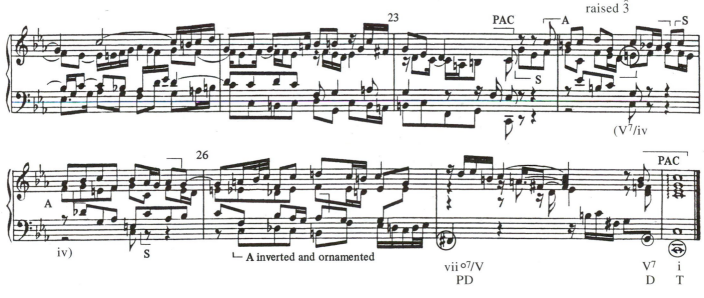

Example 11-23 employs a two-voice close stretto with S and A used interchangeably (as indeed they usually are after the exposition), with free (though of course motivic) accompaniments in the other voices, an inverted and highly ornamented A (m. 26, voice 4), an improvisatory flourish prolonging vii°7/V, and a PAC with a thickened texture. The whole final section is set off by a PAC in m. 23, and thus may be understood as a coda.

There may be a final episode based on fragments of the S, and a brief homophonic passage at the end, as in example 11-24.

Ex. 11-24   Well-Tempered Clavier I, Fugue No. 5

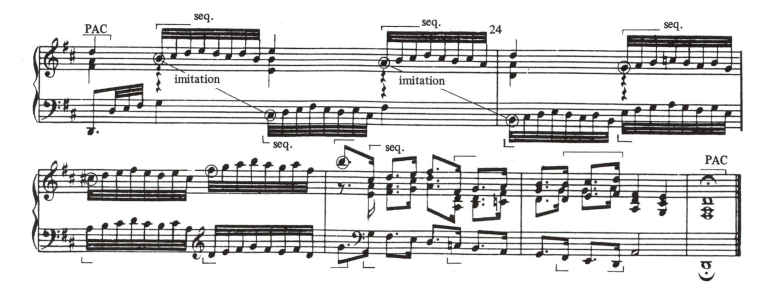

Here again, the closing section is set off by a PAC (m. 23) followed by a sequential, imitative passage based on the head of the S, and another homophonic sequence built on its tail (mm. 25–26). These dramatic, homophonic codas are not particularly common in Bach (they are much more so in the work of George Frideric Handel).

There may be a dramatic pause, using a fermata chord or rest, which sets off the closing section, as in example 11-25.

Ex. 11-25   Well-Tempered Clavier II, Fugue No. 17 (four voices)

This passage contains a dramatic pause on the climactic V$_5^6$ and a scalar flourish leading up to the final, intensely chromatic passage (climax through texture and harmony), within which the S is imbedded (mm. 48–50, voice 2).

Most fugues in *The Well-Tempered Clavier* simply "wind down" at the end, often approaching the end through a descending series of steps, as in example 11-26. Elaborate, dramatic endings, with toccata-like passage work and fermatas, are more characteristic of the fugues of Handel and of Bach's organ fugues.

Ex. 11–26   Well-Tempered Clavier II, Fugue No. 9

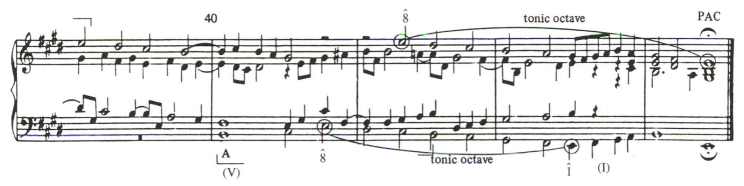

Worthy of comment is the stretto of S and A, mm. 35–38, and the highly sequential nature of the accompanying voices, which are derived from the tail of the subject by diminution and inversion. Note the very clear descending tonic octave lines (mm. 40–42, voice 4, and 41–43, voice 1), which make the ending gesture and tonality so clear and satisfying.

ANALYSIS OF A COMPLETE FUGUE

It is necessary before beginning the composition of an entire fugue to analyze several Bach fugues to discover how the techniques we have been studying operate together to produce a unified, convincing work. Here, as a sample, is an analysis of *The Well-Tempered Clavier* I, Fugue No. 2, showing thematic material, sectional divisions, and sequences. In this analysis (S) indicates episodic material derived from the S; (CS) indicates material derived from the CS.

Ex. 11–27

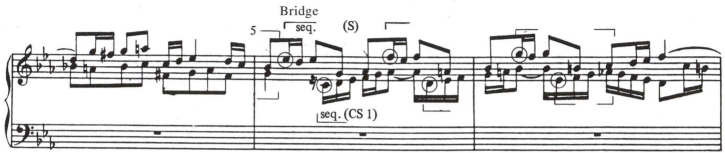

The following is a brief description of the principal thematic events in this fugue.

- mm. 1–2:   S in voice 2
- mm. 3–4:   tonal A in voice 1; CS 1 in voice 2 (double counterpoint)
- mm. 5–6:   sequential bridge, in double counterpoint; described on p. 205
- mm. 7–8:   the complete "model" for the fugue; triple counterpoint:
  CS 1
  CS 2
  S
- mm. 9–11:   episode 1; triple counterpoint
- mm. 11–12:   ME I: S
  CS 2
  CS 1
- mm. 13–14:   episode 2; voice 1 related to voice 3, mm. 9–10, by inversion
- mm. 15–16:   ME II: CS 1
  A
  CS 2
- mm. 17–19:   episode 3; a reworking in triple counterpoint of the bridge; note the voice exchange in m. 18; a three-measure phrase
- mm. 20–21:   recapitulation: S
  CS 1
  CS 2
- mm. 22–26:   episode 4; a transposition of episode 1
- mm. 25–26:   a free reworking of motivic materials
- mm. 26–28:   last full entry of model: CS 1
  CS 2
  S
- mm. 29–31:   coda (or codetta) with tonic pedal, described on p. 228

There is a multitude of marvelous details in this work; just a few will be discussed here. The interlocking of sections at m. 11 and 20 (where episodes overlap MEs) is noteworthy, as is the exchange of material between voices in mm. 18 and 26–27. The fact that the entire work is conceived in double and triple counterpoint means that the exposition and episode 1 contain virtually all the motivic/contrapuntal material for the piece; this is an extremely tightly organized fugue. The triple invertible model for this work may be found in mm. 7–8, which give rise to mm. 11–12, 15–16, 20–21, and 26–28. The bridge is the basis for episode 3, and possibly mm. 25–26. Episode 1 is the model for episode 2 (partially) and episode 4.

There are also brief passages of somewhat free thematic material (though these are motivically related to S and CS), which are necessary to prevent the fugue from becoming a dry, academic exercise. See mm. 25–26 and 29, and, to an extent, the coda.

The phrase structure is quite regular. The two-measure S imposes its length on the phrase. All phrases are two measures long (plus one arrival beat in the third measure) until episode 3, mm. 17–19, which provides a much-needed variation in the phrase length and avoids squareness. Episode 4 is four-and-a-half measures long, which means that the S enters (for the first time) on beat 3 instead of beat 1 (m. 27), and that the final cadence falls on beat 3. Thus, both phrase length and meter have been shifted. Recall that in Bach, beats 1 and 3 in a quadruple meter have roughly equal weight.

The modulations are smoothly accomplished. The modulation to the relative key may be understood as occurring by common chord in m. 10, although the sequential nature of this passage somewhat obscures the moment of modulation. The shift to G minor happens in m. 15, with the entrance of the A in the dominant key. And the return to C minor is accomplished very subtly in the sequential passage, mm. 18–20; this may be said to be a modulation by structural line and by sequence.

The derivation of materials used in the bridge and episodes is very clear. There is little transformation of themes other than some melodic inversion (mm. 13–14, voice 1) and there is no stretto. The work is based almost entirely on the technique of double and triple counterpoint.

Following is a graph of the large-scale aspects of the work.

Expos.	Ep. I	ME I	Ep. II	ME II PAC⌐	Ep. III	Recap. (ME III)
1–9	9–11	11–13	13–15	15–17	17–20	20–22

c: (g:) ──→ Eb: ──────→ (c:)   g: ──────→ c: ──────→

Ep. IV	ME IV	cadential PAC⌐	Coda IAC⌐
22–26	26–28	28–29	29–31 ‖

The overall structure is binary:

	Section I	PAC⌐		Section II (including coda)	
	1–17			17–31	
keys:	c Eb g			c	
	17 measures			15 measures	

Example 11-28 shows a reduction of mm. 1–13, showing the structural-pitch framework and the importance of the circle of fifths in episodes.

Ex. 11-28

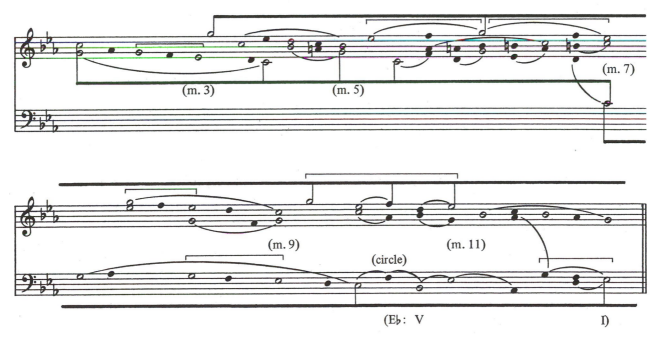

This reduction, only one of several ways of understanding the fundamental pitch structure,[5] shows how very unified and directional the linear structure is. Episodes, by virtue of their sequential nature, are typically organized this way. Throughout, one hears the importance of the ascending and descending scalar thirds, especially the pitch-class sets Eb–F–G and G–F Eb, related as noted earlier, to the structural pitches of the S. This set is shown with a bracket (⌐) in the graph. Observe the linear and tonal importance of the mediant note Eb. The principal tonic and dominant departure and arrival pitches are shown in the graph. These primary structural pitches are prolonged or filled in with the usual repertoire of secondary pitches (neighbors, passing tones, and circle-of-fifths patterns). It is as always the combination of a coherent contrapuntal and thematic surface with a highly directed linear/harmonic structure that makes such a work so convincing.

Exercises

1. Transform selected subjects from p. 209 by the processes suggested below, then treat the original form and the varied forms as the material for:
   A. episodes (some should be in canon), and/or
   B. passages in stretto, if that is workable.
   Recall that, in stretto, a combination of devices of transformation (such as fragmentation, inversion, and diminution) may be employed; that the answer may be mixed freely with the subject; and that subtle alterations of material are acceptable. If there are head and tail sections in a given S, these two may be treated as independent motifs and used in episodes and strettos.
   Play through and discuss the following example before beginning work on this exercise.

Ex. 11–29

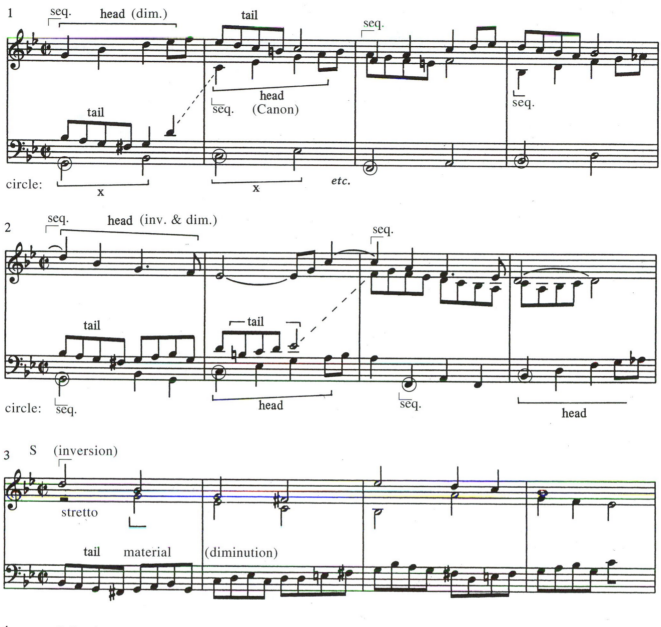

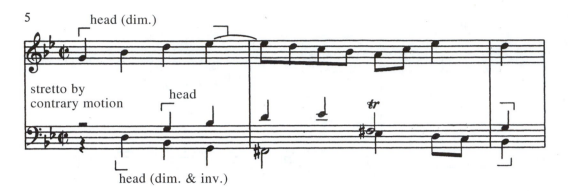

The given S is manipulated by a variety of devices (many other transformations are available). Then these altered materials are subjected to a variety of treatments, such as:

① a sequential episode in canon between the upper voices, using both head and tail of the S in diminution, and the opening interval (marked as X) in voice 3; this passage progresses around the circle of fifths

② a sequential episode by contrary motion (inversion) between voice 1 and voice 3, with a supportive voice 2 constructed from motivic material

③ a stretto imitation at one beat, at the third below, between voices 1 and 2, with a supportive, motivic bass line

④ a stretto imitation by contrary motion at one beat between voices 1 and 2; free motivic bass

⑤ a stretto imitation by diminution of the S and contrary motion, in all three voices; the effectiveness of such stretto passages rests on the invertible nature of the triad and the diminished seventh chord

2. Treat the following subjects by the processes suggested above, and combinations of these processes, in episodes and stretto passages.

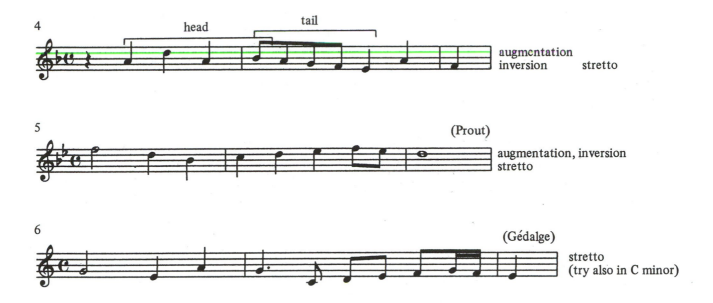

4   head   tail   augmentation
inversion   stretto

5   (Prout)   augmentation, inversion
stretto

6   (Gédalge)   stretto
(try also in C minor)

3. Next, treat selected subjects from p. 209 by the same developmental processes. Include at least one of your own subjects.

4. Select two subjects (one each in major and minor) and use them as the basis for the final section of two fugues, including the use of dominant and tonic pedal point. Make sure that the harmonies associated with both pedals are typical. Try at least one stretto episode over dominant pedal.

Example 11-30 provides a demonstration of dominant and tonic pedal, using the demonstration subject in D major.

Ex. 11–30

The dominant pedal is approached through subdominant and secondary dominant harmony (m. 1), prolonged for three measures, with the S in voice 1 and with simple harmony (I, IV, V). This is resolved into tonic, with a four-measure pedal, the S in voice 2, the usual movement toward IV (using a secondary dominant of IV), a textural thickening at the end, and a modally borrowed $ii^{\circ 6}_{5}$ in m. 7, beat 4 (with apologies to Felix Mendelssohn).

Writing a Fugue

You are now prepared to undertake the composition of a fugue. The following exercises should be done in the given order, at the discretion of the instructor,[6] who should check and approve *each stage* of the process before you proceed to the next.

Exercises

1. Analyze several more three-voice fugues from the anthology. Identify all the thematic material, episodes, middle entries, sequences, strettos, and all manipulations of the thematic material. Do a formal graph as on p. 212, and a structural-pitch graph. Show all modulations, keys, and cadences, and the harmonic organization of all episodes. Show structural harmony, and all aspects of patterning, including bass-line root patterns, sequences, and LIPs.

2. Then select one fugue as your model, and prepare a detailed bar-by-bar graph of it. A graph of mm. 1–12 of *The Well-Tempered Clavier* I, Fugue No. 2, is shown as a model.

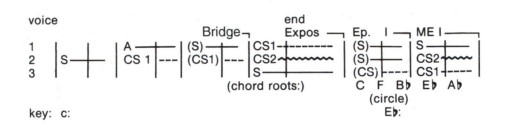

3. Compose a fugue based directly on this procedural model, including at least in part the same harmonies and cadential structure.

4. Compose a fugue in triple counterpoint based directly on *The Well-Tempered Clavier* I, Fugue No. 2. First compose your exposition model (mm. 7–8) in triple counterpoint; then compose your episode model (mm. 9–10). These measures will be the contrapuntal basis for your fugue. This is an effective way to begin fugal composition, and is recommended as a preliminary step before beginning the free composition of original fugues.

5. Compose a fugue based on a broad outline graph (as distinct from the detailed graph prepared in exercise 2) of a Bach fugue, as selected by the instructor. Refer to the sample outline graphs given on p. 212. This need only follow the general outlines, as does this partial sample, based on *The Well-Tempered Clavier* 1, Fugue No. 11.

Exposition	Episode I	Counterexposition	Episode II	ME I
1–13	13–17	17–31 (stretto)	30–36	36–
F:		d:		

6. Compose a fugue based on one of your own expositions, with episodes and strettos, from p. 209. Experiment with stretto, canon, pedal point, and the usual thematic transformations.

One possible procedure for the composition of an original fugue is shown below.

A. Write a subject and test it for suitability in stretto by writing brief stretto imitations at a variety of pitch intervals.
B. Test various transformations of its motifs in stretto.
C. Write a three-voice triple counterpoint model of the exposition, with S, CS1, and CS2; test in several possible voice-exchanged positions.
D. Write the exposition, including the bridge; write several sample episodes.
E. Prepare a general overall plan for the rest of the fugue, laying out roughly the order of events and keys.
F. Write an appropriate ending, possibly employing pedal point.
G. Write the fugue through from the beginning.

Above all, be aware of the necessity for continuity, motivic coherence, clear overall shape, and naturalness of line. Play each voice as you write it to test its integrity and musicality, and play the entire work repeatedly when it is completed, listening to it as critically as you can. Analyze every aspect of your work at every stage of the process.

Notes

1. Information on the ricercar and the other antecedents of fugue may be found in *The New Grove Dictionary of Music and Musicians,* "Ricercar," vol. 15.
2. It is possible in stretto to cut the S off after the first few notes, as long as this truncation is obscured by stretto entries in the other voices; we could call this pseudostretto. See also *The New Grove Dictionary of Music and Musicians,* "Stretto," vol. 18, and the books by Horsley, Mann, and Oldroyd cited in the bibliography.
3. To characterize pedal point as a type of nonharmonic tone, as is often done, may be misleading. Its effect is rather to sustain (prolong) a single structural harmonic root under foreground changes in harmony in the upper voices.
4. Some theorists avoid the term *recapitulation* as conflicting with its more common application in later music, preferring the term *return.*
5. It would be a very useful exercise for the class to make its own reductions of this and several other Bach fugues, either individually or as a group. The linear/harmonic reductions in the books by Gauldin and Parks (see bibliography) are also worthy of attention.
6. Most classes will not have time to do all of these exercises, but the general order of analysis and focused exercises followed by composition should be observed.

CHAPTER 12

FOUR-VOICE COUNTERPOINT

Perform the fugue expositions given below, and analyze the four-voice writing in them, focusing not on the specifically fugal aspects but on the more general features of counterpoint, as suggested on pp. 247 ff.

Ex. 12–1   Well-Tempered Clavier II, Fugue No. 7

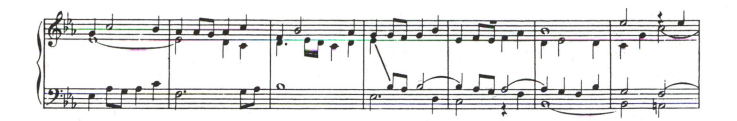

Ex. 12–2   Well-Tempered Clavier I, Fugue No. 1

Directed Study

Analyze in the preceding expositions the texture, rhythm, harmony, and counterpoint.

TEXTURE. Do the voices seem equally active? Do any seem merely accompanimental? Does the bass voice seem at any point to be functioning as harmonic support? Is there any pairing of voices? If so, which voices are paired?

What is the widest interval between adjacent voices? Which pair of voices is allowed to become farthest apart? Is there any crossing of voices? Are all notes playable by two hands?

Do the voices seem to have narrower ranges individually than in three-voice writing, or not? Are there moments of two- or three-voice counterpoint within these passages?

RHYTHM. Make a rhythmic chart of example 12-1, mm. 21–30; example 12-2, mm. 5–7; example 12-3, mm. 10–13; example 12-4, mm. 5–9. Use the format found in example 12-5. Generalize about your findings.

Ex. 12-5 (rhythm of ex. 12–3, mm. 6–7)

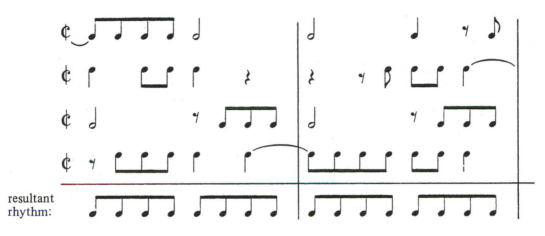

Are there homorhythmic passages in all voices? For how long are such effects sustained? Is the pulse always heard in at least one voice? Look at the use of rests, longer values, and ties. Compared to three-voice works, are they more or less commonly used here?

Perform these expositions in class, conducting and intoning the rhythm of each voice (but not the pitches) on a neutral syllable such as *ta*, to appreciate both rhythmic independence and complementarity.

HARMONY AND COUNTERPOINT. Analyze the harmony, including chord types (qualities), inversion, completeness, and doubling. Generalize about what you find. Circle the roman numerals of the structural chords.

Analyze the nonharmonic tones. Are there any new idioms? What simultaneous nonharmonic tone idioms do you find? What successive nonharmonic tones? What do the nonsuspending voices do to accompany suspensions?

Play each pair of voices. There will be six pairs (voices 1–2, 1–3, 1–4; 2–3, 2–4; 3–4). Do you find any parallel perfect consonances? Direct fifths or octaves? Unequal fifths? How many imperfect consonances are on average found in succession?

TEXTURE AND RHYTHM

Counterpoint in four voices is no different in technique from that in three, nor appreciably more difficult to write. The primary distinctions concern texture and rhythm.

You may have noticed that, due to the rests and longer note values, several brief passages above are, in effect, in three-voice texture. A glance through the four-voice fugues of Bach, espe-

---

cially those for keyboard instruments, will reveal a good deal of three- and even two-voice texture, in particular in the episodes. The fullest texture will occur at the end of the exposition, in the later episodes, in stretto passages, and at the end. In most four-voice counterpoint, the voices are treated as equals. Generally speaking, they are equally active, and there is rarely a feeling of upper-voice domination, inner-voice "filler," or bass lines that are merely harmonic support. The use of short rests, ties, and longer note values in one or two voices at a time accomplishes several ends: it avoids textural thickness and rhythmic squareness; it allows the voices to phrase individually; it avoids contrapuntal problems; and it gives the voices a feeling of rhythmic independence. Such passages lighten or "ventilate" the texture, clarify the counterpoint, and make the fuller passages more impressive by contrast. There will be few, if any, moments during which all the voices are moving simultaneously, as this effect quickly becomes homophonic. Even such a passage as in example 12-3, mm. 6ff., in which all the voices primarily move in eighth notes, is still sufficiently varied by the use of longer notes and rests. Such passages as the following are particularly fine from the point of view of rhythmic variety and complementarity.

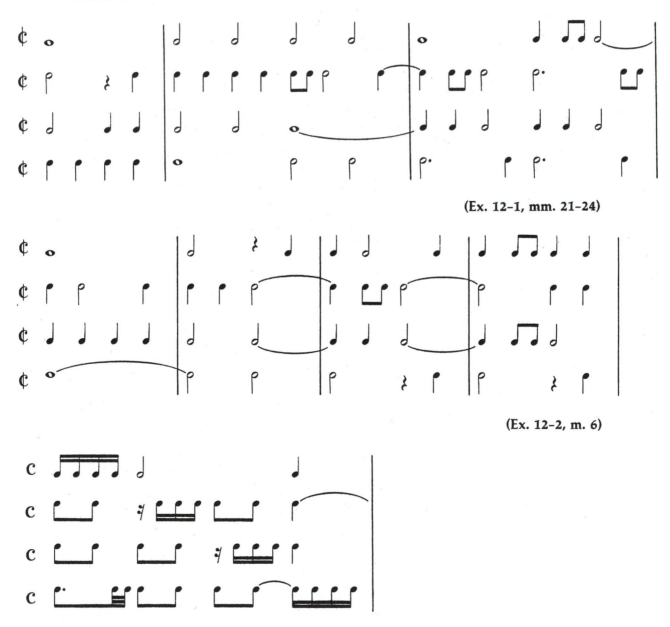

Ex. 12-6

(Ex. 12-4, mm. 5-7)

(Ex. 12-1, mm. 21-24)

(Ex. 12-2, m. 6)

The Craft of Tonal Counterpoint

Note in these rhythmic reductions that no two voices are allowed to move for more than two or three beats in the same values, that the various values are shared equally among the voices, and that the shorter values often follow a tie or short rest. At any given moment, any voice may be inactive due to rests, ties, or long notes; but such passages are typically brief, unless the voice involved is allowed to rest for an entire episode to lighten the texture. In such cases, the resting voice must have come to a natural point of rest (on a stable note) and will almost always return with important thematic material.

There is a certain amount of *voice pairing* in four-voice texture. It is important that these voices vary, in terms of the specific pairs involved. It would be a mistake, for instance, to pair voices 1 and 2 throughout. Example 12-3 is especially instructive in this regard; notice how the eighth notes involve constantly shifting voice pairings. Such pairings, when they do occur, are relatively brief and usually occur in the fastest values. Any parallel motion is of course limited to brief passages of imperfect consonances.

A texture in which a short motif in faster values is passed freely between the voices (informal or motivic imitation) is a particularly effective one. See, for instance, example 12-2, m. 3, or example 12–3, passim.

The *spacings* in four-voice texture are, of necessity, somewhat closer than in thinner textures. Bach was limited by the range of his keyboards so that the thicker the texture, the narrower the range of each voice and the closer the spacings. Adjacent voices are rarely more than an octave apart,[1] though the relation of voices 3 and 4 may occasionally exceed this. As usual, the wider spacings will generally sound best at the bottom of the texture—that is, between tenor and bass. There may be occasional voice crossings, especially between the upper voices, though these will not continue for many beats. The crossing of voices 3 and 4 is fairly rare and creates a new bass line against which chord inversions will then have to be measured.

Students at this stage of writing often fall into the trap of harmonic thinking and chorale-like textures. To avoid homophonic effects, one should always play or sing the individual lines when writing them, and never allow oneself to make a note choice on purely harmonic grounds.

HARMONY

The harmonic language is no different from that in three voices, but of course the harmony will be fuller and the chords more explicit. Complete seventh chords are now possible, although they often occur with the fifth or (more rarely) the third omitted and the root doubled. Seventh chords of all the usual types are somewhat more common in four voices than in three. A brief overview of doubling practices in four voices may be helpful at this stage.

Chord Type	Most Usual Doubling	Least Usual Doubling
Root Position Triads (M and m)	root	third
First Inversion Triads (except ii°⁶ and vii°⁶)	root	third
Second Inversion Triads	fifth	third
Seventh Chords	root	seventh, third

These are general suggestions for doubling; they are not prescriptive, as integrity of line takes precedence over doubling. A more useful way to think of doubling may be in terms of notes *not* normally doubled, which is to say chord thirds (especially in major triads and dominant seventh chords) and tendency tones (chord sevenths and ninths, leading tones and accidentals, or either note of an augmented or diminished interval). But even a tendency tone may be doubled, providing this doubling is brief and metrically weak.

As in three-voice texture, triads without thirds are extremely rare; complete major and minor triads in root position and first inversion predominate; seventh chords are used in all positions, and diminished triads are usually found in first inversion. The $^6_4$ "chord" is of course a dissonant sonority and must be treated in the usual ways (see chapter 8).

There are no new nonharmonic tone idioms, though care should be exercised with regard to their use, since multiple nonharmonic tones can obscure the underlying harmony. The usual dissonances are found, used in the ways we have studied. Bear in mind that the faster-moving notes tend to be consonant with each other, even though one or both may dissonate against the other voices. Simultaneous suspensions, neighbors, or passing tones in two voices are usable, but such effects quickly become homophonic and are best not overused. There will be virtually no cases where three voices are simultaneously dissonant against the fourth voice, except under conditions of pedal point (for example, V^7 or vii^{o7} over tonic pedal just before a final cadence, as in *The Well-Tempered Clavier* I, Fugue No. 2, mm. 30–31). Successive nonharmonic tones, either in one or two voices, are found, as long as both are treated correctly in relation to the other voices and the underlying harmony is not obscured.

As in three voices, parallel fifths and octaves are not used (even if by contrary motion), and direct fifths and octaves are not found between the outer voices, though they may occur between other pairs of voices, as may unequal fifths. In other words, each pair of voices still operates according to the principles of two-voice counterpoint, with the exceptions just noted. And the outer voices behave exactly as in two-voice writing. Each pair must be played and checked for counterpoint.

Keep in mind the usefulness of contrary motion between moving voices (especially the outer voices) and the fact that brief rests may occasionally be employed to avoid contrapuntal problems. There will be few conditions under which three voices will move in parallel motion, as this will often create problems of independence and unusable parallelisms, and in virtually no case can all four voices move simultaneously in the same direction. Recall that nonharmonic tone activity cannot be used to avoid unacceptable parallelisms.

Exercises

1. Analyze several more four-voice passages from the anthology, from both fugal and nonfugal works. Do not focus on the imitative aspects at this point, but rather on the other details of the counterpoint and harmony, including structural lines and structural harmony, scale-degree formulas (especially in the bass), sequences and LIPs, as well as rhythm and texture.
2. Locate the errors in the following examples and suggest possible corrections.
   A. Critique the following passage mainly in terms of doubling and spacing. As always, there are many errors.

The Craft of Tonal Counterpoint

B. Critique the following passage mainly in terms of counterpoint.

A Note on the Written Exercises

In all your four-voice writing, be alert to these aspects:

- motivic unity and balance between the voices (motivic imitation is helpful)
- equal rhythmic activity among voices
- regular resultant rhythm, with no breaks in the pulse
- appropriate and consistent nonharmonic tone activity
- clear harmony
- clear texture (good-sounding spacing, minimal crossing, and appropriate use of ties and short rests)

Suggestions:

1. Work three to four beats ahead in one voice at a time, then catch the other voices up, adjusting as you write.
2. Play or sing each voice as you write it, and again after it is completed, to check shape, flow, and coherence.
3. *Never write a note for purely harmonic reasons*; it must make linear sense.
4. Always play and analyze your work.

Exercises

3. Fill in the indicated missing voices in the following excerpts by Bach. Be attentive to motivic coherence and balance of rhythmic activity. Play and check your lines and counterpoint with care (check each of the six pairs of voices for problems of parallel or direct intervals and unresolved dissonances). Analyze the harmony before you write, and analyze all the non-harmonic tones when you have finished.[2]

a.

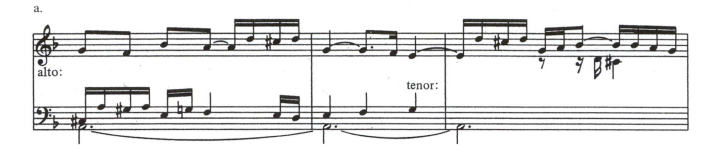

b.

c.

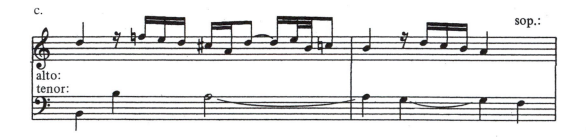

The Craft of Tonal Counterpoint

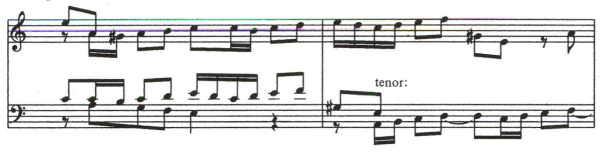

4. Work out the following figured and unfigured basses in four contrapuntal voices, using a mixture of note values, including sixteenths. Work for evenness of both motivic distribution and rhythmic activity. The given bass voice may be slightly elaborated for rhythmic and motivic interest. Check carefully and analyze fully.

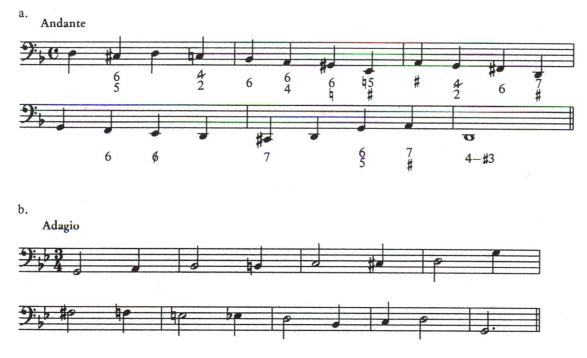

a.

Andante

b.

Adagio

5. Use the following chord formats as the basis for counterpoint in four voices. Employ a texture of four equal voices and a limited motivic content. Check your counterpoint; analyze fully. See the demonstration below for process.

a. A: 4/4 I V | vi iii | IV I | V HC ⌐ | V⁶₅/vi vi |

V⁶₅/ii ii | V V⁷ | I PAC ⌐ ‖

b. e: 6/8 i | v⁶ | iv⁶ | V♯ | i | ii°⁶ | V⁷♯ | i ‖

Demonstration

Given format: g: $\frac{4}{4}$ i vii^{o7} |i iv |V♯

1. Write four-voice framework; bass first, then soprano. Check: lines, counterpoint, resolutions.

2. Articulate.

3. Analyze:

g:	i		vii^{o7}	i	i$_6$	iv	V♯		i$_6$	V♯	i
or:	T	prolonged				PD	D				T

Exercise

6. Articulate the following four-voice frameworks in any meter and tempo. Each should be at least eight measures long. Tonic or dominant harmony may be prolonged as that seems appropriate. Use contrapuntal texture and motivic imitation. Provide figured bass, then analyze the harmony. Analyze fully when the work is completed and check your lines and counterpoint with care. See the demonstration below.

a.

(exchange pattern)

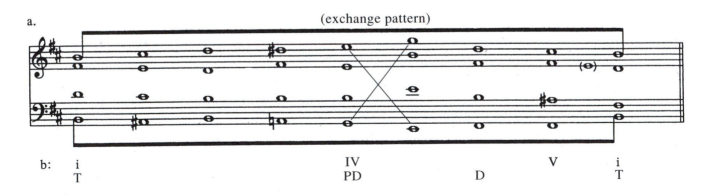

b:	i					IV		V	i
	T					PD	D		T

b.

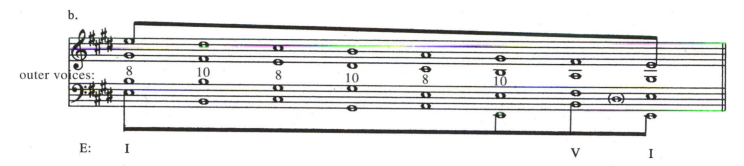

outer voices: 8   10   8   10   8   10

E: I   V   I

Demonstration

Given framework:

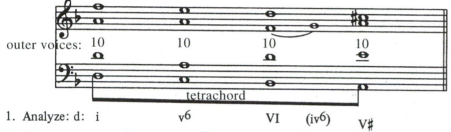

outer voices: 10   10   10   10

tetrachord

1. Analyze: d: i   v6   VI   (iv6)   V♯

2. Choose a meter and tempo; articulate voices.

3. Check and analyze.

Adagio

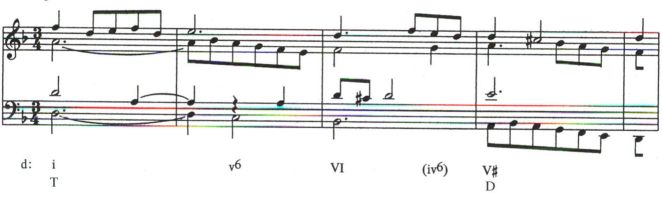

d: i   v6   VI   (iv6)   V♯
      T   D

Exercise

7. Analyze a complete four-voice (nonfugal) suite movement or prelude and use it as a model for a comparable original work. Include in your model the main cadence points, key scheme, and harmonic structure.

Passacaglia (chapter 13) or chorale prelude (chapter 14) may be taken up at this point, before or instead of the study of four-voice fugue.

Four-Voice Fugue

Analyze the fugal excerpts beginning this chapter. Identify S, A, CS (if any), bridge (if any), and locate the end of the exposition. What is the order of voice entries in each? Do you notice any procedural differences from three-voice fugue expositions? Graph each excerpt as shown on p. 256.

Discussion

While four-voice fugue is common in the choral and ensemble music of Bach, as well as in his organ music, his other music exhibits a slight preference for three-voice fugues. *The Well-Tempered Clavier*, for example, has one fugue for two voices (*The Well-Tempered Clavier* I, Fugue No. 10), two for five voices (*The Well-Tempered Clavier* I, Fugue Nos. 4 and 22), nineteen for four voices, and twenty-six for three voices. Four-voice fugues are not very different procedurally from those with three voices. There are some differences: fugues in four or five voices tend to be weightier and graver in character; their subjects are often shorter, slower moving, and narrower in range (see the subjects in examples 12-1 to 12-4); they are also often slightly more homophonic in texture, with more voice crossing and more typically chordal endings. Four-voice fugues are not necessarily longer than those in three; this is more a matter of the length of the subject and the nature of the working-out processes.

Procedurally, four-voice fugues tend to avoid the more complex contrapuntal treatments. Passages in three- or four-voice canon or stretto are fairly rare and usually brief. The counter-subject (CS) material is often less consistent, and while double counterpoint is common, triple and quadruple are not. Because of the ineffectiveness of unrelieved textural thickness, the episodes are often reduced to three voices. There may even be brief two-voice passages, for instance, at the beginning of a stretto section. As mentioned above, when a voice drops out for more than a few beats, it must have come to a point of completion, on a stable note; and when it reenters, it will normally have important material, such as the subject (S) or answer (A). Structurally, the four-voice fugue exhibits no schemes not found in three voices, though counter-expositions are rare, and the bridge when present is more variable in placement.

Since there is one more voice to bring into the exposition, we will focus on this section. Following is a graph of the exposition of *The Well-Tempered Clavier* II, Fugue No. 7 (example 12-1).

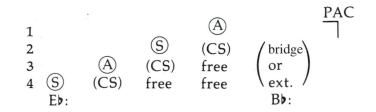

There is a fragmentary CS (first heard in mm. 10–12, voice 4). There is no bridge, though there is a linking measure (m. 13, m. 20) heard twice, and a bridge or extension-like passage after the end of the exposition (m. 27), reaching a cadence in m. 30. The order of voices is regular (4-3-2-1), as are the time intervals of the entrances.

The exposition of *The Well-Tempered Clavier* I, Fugue No. 1 (example 12-2) also lacks a bridge (as it is a stretto fugue, it lacks episodic passages generally). There is no consistent CS, but there are fragments of recurring CS material (m. 4, voice 1, by inversion of m. 2, voice 2; mm. 5–6, voice 1, also has a fragment of this sixteenth-note figure). This exposition contains one anomaly: the entrances are S–A–A–S, the only such case in *The Well-Tempered Clavier*. The voices enter in the order 2–1–3–4.

The Well-Tempered Clavier II, Fugue No. 5 (example 12-3) also makes considerable use of stretto. Its subject is brief and the exposition thus very short. There is no consistent CS, but the free counterpoints are very consistent on a motivic level. There is a brief bridge or link (m. 4), and the first episode, by stretto, follows immediately on the end of the exposition (mm. 7–10). The order of entries is 3–2–1–4.

The Well-Tempered Clavier II, Fugue No. 9 (example 12-4) likewise lacks a bridge. It also has a short, simple subject suitable for stretto and diminution (as well as inversion). There is a short CS (m. 3, voice 4, is the first instance). The order of entries is 4–3–2–1.

It is possible to generalize somewhat about the expositions of four-voice fugues. The voices enter with S–A–S–A (except for *The Well-Tempered Clavier,* Fugues Nos. 1, 12, and 14) and in any one of various voice-entry orders. The orders most often chosen by Bach are 3–2–1–4 and 4–3–2–1; any succession is possible as long as the first two entries are in adjacent voices, as in three-voice fugue. Voice 1 rarely begins (it never does in the *The Well-Tempered Clavier*), and voice 4 is the most likely to enter last. There may be a brief link between entrances, depending on the harmonic implications of the S and A, as in three-voice fugue. If there is a bridge, it may be placed between entrances 2 and 3, or (less often) between 3 and 4. The countermaterial is in general not very consistent, though there may be one CS, in double counterpoint, and occasionally two CSs. Two variant schemes are briefly noted below.

The Well-Tempered Clavier I, Fugue No. 1 was mentioned above for its unusual entrances (S–A–A–S). Fugue No. 12 also has an unusual exposition, which could be graphed as follows:

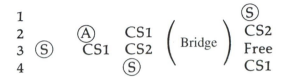

Here we find the entries S–A–S–Bridge–S, along with two quite consistent CSs. The bridge, when placed between entrances 3 and 4, gives the effect of a three-voice fugue with one episode, followed by a final entrance of the S, almost as if there were to be a counterexposition. *The Well-Tempered Clavier* I, Fugue No. 14 also has a variant exposition.

$$
\begin{array}{l}
1 \\
2 \qquad\quad \text{(A)} \quad \begin{pmatrix}\text{Bridge}\\ \text{or}\\ \text{link}\end{pmatrix} \quad \text{CS} \qquad \begin{pmatrix}\text{Bridge}\end{pmatrix} \quad \begin{array}{l}\text{(S)}\\ \text{free}\\ \text{(CS2)}\\ \text{CS}\end{array} \\
3 \quad \text{(S)} \quad\ \text{CS} \qquad\qquad\qquad \text{(CS2)} \\
4 \qquad\qquad\qquad\qquad\qquad\ \text{(S)}
\end{array}
$$

This pattern is similar to that of *The Well-Tempered Clavier* I, Fugue No. 12, with S–A–Link–S–Bridge–S. Here again the last entry is of S rather than A, and the bridge is placed between entries 3 and 4. There is one consistent CS and a very fragmentary second one.

Exercises

1. Play and analyze several four-voice fugues from the anthology. Analyze these in detail, showing their thematic structure and overall layout. Identify all the thematic material, episodes, middle entries, strettos, sequences, and so on. Do a formal graph, as on p. 212, and a structural-pitch graph. Show the harmonic scheme, including all keys and cadences, and the harmonic plan of the episodes. A detailed, bar-by-bar analysis, as suggested on p. 236, may also be helpful.

2. Compose a four-voice fugue on an original S, according to the processes suggested under three-voice fugue, pp. 238 ff. It is a good practice to compose *models* of stretto passages (it is suggested that you use a subject that will permit at least two-voice stretto), the exposition (with at least one consistent CS), several episodes, and perhaps also the ending section, with pedal points. This should be done in stages, with the instructor checking and approving all stages. Each stage should be fully analyzed for all aspects.

Other Fugal Variants

Fugato

This term, which simply means "fugue-like," refers to a fugal section within a larger nonfugal work. Such passages occur frequently in the development sections of instrumental works by the Viennese classical and romantic composers.

Fughetta

A *fughetta* (literally, "small fugue") normally contains one exposition, one episode, and a second, balancing section, which may consist of one or two more entries of the S (or A), or an extended episode or coda. The distinction between a modest fugue and a fughetta is not always clear, and these terms (like many others) were used loosely at the time of Bach. There are several fughettas in the organ works, including some based on chorale melodies. The fughettas for solo harpsichord (such as BWV 899 and 961) are of doubtful authenticity. Some of the shorter fugues from *The Well-Tempered Clavier* (for instance, *The Well-Tempered Clavier* II, Fugue No. 15) may be classed as fughettas. The fughetta for organ based on the chorale melody *Allein Gott in der Höh sei Ehr* is given in the anthology.

Double Fugue

A fugue with two more or less equal subjects is a *double fugue*. These subjects will appear either together in the exposition (as if they were S and CS), and subsequently through the fugue, or with two separate expositions and combined toward the end of the fugue. The two subjects must be written in double counterpoint.

In the first category, the second subject (S2) is heard as a normal though prominent CS in the exposition. It is associated throughout with S1, and may be used as the basis for episodes. It often assumes increasing importance as the fugue progresses. *The Well-Tempered Clavier* I, Fugue No. 12 (in the anthology) is a good example of this procedure.

A subcategory of the first category has the two subjects appearing together from the very beginning (usually m. 1). They are always associated, in double counterpoint, in the course of the fugue, and either or both may form the basis for episodes. If one of these subjects seems distinctly less important, it may better be understood as a CS. This type does not appear in *The Well-Tempered Clavier*, but it may be found in some organ fugues, such as the fugue from the Toccata in E Minor.

In the second category, one finds in effect two expositions in succession, the subjects of which are later combined in a climactic way toward the end of the fugue. S2 often seems, when first heard, to be merely a new CS (as it is normally heard against counterpoints derived from S1), but it then receives an exposition-like series of imitations and is finally combined with S1. *The Well-Tempered Clavier* II, Fugues Nos. 4 and 18 have such a scheme, as does Fugue No. 9 from *The Art of Fugue*. Again, the association of S2 with motivic material from S1 may obscure the identity of the second exposition and the importance of S2.

Triple Fugue

There are two principal options in triple fugue:

- a normal exposition of S1, followed by separate expositions of S2 and S3 (usually in combination with material from S1, which is momentarily subordinate)
- a first exposition in which S1 and S2 are heard simultaneously (as in some double fugues), and a second in which they are associated with S3, which initially appears to be a new CS (and in fact may be so understood).

The first type is the more common. The best-known examples are *The Well-Tempered Clavier* I, Fugue No. 4, and Fugues Nos. 8 and 11 from *The Art of Fugue*. *The Well-Tempered Clavier* I, Fugue No. 4 is given in the anthology. It is a wonderfully expressive work, clearly conceived in terms of a triple counterpoint model. The three subjects enter in mm. 1, 36, and 49. It might be possible to understand this as a fugue with two prominent CSs (or possibly as a double fugue with S3 as countermaterial), but the focus and weight given to S2 and S3 would appear to make the label of triple fugue the most appropriate. On the other hand, to regard certain more modest fugues with two consistent CSs as true triple fugues (for instance, *The Well-Tempered Clavier* I, Fugue No. 21) may be a misapplication of the term, as the CSs of such fugues lack the weight and independence to be considered subjects. True triple fugues are very rare.

Exercises

1. Analyze any double fugue (such as the one on p. 344) and use it as a procedural model. Your own fugue must have two equally strong and interesting subjects, of somewhat independent character and rhythm, written in the best possible double counterpoint.
2. Analyze *The Well-Tempered Clavier*, Fugue No. 4 (p. 350) and use it as the model for a comparable triple fugue. You should compose three equally strong subjects that have distinctive individual character and rhythmic identity (each should move in somewhat different note values from the others, as in the model fugue), and that form solid triple counterpoint, as this will be the contrapuntal model for the entire work. The analogous measures of this fugue are mm. 49–51 (or 52–54 or 59–61). Write this in stages, as assigned by the instructor, with each stage checked and approved. Analyze fully.

Notes

1. Of course, in keyboard music the span of the hand imposes spacing limits on adjacent voices, as well as on the range and intervals of each individual voice. The music is very well calculated to "fit under the hand."
2. The additive process in these exercises is analogous to one Bach himself employed occasionally when reworking an earlier composition; for example, his addition of a fourth voice to the slow movement of the Trio Sonata for organ, BWV 527, which became the slow movement of the Triple Concerto, BWV 1044.

CHAPTER 13

VARIATION FORMS

As variation forms are sectional and somewhat homophonic in nature, they are tangential to our study. Yet several of Bach's major works are variations, so that a brief discussion is appropriate.

THE PASSACAGLIA

A *passacaglia* is a variation set based on a repeating bass-line pattern (*basso ostinato* or *ground bass*), normally in minor mode and triple meter, with a slow and regular harmonic rhythm. The various available bass patterns almost all involve the descending tetrachord, moving from tonic to dominant in four or eight measures.[1]

Ex. 13-1

The simplest diatonic version is the oldest, and the basis for all subsequent versions.

The aesthetic dangers in a process based on the manifold repetition of the bass line are obvious:

- squareness and discontinuity of form
- repetitive phrase structure and harmony
- too much tonic harmony and too many authentic cadences
- a homophonic tendency in the process itself
- aimlessness (no sense of overall structure)

These problems can be overcome by:

- melodically eliding the upper voices over the phrase break, and making sure the upper-voice phrase endings do not always coincide with the bass line cadences (Henry Purcell was the great master of this technique)
- covering the phrase break by motion and suspensions
- choosing an eight-measure in preference to a four-measure pattern
- varying the harmony as much as possible, given the limitations imposed by the implications of the bass
- using as much motivic imitation and rhythmic independence as possible to achieve the effect of a contrapuntal texture
- avoiding authentic cadences and tonic harmony by suspending notes into the tonic triad, by substituting VI^6, ii_2^4 or V_2^4/V for I, or by choosing a pattern that places the dominant rather than the tonic harmony on the first strong beat (see the Henry Purcell and Dietrich Buxtehude versions, examples 13-1, C and D)
- thinking through the entire work as a single shape (or series of shapes), building throughout in terms of textural density, rhythmic activity, harmonic complexity, use of extreme registers and intricacy of counterpoint
- allowing the bass line to move to another voice, to be ornamented, or to be transposed to one or two other keys

Most of these devices may be seen in example 13-2, and may be observed in the Passacaglia in C Minor, pp. 376 ff.

There may be an overall tonal plan in larger passacaglias, especially those for organ. The organ is the most appropriate instrument for this form, as the bass, with its long notes, can easily be taken by the pedals. Longer organ passacaglias may be organized in a broad symmetrical design such as the following, taken from Buxtehude[2]:

Section	Repetition of Bass Pattern	Key
1	7	tonic
2	7	relative
3	7	dominant
4	7	tonic

In this scheme there will be a textural and rhythmic intensification within each section, and through the set. There may also be brief modulating interludes between the sections. Within each section, variations will be paired or grouped together by the use of a motif or rhythmic figure.

Bach must have been aware of both the dangers and the opportunities in the passacaglia. In the extremely affecting "Crucifixus" from the *B-Minor Mass* (example 13-2) he uses a chromatic version of the tetrachord, and elides the cadences (mm. 9, 13) by suspending voices and by bringing in the next voice on the next weak beat. The harmony is intensified from one variation to the next (for instance, in m. 5, VI^6 substitutes for I, avoiding the expected cadence; $vii^{°7}/iv$ in m. 6 substitutes for the v^6 of m. 2; the ii_3^4 in m. 7 replaces the iv^6 of m. 3), and becomes more and more expressive and dissonant as the movement progresses. The use throughout of suspensions also contributes an important element of tension and continuity. The voices have their own motivic material, independent of the bass line, which they share in a process of motivic imitation. The entire movement (to be found on p. 394) builds from beginning to end, with the textural density increasing, the counterpoint increasing in complexity and the harmony in intensity, and the soprano rising to a high point (e²) near the end. There are three internal cadences, which provide momentary textural and harmonic relief, and at the end there is a modulation to G major, via a root position German augmented-sixth chord. The overall shape could be graphed as:

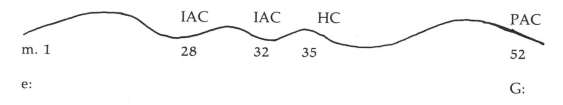

This graph shows a main climactic section, with three preceding but subsidiary upward curves that mirror its shape. The principal climactic moment surrounds m. 42, close to the end; this late climax makes for a dramatic contour.

Ex. 13–2   Mass in B Minor, "Crucifixus"

The *Passacaglia in C Minor* for organ uses a longer (eight-measure) bass pattern, but it exhibits many of the same techniques as the "Crucifixus." In addition to the variation processes used there, Bach also ornaments the bass pattern, and allows it to move into the upper voices. The entire work should be listened to and studied for its large-scale shaping processes. The sense of continuity, motivic coherence, rhythmic acceleration, and textural accretion, as well as the brilliant writing for organ, are extremely impressive in this grand work.

The Chaconne

The *chaconne* is a variation procedure closely allied to that of the passacaglia. The distinction often made between the two—that passacaglia depends on the presence of an invariant bass pattern while the chaconne depends more on a succession of repeated harmonies—does not hold up well under scrutiny. Composers of Bach's time and earlier used these two terms somewhat inter-changeably. And it is obvious that a given bass line in this style implies a fairly limited number of harmonic progressions, just as a given set of harmonies allows very few possible bass lines. Bach's great contribution to the genre is the *Chaconne in D Minor* for solo violin, the opening of which is given in example 13-3.

The work is based on a four-measure harmonic pattern:

$$\text{d:}\ \tfrac{3}{4}\quad i\ \left|\ ii_2^4\quad V_5^6\ \right|\ i\quad VI\ \left|\ iv\ (i_4^6)\quad V^7\ \right|\ i\ \right|$$

Associated with the progression is the tetrachord bass $d^1 \longrightarrow a$, filled in initially as follows:

But as the work progresses, the harmonies are permitted to vary considerably, until finally only the tonic-to-dominant outline is still clear and the bass line has become thoroughly obscured. In addition. Bach modulates to D major in the middle, returning finally to D minor. Again there is a strong feeling of continuity and overall shape, achieved here by increasing rhythm activity, harmonic intensification, range, texture, and instrumental virtuosity.

The entire movement should be heard, both as a fine example of variation technique and as a great example of counterpoint written for a single non-keyboard instrument.

THE GOLDBERG VARIATIONS (CLAVIERÜBUNG, PART IV)

Several of the *Goldberg Variations* have been used earlier as examples. The set is based on a theme (an "aria") from the *Notebook [1725] for Anna Magdalena Bach*. The aria is a symmetrical binary form of thirty-two measures.

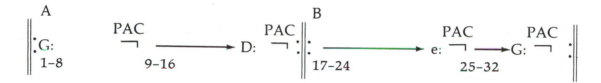

The variations are organized not around the melody of the aria, but around the harmonies and bass line. The first eight measures of the bass, a standard bass line for the time, are given here, with the harmonization from the aria.

Ex. 13-5

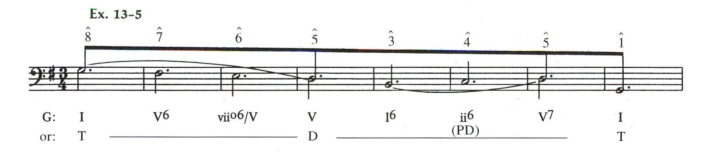

The *Goldberg Variations* form a massive passacaglia or chaconne, in the form of thirty variations, though they differ from a typical passacaglia by being sectional rather than continuous. As mentioned earlier, each third variation (Nos. 3, 6, 9—through to 27) is a canon at an increasing pitch interval, from the unison up to the ninth, between the upper voices, with supporting bass (except for Variation No. 27). At the same time, the bass line and harmonies are to a large degree those of the theme.

There is a feeling of intensification through the set: the canons generally become more and more elaborate, the virtuosic variations increasingly so, and their texture becomes thicker; the expressive variations become increasingly chromatic and complex, including the three variations in G minor (Nos. 15, 21, and 25). This magnificent variation set demands long and detailed study.

It is hoped there will be an opportunity in the course for at least an introduction to it. The aria and a few of the variations are included in the anthology.

Exercise

1. Use one of the following unfigured basses, as assigned by the instructor, as the ground bass for a passacaglia. Before you start, write figured bass symbols and/or roman numerals below the bass lines, giving every stylistically possible harmonization for each bass note. As you compose, keep in mind the necessity for motivic unification, rhythmic continuity and overall shape.

It may be wise before starting this project to study in detail the *Passacaglia in C Minor* (pp. 376 ff.), paying particular attention to motivic consistency and development, and the overall process of intensification achieved through rhythmic and textural accretion. You may also wish to study and follow the process demonstration below. A five-stage process is suggested.

1. Bass is given.
2. Add appropriate figures or roman numerals.
3. Write the upper voice, working for a clear shape and strong outer-voice framework.
4. Part-write the inner voices, working for clear harmony and smooth voice-leading.
5. Articulate the four-voice skeleton, working for flow and motivic unity.

Process Demonstration

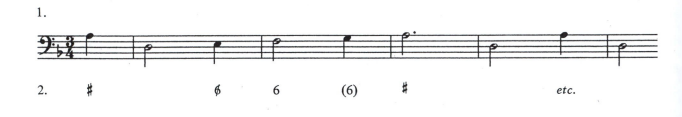

2.   #   ♭   6   (6)   #   *etc.*

3.

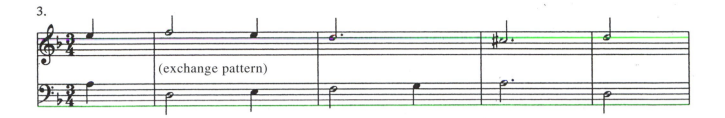

(exchange pattern)

4.

5.

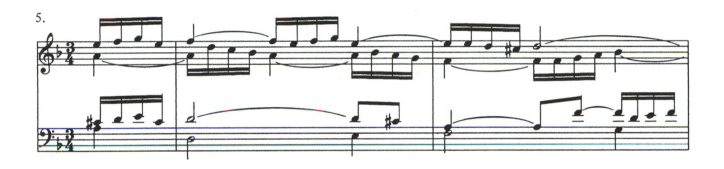

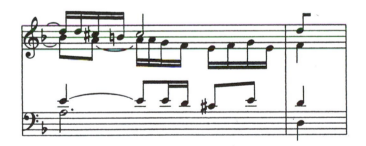

Exercises

2. Compose a passacaglia in the minor mode for organ or for instruments available in class, on a newly composed bass.[3] One of the following two formats for the whole work may be used, at the discretion of the instructor. Analyze the completed work fully, and perform.

	Section	Number of Bass Repetitions	Key
A.	1	4	tonic
	2	4	relative
	3	4	tonic
B.	1	4	tonic
	2	4	relative
	3	4	dominant
	4	4	tonic

3. For students adept at the keyboard, the improvisation of passacaglias and chaconnes will be an interesting and challenging exercise. Bach and his great contemporaries were, to all reports, superb improvisors. The improvisation of variations over a given bass is far less daunting than the playing, *ex tempore*, of more rigorous genres such as the fugue. Group improvisations, jazz-like, over a given harmonic framework, will be entertaining for classes and excellent ear and musicianship training in the style.

Notes

1. For further historical background, see *The New Grove Dictionary of Music and Musicians,* "Chaconne" (vol. 4), "Ground" (vol. 7), "Ostinato" (vol. 14), and "Passacaglia" (vol. 14).
2. Bach's *Passacaglia in C Minor* has no such key scheme, as it does not modulate. The "Crucifixus" from the *B-Minor Mass* likewise does not modulate (until the end).
3. A brief introduction to writing for the organ may be found in the Appendix. A demonstration of organ-playing techniques will be helpful and interesting, if an instrument is available.

CHAPTER 14

Cantus Firmus Procedure: The Chorale Prelude

Cantus firmus technique forms an important category for contrapuntal study. In works employing this technique, a previously existing melody (*cantus* or *cantus prius factus*) is used as the basis for contrapuntal elaboration. This melody appears in one voice, in longer note values than the other voices, which form counterpoints against it. A great deal of sacred vocal part-music of the late medieval period (13th to 14th centuries) and Renaissance uses cantus firmus procedure, employing plainchant melodies or popular songs of the period. In such music, the cantus most often appears in the tenor voice, unornamented.

Cantus firmus survives as a technique in the Baroque period principally in the form of the organ chorale prelude of the Protestant Church, used to prelude the singing of hymns (chorales) and in some cases to act as interludes between verses of the hymns. These hymn melodies came from a variety of sources: plainchant (sometimes with its modality obscured by accidentals), popular songs of the Renaissance with sacred texts substituted, and newly composed sacred melodies from the Reformation and later. These tunes are simple and easy to sing and remember; many are ideally suited to contrapuntal elaborations of all kinds.[1]

Bach composed a wide variety and large number of works based on chorale tunes, including chorale fugues, fantasias, variations (partitas), and preludes. These are primarily works for organ, but he also applied the same techniques to the choral writing in many of the cantatas. Such works vary widely in technique; we will focus in this chapter exclusively on the chorale preludes that employ the whole chorale melody (the cantus) in one voice, decorating it with counterpoints in the other voices.

There are many variant procedures. Bach was always extremely inventive with his compositional options, and the categories suggested below must be understood as fluid and overlapping. For instance, the tune may be slightly or highly ornamented; it would presumably have been familiar to the Lutheran congregations of Bach's time, who would have recognized it even when ornamented. Further, the tune may appear in the upper voice, the tenor voice, or in the pedals, sometimes with a 4' stop (which makes it sound an octave higher than notated). It should also be noted that Bach's chorale settings of all types are always expressive of the chorale text, in both general and sometimes specific (text painting) ways, so that in setting a chorale tune one needs to be aware at least of the general character and mood of the text.[2]

The Ornamented Chorale Harmonization

This category provides a natural middle ground between plain chorale harmonizations and the more elaborate kind of chorale prelude. Here, the lower three voices of the harmonization are only slightly ornamented; the chorale tune (in the soprano) may be given plain or slightly ornamented (as below).

Ex. 14-1   Herzlich tut mich verlangen

The first two phrases of the original chorale tune on which this prelude is based are:

In example 14-1, the chorale melody in the first phrase is placed by itself on a separate manual, so that it can be given an organ registration (color) to distinguish it from the voices around it.

For a complete example of this type of chorale prelude, see the anthology, p. 383.

Cantus with Motivic Counterpoints

There are two subcategories here. In Bach's usage one is not always clearly distinct from the other.

In the first type the chorale tune is accompanied by free motivic counterpoints not clearly related to the cantus itself. The voices may relate motivically to each other, or they may not. The following examples are selected mainly from the *Orgelbüchlein*, which is rich in this type of procedure.[3]

Example 14-2, a relatively simple chorale prelude for manuals only, uses a figural accompaniment unrelated to the tune, which is found in voice 1.

In example 14-3 the counterpoints are motivically interconnected, but they are not derived in any obvious way from the chorale melody. The pedal participates in the motivic content. Note the alternating-feet figure in the pedal; the choice of this motivic figure may have been suggested by performance considerations.

Ex. 14-4   Durch Adam's Fall ist ganz verderbt

In example 14-4 the remarkable pedal part is unrelated to both the cantus and the other counterpoints; it may instead have been suggested by the text: "Through Adam's fall all is corrupted".

In the second category, shown in the next two examples, the counterpoints are motivically derived from the cantus.

The rising-third motif in example 14-5, A–C♯, is probably heard as a reference to the opening of the melody, as is the rising scalar figure () in the alto voice.

Ex. 14–6   Helft mir Gottes Güte preisen

Example 14-6 employs motivic imitation based on the first two phrases of the chorale melody.

In many chorale preludes of this type, the relationship of the counterpoints to the cantus is well hidden; the process of motivic derivation in these works will require close study.

CANONIC TREATMENT OF CANTUS AND/OR ACCOMPANYING PARTS

The *Canonic Variations on "Vom Himmel hoch"* have already been discussed. The double canon in "In dulci jubilo" has also been mentioned (p. 119). The following excerpt contains a canon between voices 1 and 4 at the octave, at one measure, on the chorale tune. The inner voices have free, though motivically related, counterpoints. In such works the chorale tune may be involved in the canon or in the other voices, or (as in 'In dulci jubilo") both may be canonically treated.

Ex. 14–7   Gottes Sohn ist kommen

CHORALE PRELUDE INVOLVING "VORIMITATION" (PREIMITATION)

In many of the longer chorale preludes, the chorale is preimitated by the other voices before the entrance of the melody per se in long notes. Each phrase of the chorale will be separated by several measures (often one to four, but even more in longer works), during which the accompanying voices continue their counterpoints. The imitations are not usually rigorous (canonic); they are likely to be brief and informal, and may ornament the melody. Imitations are usually at the octave or the fifth (fugal preimitation). There are two subcategories.

In the first type, the imitations are usually informal and are based on only the first phrase (or just the head motif) of the melody.

Ex. 14–8   **Auf meinem lieben Gott**

In example 14-8 the accompanying voices are based on the first three notes of the cantus and treat it in a manner similar to a two-voice invention prior to its entrance in the pedal (at 4') in m. 6.

In example 14-9 the two upper voices have an extensive imitation based on an ornamented version of the chorale tune, supported by a nonimitative (though motivically related) bass. The melody appears in the pedal, with a 4' stop.

In the second type, the imitative voices are based successively on each phrase (or only its head) of the melody before it enters in long notes. As these works are lengthy, none is shown here, but one (Jesus Christus unser Heiland) is given in the anthology (p. 387). This category is often referred to as a *chorale motet* or *chorale ricercar*. The *motet* (vocal) and *ricercar* (instrumental) were Renaissance forms consisting of successive imitative sections ("points of imitation"), each section based on a new phrase of the melody, rather like a series of fugatos, and are the principal forerunners of the fugue.

Chorale Prelude with "Obbligato" Melody

("Ritornello" Procedure)

Here, a clearcut and independent theme, usually regular in phrase structure and even periodic, precedes the entrance of the cantus. This theme, which may or may not be related motivically to the cantus, recurs throughout in the soprano voice in a rondo-like manner, either whole or in part, between and against successive phrases of the chorale melody, which is usually placed in the tenor or pedal. A complete restatement of the theme follows the last phrase of the chorale. Perhaps the best-known example of this type is Bach's setting of "Wachet auf, ruft uns die Stimme," given complete in the anthology, on p. 391.

Exercises

1. Analyze several of the chorale preludes in the anthology, starting with the simpler varieties.[4] Consider the motivic relationship (if any) of the accompanying voices to the chorale melody; such relationships are often obscured by filling in, inversion, and/or ornamentation. Analyze the implied harmony of the melody first, or Bach's own harmonization of the chorale (as found in the *371 Chorales*), and compare this to the harmonization used in the prelude. Consider the relations between the accompanying voices: are they unrelated, motivically related, or imitative?
2. Analyze the Bach chorales below in terms of keys, cadences, chords, nonharmonic tones, and motifs in the melody (the soprano voice).

Du Friedensfürst, Herr Jesu Christ

A.

Werde munter, mein Gemüte

B.

Ach wie nichtig, ach wie flüchtig

C.

The Craft of Tonal Counterpoint

3. Compose chorale prelude excerpts based on the first phrase of one or more of the chorales above, exemplifying the principal types of chorale preludes.
    A. Ornamented harmonization. This type, if heavily ornamented, will become indistinguishable from the next type.
    B. Free motivic. The accompanying voices will not be clearly related motivically to the chorale melody; they may share motifs between themselves, or they may not.
    C. Derived motivic. The motifs should relate clearly to the *cantus,* which should be analyzed for motivic content first.
    D. *Vorimitation.* You may try either subcategory of this type; the first is somewhat easier to handle. The imitations may be brief and informal.
    E. *Obbligato* melody (*ritornello*). Study p. 391 in the anthology, and base your chorale prelude on this model.

These excerpts may be written for three or four instruments in the class, or, if possible, for the organ, using two manuals and pedals. The *cantus firmus* should not be highly ornamented.

Process Demonstration

Given chorale phrase:

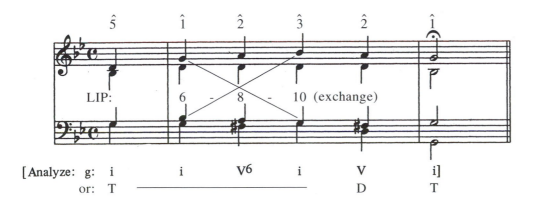

- slightly ornamental chorale, unornamented cantus in voice 1

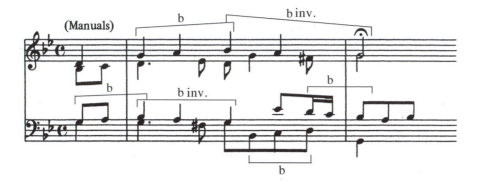

- free motivic type (may be subtly related to cantus), unornamented cantus in voice 1

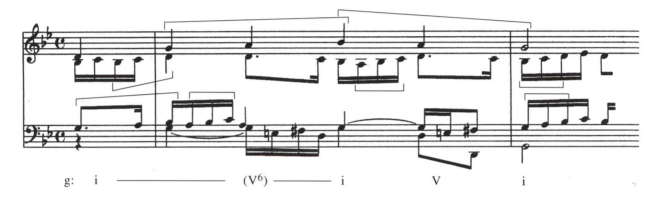

g: i ——————— (V⁶) ——— i   V   i

- related (derived) motivic type; unornamented cantus

- Vorimitation type; cantus in pedals, at 4'

4'   (sounds octave higher)

(chorale)

Exercises

4. Select your most successful result from exercise 3 above, and continue it through to the end in the same style. Especially if you choose to compose the Vorimitation or *obbligato* type, you may wish to refer again to one of the models in the anthology. Analyze fully.

5. Harmonize one of the chorale melodies below in the Bach style. After it has been checked for correctness of harmony and counterpoint, use it as the basis for a chorale prelude of any type, as suggested in exercise 3. Analyze the melody carefully for motivic content and commit it to memory before starting to write. There may be three or four voices, and it may be written for instruments from the class or for organ, as specified by the instructor. You may choose to ornament the cantus slightly. The cantus may appear in soprano, tenor, or bass (pedal).

For keyboard performers, especially organists and harpsichordists, the exercise of improvising chorale preludes will be excellent training in harmonization, style awareness, ear training, and musicianship.

Notes

1. For further background and historical information, see *The New Grove Dictionary of Music and Musicians,* "Chorale" (vol. 4), "Chorale Settings" (vol. 4), and "Cantus firmus" (vol. 3).
2. Incidentally, the fermata signs ⌢ in the chorales are not necessarily intended to indicate that the affected note be held, but to show phrase endings.
3. The *Orgelbüchlein* is a collection of forty-six chorale settings dating mainly from the years 1713–17.
4. Those wishing to compose any of these projects for the organ are referred to appendix 2.

Conclusion

We return, at the end of our study, to some thoughts expressed at its outset. Your intensive investigation of Bach's style and technique should be a lasting source of pleasure and instruction to you. It will already have made you a better musician—a more understanding performer and listener, a more skilled composer—and will have reinforced your admiration for the intellect and spirit of a great human being. In addition, you will have gained a renewed respect for your own creativity, musical intuition, and ability to master a complex craft. I hope you will carry these possessions with you always.

APPENDIX 1: HARMONY

One of the principal reasons for the solidity of Bach's music is its strong, functional harmonic basis.[1] Chords are placed, and resolve, in predictable ways (that is, to ears at all familiar with tonal music). Bach's harmony, while rather more chromatic than that of his contemporaries, is still mainly diatonic. This book focuses primarily on his diatonic style, since the more contrapuntally complex a texture is, the simpler the harmony usually becomes.[2] The chart below is intended simply as a review and for quick reference.

Chord Functions in Tonal Harmony

Most common progressions ↓	Diatonic Repertoire	Chromatic Repertoire[3]
		/iii
	iii$^{(7)}$	/vi
	vi$^{(7)}$	/ii, /IV, /N
	ii$^{(7)}$, IV$^{(7)}$	/V, N, Augmented Sixth Chords
Pre-Dominant (PD)		
Dominant (D)	V$^{(7)}$, vii$^{\circ(7)}$	
Tonic (T)	I	

*The symbol / indicates a secondary dominant chord, so that the symbol /iii reads "any secondary dominant of iii."

GENERAL COMMENTS ON CHORD PROGRESSION IN BACH

Common progression (down the chart, chord-to-chord) predominates in Bach. The tonic chord may progress to any other chord.

Other progressions are found often but rarely two in a row. In other words, a less common progression is normally followed by a common one. Of the less common progressions, some of the most characteristic are iii–IV, vi–V, V–vi, and ii–vi.

Since in this music, especially in the thinner textures, it is often difficult to distinguish ii from IV, and V from V[7] or vii°[7], the symbols T (tonic), D (dominant), and PD (predominant) may prove very useful.

The chords toward the bottom of the table above are found most often. Some simpler works use only tonic, dominant, and predominant chords. The higher one goes in the chart, the rarer the chords, in most works. The chords near the bottom of the chart are also most frequently prolonged, and function as departure and goal harmonies, (*structural harmonies*), especially I and V. Chords other than I and V may be thought of as linear (contrapuntal, decorative), rather than structural, in function.

Works usually begin on tonic harmony and always end on it. The feeling of a tonal center is rarely suspended. Tonic harmony is most often placed on a strong beat, at the beginning and/or end of a phrase.

The note forming the chord seventh is often short and metrically weak, casting some doubt as to whether these notes are best considered chord tones or nonharmonic tones in such instances.

Chord progressions (chord functions) are largely the same for both major and minor modes, although there are a few special cases in minor, involving the descending tetrachord or harmonic sequences.

Harmonic rhythm is usually patterned and regular. The faster the tempo, the slower the harmonic rhythm will tend to be, avoiding a feeling of nervousness in the harmony. Chords usually change from a weak into a strong beat, and thus the bass line moves over the barline (unless the bass is suspended). Thus, *harmonic rhythm supports meter*. The harmonic rhythm may accelerate in mid-phrase; at phrase endings it may either speed up or (less often) slow down.

Cadences (breathing or resting places, phrase endings, harmonic arrival points) are a principal means of clarifying form in this music. The harmonic goal of the cadence arrives on a strong beat (the exception is at a half cadence, where the V may be preceded by a (I $^6_4$) with a suspension- or appoggiatura-like effect. Following is a brief overview of the four available cadence types in this style.

1. *Authentic (full) cadence:* dominant moving to tonic harmony.
   A. *Perfect authentic cadence* (PAC): root position V or V7 progressing to root position I, tonic note in upper voice with I. This is the strongest cadence type, almost always found at the main formal articulative points.
   B. *Imperfect authentic cadence* (IAC): a less final-sounding version of the PAC, appropriate to internal but not usually final cadences. Either the V or the I may be in first inversion, or the mediant rather than the tonic note is placed in the upper voice with the I.
2. *Half (semi-) cadence* (HC): an internal (medial) cadence type only, with tonic or subdominant (or much more rarely vi or a secondary dominant of V) moving to dominant. The goal chord is almost always a root position V.
3. *Deceptive cadence* (DC): replaces an expected PAC, usually very near the end of a work, with the expected tonic chord being replaced by a vi or, more rarely, a IV⁶ or V $^3_4$ /V, with $\hat{5} \rightarrow \hat{6}$ in the bass.
4. *Plagal cadence* (PC): the so-called Amen cadence, with subdominant moving to tonic harmony. These may occur at the ends of relatively substantial works (such as a fugue) following a strong PAC.

Chord inversion is taken up in detail in the text. It should be pointed out here that first-inversion triads are freely used, except at beginnings and ends of phrases, where the more stable root position sound is needed. The use of inversion is an essential ingredient of good bass-line writing; it has the effect of "lightening" the harmony by avoiding the stable root position in mid-phrase. The use of second inversion triads ($^6_4$ chords) is highly restricted. Indeed, "$^6_4$ chords" are best understood and heard as *linear*, dependent, and embellishing effects and not as stable harmonies; they should always be analyzed in terms of their usage (cadential, passing or neighboring: cad., P, or N).

Dominant ninth chords are rare in Bach, though they may occasionally be found in arpeggiations. Clear nondominant ninths are not found. The note forming the ninth can usually be analyzed as a nonharmonic tone.

Diminished seventh chords, both dominant and secondary dominant in function, are more common in Bach than in other composers of his time and are an important characterizing element of his music. They are quite often outlined by melodic lines, either by scales or by arpeggios. The fully diminished seventh is far more common than the half diminished.

Altered chords are nearly always functional; for instance, secondary dominants of vi, such as V^7/vi or vii^{o7}/vi, resolve to vi.

The *Neapolitan chord* is almost always used functionally, as a dominant preparation chord, usually resolving to i^6, i^6_4, V, V^7, or vii^{o7}. It is used only in the minor mode, most often approaching a cadence.

Augmented sixth chords are not common in Bach. When used, they are employed as dominant preparation chords (going to V, sometimes through a cadential i^6_4 effect), nearly always in the minor mode. The Italian sixth is the most common type in Bach.

Harmonic tendency tones, like melodic tendency tones, are resolved with great care in this style. These tendencies can be summarized as follows:

- diminished intervals resolve inward by step
- augmented intervals resolve outward by step
- chord sevenths (and the rare ninths) resolve down by step

Naturally, these tendencies are subject to the same variations as are the melodic forms of these intervals, including delayed and transferred resolution.

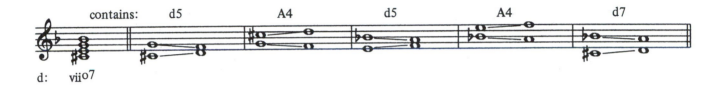

MODULATION

While modulation can be viewed as a large and complex topic, our discussion here will be confined to Bach's most typical usages. Bach normally restricts his modulations to closely related keys, that is, to the following set of relationships:

The most common modulations are to the relative and dominant keys. Note that all closely related keys are diatonic *chords* in the main key, and that all differ from the main key by a signature difference of no more than one accidental.

Modulation is most often accomplished by common (pivot) chord. The first key is clearly tonicized, and after the common chord the new key is carefully tonicized by harmony, line and scale before its cadence. The new key is nearly always established by a PAC. Lacking such a cadence, there may be a question to the ear whether a modulation has occurred. The common chord in Bach is diatonic in both keys and is typically a predominant chord in the new key, followed immediately by the first dominant chord in that key. A typical common chord modulation could be graphed thus:

First key established		Common chord ↓		PAC (2nd key)	⌐
		2nd key: IV (ii)		V⁷	I
	or:	PD		D	T

A circle-of-fifths sequence is sometimes used to modulate, though these modulations can often just as well be understood in terms of a common chord.

Phrase modulation, in which the new key is begun abruptly following an authentic cadence in the old key, is possible in the style, though less common than in later styles. Chromatic modulation is not characteristic of Bach, except in some highly chromatic works.

NONHARMONIC TONES (GENERAL DEFINITIONS)

Any note not heard as a member of the harmony at any given moment is a nonharmonic tone.[3] Not all nonharmonic tones are dissonant, nor are all dissonances nonharmonic (for example, the m7 or tritone in a dominant seventh chord). The definitions given here should not be taken to imply that line is subservient to harmony, as line and chord are inseparable. Depending on the style, any nonharmonic tone can be short or long, metrically weak or strong, diatonic or chromatic. Bach's usages tend to be diatonic and relatively short.

a. *Passing tones* fill in by step between chord tones. Some theorists refer to an accented passing tone as an appoggiatura.

b. *Neighbor tones* (auxiliaries) embellish a repeated chord tone by moving away and back by step.

c. *Escape tones* are approached by step and resolved by leap, usually downward. They are often cadential, as in the last example.

d. *Anticipations* occur immediately before an expected chord tone. They are most often used at cadences, anticipating the tonic note.

e. *Appoggiaturas* are approached by leap and resolved by step, usually downward. They are accented and often relatively long.

f. *Incomplete neighbor tones* are like brief, unaccented appoggiaturas, approached by leap and resolved by step. They are sometimes termed cambiatas.

g. *Suspensions* are prepared on the same pitch and resolved by step, usually downward. They are placed on a strong beat. The suspension idiom involves three facets: *preparation, suspension,* and *resolution* by step.

Ex. A–1

a.

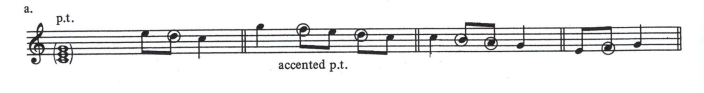

b.

The Craft of Tonal Counterpoint

Figured Bass Symbols

Figured bass symbols were used by Bach and his contemporaries to indicate intervals above a given bass line. These symbols were converted into harmonies by the continuo (harpsichord or organ) player, improvising with the right hand on the intervals indicated by the symbols, while the left hand played the bass line. Bach composed—and taught—in terms of these interval combinations, not of the roman-numeral chordal system, which postdates him.

The arabic figured bass numerals show which intervals (and their compounds) are to be played above each bass note. They do not specify spacing, register, doubling, or texture. These are the standard symbols:

- root position triad: no numerals, except when a figure of $\frac{5}{3}$ is needed to cancel an immediately previous $\frac{6}{4}$ under the same bass note.
- first inversion triad: 6 or $\frac{6}{3}$
- second inversion triad: $\frac{6}{4}$
- seventh chords:
  - root position: 7
  - first inversion: $\frac{6}{5}$
  - second inversion: $\frac{(6)}{\frac{4}{3}}$
  - third inversion: $\frac{(4)}{2}$

- an accidental beneath a bass note, if not next to a numeral, affects the third (tenth, seventeenth) above that note
- any accidental in the music (except an accidental affecting the bass note itself) must appear in the symbols. The slash (⑥) has the effect of chromatically raising the affected note.

Ex. A–2

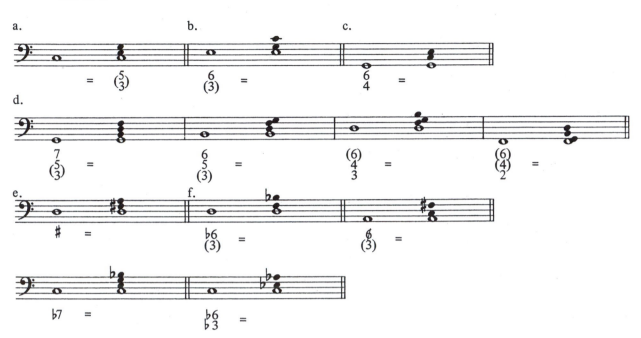

Any interval above the bass note can be shown in the figures, including nonharmonic tones. I have chosen to indicate only chord tones in my use of the figures, with the exception of the $\frac{6}{4}$.

Notes

1. In introducing this material the instructor may wish to discuss the fact that Bach thought—and taught—in terms of figured bass symbols, not roman numerals. Because of the problems a purely figured-bass approach could create for students trained in roman-numeral thinking (and implicitly in Jean-Philippe Rameau's chordal-identity concepts), this text suggests using the chord-functional approach. An instructor preferring the figured bass approach will find this text compatible.

   The sections on harmony, modulations, and nonharmonic tones are primarily intended as a brief review, but even well-prepared classes will benefit from going through them. See Notes to the Instructor, p. xiii, and the entries "Harmony" (vol. 8) and "Modulation" (vol. 12) in *The New Grove Dictionary of Music and Musicians.*

2. There are, of course, some fascinating exceptions, especially in the fugues and canons with chromatic subjects.

3. This section discusses nonharmonic tones in general. Bach's characteristic nonharmonic tone usages are taken up on pp. 23 ff.

APPENDIX 2: COMPOSING FOR THE ORGAN

For students wishing to write any of their composition projects for the organ (especially the projects involving fugue, passacaglia and chorale prelude), the following brief comments may prove helpful.

Bach's pedalboard has a range of from C to d[1] (or f[1]); the two or three manuals range from C to d[3] (or c[3]). The pedals are ideal for sustained notes.[1] Rapid scalar patterns are difficult for the pedals. Leaping patterns that alternate the feet are more practicable (see the following example). Pianists will have to remind themselves that there is no damper pedal on the organ or harpsichord. A key must be held down to sustain that note; therefore, pianistic figurations such as wide arpeggios are ineffective, and are in any case not characteristic of the rigorously contrapuntal side of the Bach style. An ideal texture for organ writing, and one in which Bach excels, is the trio-sonata texture of two equal upper voices and a linear bass in three-voice counterpoint. Four-voice writing is also typical, but keep in mind that if two voices are played on one manual, the notes must fit within the compass of the hand (in other words, must "lie under the hand") to be performable. The best course is to study several characteristic passages from the organ music, as found in the anthology.

Observe in the following passage from the Passacaglia in C Minor the three equal and linear upper voices, and the sustained notes and alternating-feet patterns in the pedal part.

Notes

1. It should be understood that the bass voice, when played by the pedals, will normally be doubled at the lower octave by the addition of a 16' stop. To avoid this effect, one would have to specify 8' (sounding at the written pitch) or 4' (sounding an octave higher, as in some chorale preludes where the chorale melody is in the pedal).

GLOSSARY

This glossary gives very brief definitions of principal technical terms used in this text, and is based on the usages found in Bach. It is not intended to cover all possible cases, just the most common ones. The reader is referred to the index page references for fuller coverage of each topic, as well as to the resources cited in the bibliography.

Affect (*Affekt*, in German) Expressive character of a given work or movement, inherent in its tempo, mode, intervals, gestures, genre, and musical figures. Baroque movements are highly unified in affect and musical figure, and each figure embodies an affective or rhetorical meaning. These concepts were variously classified in the seventeenth and eighteenth centuries into the Doctrines of the Affections (*Affektenlehre*), and of the Figures (*Figurenlehre*), but were never firmly codified nor universally agreed upon.

Answer (response) In a fugue exposition, the second statement of the subject, usually transposed to the dominant key.

Augmentation Statement of a musical idea (such as a fugue subject) in slower note values, usually in a 2:1 ratio, compared to the initial statement.

Basso continuo See figured bass.

Basso ostinato See ground bass.

Bridge Transitional passage, as in a fugue exposition—typically of two to four measures and usually following the end of the answer—that remodulates to the tonic key preceding the next entrance of the subject.

Cadence Resting or breathing place in music, marking the end of a phrase, section, or composition; in tonal music cadences are often classified by the final two harmonies at the point of cadence.

Canon Composition or extended passage in which the voices imitate each other strictly. See *imitation*.

Canon cancrizans (crab canon, or retrograde canon) Canon in which one voice imitates the other by retrogression (backward from end to beginning).

Canon per motu contrario (canon by contrary motion, canon by inversion) Canon in which one voice imitates by melodic inversion.

Canon per augmentationem Canon in which one voice imitates by rhythmic augmentation, usually in a 2:1 or 4:1 ratio.

Cantus firmus Preexisting melody, such as a Lutheran chorale, used as the basis of a contrapuntal work, such as a *chorale prelude*.

Chaconne Variations based on a repeated chord progression, most often I–IV–V–I and variants. Closely related to the *passacaglia*, and often indistinguishable from it, though chaconnes are more usually in major mode. May be sectional or continuous.

Chorale prelude Composition based on a preexisting chorale melody, most often heard in the upper or tenor voice, or in the organ pedals; for organ or (more rarely) chorus. See *cantus firmus*.

Codetta Brief (two- to six-measure) ending section of an invention or fugue.

Composite rhythm (macrorhythm or resultant rhythm) Overall pulse, the combined effect of the rhythms of all voices.

Compound line Single musical line that gives the effect of embodying several voices, most often through registral differentiation of these voices.

Counterexposition In a fugue, a second exposition, in tonic and dominant keys, that follows the first exposition.

Countersubject In a fugue, a consistent counterpoint heard against the subject and answer in the exposition and often throughout the fugue.

Cross-relation (false relation) Relationship between a scale degree in one voice closely followed by a chromatically altered version of that pitch in another voice; these alterations most often involve degrees 6 and 7 in minor.

Diminution Statement of a musical idea (such as a fugue subject) in quicker note values, usually in a 1:2 or 1:4 ratio, compared to the initial statement.

Direct (hidden, covered) fifths and octaves Voice-leading situation in which two voices move by similar motion into a perfect fifth or octave. This effect is generally avoided in Bach, especially when both voices leap, particularly in two-voice (and outer-voice) writing.

Double canon Procedure in which two different canons occur at the same time.

Double (invertible) counterpoint Relationship between two voices such that the counterpoint is equally effective when either voice is placed above (or below) the other.

Double fugue Fugue with two distinct subjects, which may be presented together in the exposition or may receive separate expositions, and are later combined.

Episode Transitional and/or development passage (as in an invention or fugue), typically modulatory and sequentially organized.

Exposition Opening section of a work (such as an invention or fugue), containing the principal musical materials of that work; in a fugue, this will include the initial statements of subject and answer in tonic or dominant keys in all voices. In many fugues it also includes a brief episode, called a *bridge*.

Figures See *affect*.

Figured bass (thoroughbass) Bass line under or over which arabic figures have been placed to indicate intervals above the bass notes, and by implication the harmonies. In Baroque music, the indicated harmonies would be filled in (realized) by the keyboard player; figured bass is often employed in music theory instruction, and was so used by Bach.

Follower Second voice to enter in an imitative work or passage.

Fugato Developmental passage in a larger work (as in development sections in sonata form) written in an imitative style similar to a fugue but not carried out as rigorously.

Fughetta Brief fugue, usually with only one episode and one modulation at most.

Fugue Imitation-based contrapuntal genre, in which the entire work is developed from its initial materials (subject and countersubject), as found in the exposition. Developmental *episodes* and *middle entries* may alternate, unless the work is a *stretto fugue* or *double fugue*. There will usually be modulations to closely related keys.

Ground bass (basso ostinato) Repeated bass-line pattern (and thus the harmonic patterns implied by it) used as the basis of a set of variations. See *chaconne* and *passacaglia*.

Harmonic rhythm The speed of and rhythmic patterns formed by chord changes. Harmonic rhythm in tonal music is usually regular and supports the feeling of meter.

Hemiola As applied to musical rhythm, the ratio of 3:2 between note values either successively within one voice or simultaneously between two. This effect is often found in Baroque music in certain dances such as the minuet, approaching cadences.

Hidden fifths See *direct fifths*.

Imitation Relationship between voices such that voices enter successively using the same melodic material. The first voice, or *leader* establishes the musical materials, which are then replicated in the other voices or *followers*. In analyzing imitative passages or works, the time and pitch intervals between successive voice entries are noted, as well as the length for which the imitation is carried out in each voice.

Invention Imitation-based two-voice contrapuntal genre in which the entire work is developed from the initial idea or theme, and sometimes from its counterpoints (counterthemes). Very like a two-voiced fugue in procedure and overall layout, with developmental, modulatory episodes and recurring entries of the theme.

Invertible counterpoint See *double counterpoint*. Three or four voices may also be written in invertible counterpoint (thus, triple or quadruple invertible), such that many or all possible repositionings (top to bottom) of the voices will be effective.

Leader The first voice to enter in an imitative passage or work.

Linear-intervallic pattern (LIP) Recurrent pattern of intervals formed between pairs of voices, most often in sequential passages.

Macrorhythm See *composite rhythm*.

Middle entry Complete entry of the subject or theme in a fugue or invention, anywhere after the end of the exposition. Such entries will typically be in closely related keys, and may use melodic inversion or (rarely) retrogression, augmentation or diminution.

Motive (motif) The smallest unit of melodic and/or rhythmic thematic material, used as the basis for development as a composition unfolds. Motives in Bach are often very short, always shorter than a phrase and often of three to four notes or rhythmic values. They are spun out in the course of a composition by the processes of repetition, fragmentation, extension, sequence, inversion and so on.

Neapolitan chord Harmonic structure with predominant function; a major triad built on the lowered-second scale degree. In Bach, used mainly in minor mode, as a cadential-preparation harmony.

Ostinato Regularly recurrent pattern, used as the basis of a composition. See *ground bass*.

Parallel (consecutive) fifths and octaves Voice-leading situation in which perfect fifths or octaves are found in succession between any pair of voices. This effect is universally avoided in tonal (and much pretonal) music, as it detracts from linear independence. The prohibition on parallel octaves is not to be confused with the consistent doubling of a melody or bass line for acoustical emphasis. See *direct fifths* and *unequal fifths*.

Passacaglia Variations based on a basso ostinato or *ground bass* pattern, usually involving a descending tetrachord from tonic to dominant scale degrees. The bass line may be diatonic or chromatic, and the work will tend to be seamless rather than sectional. Typically minor mode and triple meter, often slow and expressive in affect. See *chaconne*.

Pedal point Sustained pitch, normally a tonic or dominant note in the bass, over which the surface harmony changes. Pedal is a principal means of prolonging and stabilizing underlying harmony. Dominant pedal is most often found in the middle or nearing the end of compositions such as fugues, in places where an increase in tension is desired; tonic pedal may begin or end works, to clarify and stabilize the key center.

Period (periodic) structure Phrase-level formal unit consisting of two successive phrases of equal length, in a question-answer (or antecedent-consequent) relationship. The medial (middle or internal) cadence (usually half cadence or imperfect authentic cadence) is less final sounding than the final (usually a perfect authentic cadence). Periods are often classified in terms of the melodic relationship between the two phrases.

Prolongation Emphasis on a particular scale degree or harmony (see structural harmony and structural pitches). Prolongation can be accomplished in a variety of ways, through various linear ornamentations (passing, neighboring or arpeggiated), pedal point, reiteration and so on. Principal prolonged pitches form the fundamental melodic line *(Urlinie)* and underlying harmonic structure.

Real answer Imitative *answer*, as in a fugue, in which the exact interval structure of the leader is preserved in the follower, transposed to a different degree of the scale, most often the dominant degree (and thus temporarily to the dominant key). Compare *tonal answer*.

Reduction, graphic (linear reduction, Schenkerian analysis) System of analysis showing in musical notation and related symbology the principal melodic and harmonic events in a tonal work. Based on the work of Heinrich Schenker and his followers, this way of thinking about musical structure focuses on the overall shaping of a work's principal lines and harmonies, within the context of tonality (though the methodology has been applied to other repertoires). See *prolongation, structural harmony, structural pitches*.

Response See *answer*.

Ritornello Returning section, as in a rondo structure, that stabilizes a work. Ritornello form is found in some chorale preludes.

Sequence Melodic or motivic pattern transposed successively to different scale degrees; such patterning, a principal means of unification, usually affects all voices simultaneously.

Stretto Imitation, as in a fugue, in which successive imitative entries occur at shorter time intervals than those found earlier in the same work (for example, in the exposition). A common device for building tension in an imitative work.

Stretto fugue Fugue based on extensive use of stretto, which may replace sequential episodes. Stretto entrances near the end may be at closer time intervals, to increase tension and drive.

Structural harmony Principal harmony, underlying more localized surface harmonic changes, and thus stabilizing and clarifying tonal centers. The principal structural or prolonged harmonies in tonal music are tonic and dominant and to a lesser extent predominant, and are often expressed as prolonged pitches in the bass.

Structural pitches Principal scale degrees in a line, points of departure and arrival, giving a musical line its sense of shape and direction. In tonal music, notes of the tonic triad, emphasized by metric placement, length and other means of prolongation, may be heard as more fundamental than other (decorative) pitches. In Schenkerian terms, the principal structural pitches form a composition's fundamental line or *Urlinie,* which in this view always descends from an upper note of the tonic triad to the tonic pitch.

Table canon *(Tafelkanon)* Two-voice canon in which one performer reads from one side of the music and the other from the opposite side (with the music, by implication, placed between them on a table). Thus, a canon by retrograde inversion.

Theme In an invention, the principal musical idea, as given first in the upper voice in the exposition. Analogous to a fugue subject.

Tonal answer Imitative *answer*, as in a fugue, in which a prominent dominant pitch at or near the head of the subject is replaced by the tonic pitch (in the principal key) at the corresponding place in the answer. Thus, a tonic-to-dominant leap in the subject is replaced by a dominant-to-tonic leap in the answer, and vice versa, preserving the tonal center.

Tonal framework (tonality frame) Principal highest and lowest pitches of a melody that emphasize its tonal center. The tonal framework normally involves pitches of the tonic triad.

Triple fugue A fugue with three distinct subjects. Compare *double fugue.*

Unequal fifths In voice-leading practice, a diminished fifth between two voices followed by a perfect fifth; this is not usually found in two-voice writing, or between outer voices of a thicker texture. A diminished fifth may follow a perfect fifth as long as the diminished fifth resolves normally, but again this is very rare in two voices.

BIBLIOGRAPHY

David, Hans T., and Arthur Mendel. *The Bach Reader.* New York: W.W. Norton, 1966.

Forte, Allen, and Steven E. Gilbert. *Introduction to Schenkerian Analysis.* New York: W.W. Norton, 1982.

Gauldin, Robert. *A Practical Approach to Eighteenth-Century Counterpoint.* Englewood Cliffs, N.J.: Prentice-Hall, 1988.

Horsley, Imogen. *Fugue.* New York: The Free Press, 1966.

Kennan, Kent. *Counterpoint.* Englewood Cliffs, N.J.: Prentice-Hall, 1987.

LaRue, Jan. *Guidelines for Style Analysis.* New York: W.W. Norton, 1970.

Mann, Alfred. *The Study of Fugue.* New York: W.W. Norton, 1965.

Naldin, Charles. *Fugal Answer.* New York: Oxford University Press, 1969.

Oldroyd, George. *The Technique and Spirit of Fugue.* New York: Oxford University Press, 1948.

Parks, Richard. *Eighteenth-Century Counterpoint and Tonal Structure.* Englewood Cliffs, N.J.: Prentice-Hall, 1984.

Randel, Don, ed. *The New Harvard Dictionary of Music.* Cambridge, Mass.: Harvard University Press, 1986.

Sadie, Stanley, ed. *The New Grove Dictionary of Music and Musicians.* 29 vols. London: Macmillan, 1980.

ANTHOLOGY

(Note: all works are by J. S. Bach)

1. Solo Cello Suite I, Prelude

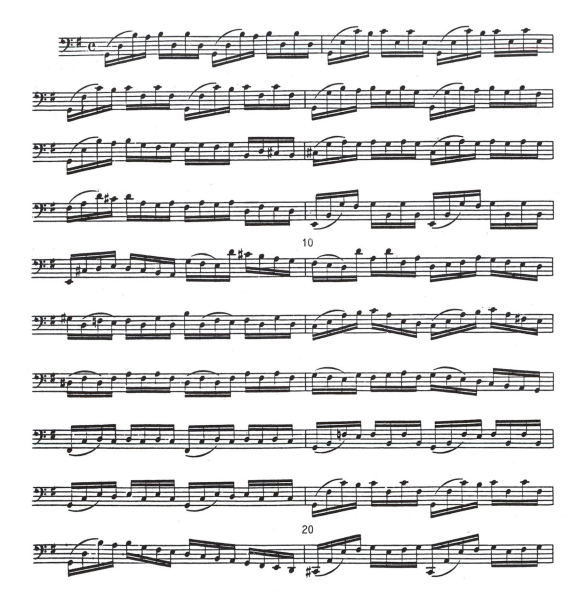

The Craft of Tonal Counterpoint

2. Solo Cello Suite I, Courante

The Craft of Tonal Counterpoint

3. Partita I, Menuet I

4. Partita II, Sarabande

5. French Suite I, Allemande

6. French Suite I, Menuet I

7. French Suite II, Sarabande

8. French Suite III, Sarabande

Trio

9. French Suite V, Courante

10. French Suite V, Gavotte

11.   French Suite V, Sarabande

40

12. English Suite V, Gigue

13. English Suite V, Passepied II

15. Fughetta on Allein Gott in der Höh sei Ehr

The Craft of Tonal Counterpoint

17. Sechs kleine Präludien, No. 4

The Craft of Tonal Counterpoint

18. Invention No. 1

20. Invention No. 3

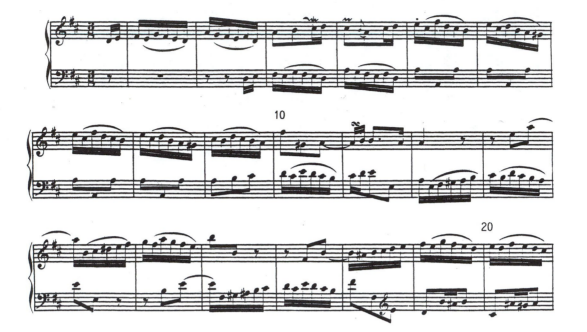

30

40

50

21. Invention No. 6

10

20

30

23. Invention No. 8

24. Invention No. 9

27. Sinfonia No. 1

Sinfonia No. 3

29. Sinfonia No. 9

Sinfonia No. 9

30. The Goldberg Variations, Aria (Theme)

The Craft of Tonal Counterpoint

31. The Goldberg Variations, Variation No. 4

33.   The Goldberg Variations, Variation No. 9

The Craft of Tonal Counterpoint

37. The Art of Fugue, Fugue No. 9

38. WTC I, Fugue No. 1

The Craft of Tonal Counterpoint

The Craft of Tonal Counterpoint

10

The Craft of Tonal Counterpoint

The Craft of Tonal Counterpoint

51. Passacaglia in C Minor

53. Durch Adam's Fall

10

54. Ich ruf' zu dir, Herr Jesu Christ

55. Herr Gott, nun sei gepreiset

56. Jesus Christus unser Heiland

10

30

40

50

57. Wachet auf, ruft uns die Stimme

30

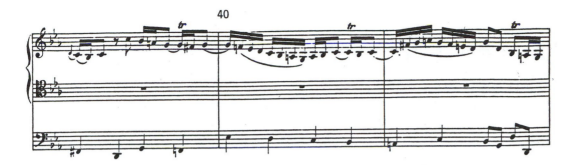

58. Mass in B Minor, Crucifixus

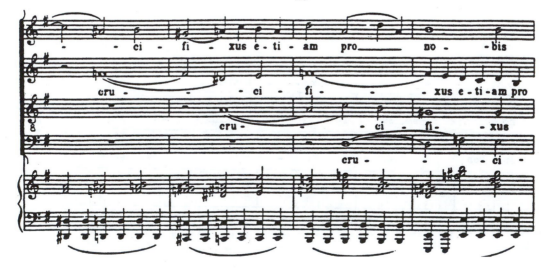

50

H

Harmonic
  framework, 69, 229–31
  intervals, xxii, 49–52
  progression, 36, 191, 214, 263–65, 284
  rhythm, 119, 173, 260, 284, 292
  tendency tones, 285
Harmony (*see also* Cadences; Chromaticism;
      Doubling; Figured bass symbols; Inversion),
      283–88, 288n. 1
  chorale, 270
  general, 20
  in four voices, 247, 249–50
  in three voices, 142–69, 173–74
  in two voices, 52–61, 64, 158
  progression (chord functions), 78–83
  structural, xv, xx, 283, 293
  tonic, 114, 230, 261
Haydn, Franz Joseph
  Symphony No. 104, first movement, 11
Hemiola, 14, 292
Hidden fifths and octaves. *See* Direct fifths and
      octaves

I

Imitation, 107–22, 217, 261, 292
  by augmentation, 117–19
  by contrary motion, 115–16, 118
  by diminution, 119
  canonic, 111–14, 129
  in fugues, 192, 232, 254, 258
  in inventions (*see* inventions, imitation in)
  in three voices, 149, 163
  in two voices, 39–75, 109–10, 123
  intervals of, 109, 111, 223
  motivic, 261–62
  real, 114
  stretto, 218, 223–27, 240, 243
  tonal, 114
Interval(s), 285
  consonant, 50–51
  dissonant, 50–51, 114
  double counterpoint, 102–103
  harmonic, 49–52, 158
  melodic, 104, 114, 129
  parallel harmonic, 102–103
  pitch, 226, 227, 243
  structural, 16
  treatment of in line, 17–18, 28
  vertical, 76n. 9
Invention(s), 292
  analysis of, 134–35, 137–40
  bridge, 141n. 4
  cadences in, 134, 135
  countertheme in, 124–26, 141n. 2
  ending of, 136, 141n. 4
  episode in, 128–32, 134, 135, 136, 137
  exposition in, 123–28, 137
  form in, 135
  imitation in, 107, 123, 125–26, 135, 140, 192
  middle entry in, 134, 136
  theme in, 124–26, 134, 136, 141n. 2
  two-voice, 123–41
Inversion(s) (*see also* Contrary motion), 26–27
  in fugues, 191, 221, 222, 236–37, 247, 256
  of chords, 56–57, 249, 284

of intervals (*see* Invertible counterpoint)
Invertible (double) counterpoint, 97–106, 106n. 1,
      179, 291, 292
  at the octave, 98–99, 103
  at the tenth, 102–104
  at the twelfth, 100–102, 103
  generalizations, 98
Invertible (triple) counterpoint. *See* Triple invertible
      counterpoint

K

Key scheme
  in dance-suite movements, 89–96
  in fugues, 192, 194–96, 211–12, 236, 257
  in inventions, 134
Keys
  closely related, 211–12
  dominant, 129, 192, 199, 211, 217, 220, 285
  major, 285
  minor, 228, 285

L

Leaps
  treatment of, 16–17, 114, 160, 191, 223, 225, 289
Linear Intervallic Patterns (LIPs), xvi, xx, xxii–xxiv,
      66, 130, 163, 184, 212, 214–16, 219, 242, 250,
      292
Link
  fugal, 201, 205, 209, 256

M

Macrorhythm, 152, 290
Melodic line
  figures in, 15–17
  intervals in, 15–18, 129
  motifs in, 7–9
  range of, 6
  rhythm in, 14
  sequence in, 28
  shape of, 5
  structural pitches in (*see also* Structural pitches),
      6–7
  tessitura of, 5–6
  tonal framework of, 140
Melodic writing, 32–38, 122n. 2
Meter
  compound, 61–62
  in dance-suite movements, 95
  in melodic line, 13
Middle entry
  in fugues (*see* Fugues, middle entries in)
  in inventions (*see* Inventions, middle entries in)
Minor scale, 19–23, 38n. 6, 228
Modulation, 288n. 1
  chromatic, 286
  general, 92–93, 285–86
  in canons, 183, 186
  in keys, 211, 236
Motion
  relative, 153–54
Motive (*see also* Figures, motivic), 292
  development processes, 26, 132–34, 242–43
  in inventions, 123, 125, 134, 136, 141n. 2
  in melodic line, 19, 26, 38n. 3, 231, 236
Motivic

coherence, 27–28, 243, 251
counterpoints, 270–74
figures, 7–8, 27, 38n. 3

N

Neapolitan chord. *See* Chords, Neapolitan
Non-harmonic tones, 283, 288n. 1
  chromatic, 82
  definitions of, 24–25, 38n. 8, 286
  in four voices, 247, 250
  in line, 24
  in three voices, 161–62, 170–73, 179
  in two voices, 46, 52–61

O

Obbligato melody (in chorale prelude), 277–79, 281
Organ
  pedals, 169n. 2, 272, 289
  writing for, 263, 268n. 3, 281n. 4, 289
Ostinato. *See* Basso ostinato
Overlapping of voices, 48–49

P

Parallel
  fifths and octaves, 44–45, 102, 153, 250, 292
  motion, 44–45, 153, 250
Passacaglia, 255, 260–63, 265, 266, 268, 289, 293
Pedal(s)
  dominant, 230–31, 241–42
  organ (*see* Organ, pedals)
  points, 24, 149, 211, 227–31, 242–43, 243n. 3, 250, 257, 293
  sequence, 28, 29, 31
  tonic, 228–29, 236, 241
Perfect fifths or octaves, 45, 79, 99, 100, 153, 179–80, 214, 216
Period structure, 10, 38n. 5, 293
Phrase structure, 9–11, 172–75, 236
Picardy third, 227–29
Pivot chord modulation, 285–86
Progressions
  chord, 284
  circle-of-fifths, 79–81, 213, 216, 240
  harmonic, 283–85

R

Range
  in three voices, 152
  in two voices, 48–49
  melodic, 5–6
Real answer. *See* Answer, real
Recapitulation
  in fugues (*see* Fugue, recapitulation in)
Relative motion
  in three voices, 149, 152, 153
  in two voices, 43–46
Repetition
  use of in melody, 130
Response. *See* Answer
Retardation. *See* Suspension
Retrograde canon. *See* Canon, retrograde
Rhythm
  in dance-suite movments, 14, 92
  in four-voice writing, 247–49

in melodic line, 13, 27, 32–38
in three-voice writing, 147
in two-voice writing, 47–48
Ritornello (in chorale prelude), 277 79, 293

S

Scale, 33, 116, 214, 238
  chromatic, 7, 19–23
  major, 21, 228
  minor, 19–23, 228
Second inversion of triads (*see also* Triads), 57, 157, 249, 284, 287
Secondary dominants (*see also* Altered chords; Chords; Seventh chords), 78–81, 82, 111, 171–72, 186, 229
Sequence(s), 293
  circle-of-fifths, 57–58, 78, 80–81, 131–32, 139–40, 183–84, 216, 229, 237
  in fugues, 212, 215, 217, 219, 232, 236–37, 250, 257
  in melodic line, 27–32, 34–36, 38n. 9, 82, 104, 129, 140
  pedal (*see* Pedal sequence)
  pseudo-, 29–30
Seventh chords
  diminished, 81, 191
  dominant, 154, 249, 286
  doubling, 156
  in four voices, 249–50
  in three voices, 154–56, 169n. 5
  in two voices, 55
  inversion of, 57–58, 76n. 13, 156, 287
  secondary dominant, 81
Spacing
  in four voices, 249, 251
  in three voices, 152
  in two voices, 48–49
Stretto, 122n. 1, 293
  in fugues (*see* Fugues, stretto in)
  in inventions, 132, 135, 136
Structural harmony. *See* Harmony, structural
Structural pitches
  definition of, 294
  in fugues, 204, 208, 212, 216, 218–19, 237–38, 242, 257
  in lines, xx, 6–7, 26, 35–36
Subject
  in three-voice fugues, 177, 188–90
  modulating, 190–91
Suspension(s), 286
  in four voices, 247
  in three voices, 148, 161–62
  in two voices, 59–61
Syncopation, 14

T

Table canon (*Tafelcanon*), 120, 294
Tendency tones, 19–23
  harmonic, 22
  melodic, 20–21
Texture
  in four-voice writing, 247–49
  in fugues, 221, 226, 227, 231–33, 242, 247–49, 256
  in three-voice writing, 147, 150, 248, 250
Thematic manipulation. *See* Motive, development processes